CLARENDON MEDIEVAL AND TUDOR SERIES

General Editor

J. A. W. BENNETT

CLARENDON MEDIEVAL AND TUDOR SERIES

—

Already published

PASTON LETTERS. Selected and Edited with an Introduction, Notes, and Glossary by NORMAN DAVIS. Critical Comment by Horace Walpole, Virginia Woolf, and others. 1958

WILLIAM DUNBAR POEMS. Selected and Edited with an Introduction, Notes, and Glossary by JAMES KINSLEY. Appreciations by John Pinkerton, John Merry Ross, Agnes Mure Mackenzie, W. L. Renwick, C. S. Lewis. 1958

A SELECTION OF ENGLISH CAROLS. Edited with an Introduction, Notes, and Glossary by R. L. GREENE. 1962

SELECTIONS FROM LAƷAMON'S *BRUT*. Edited by G. L. BROOK. With an Introduction by C. S. LEWIS. 1963

SELECTIONS FROM GAVIN DOUGLAS. With an Introduction, Notes, and Glossary by DAVID F. C. COLDWELL. Appreciations by Thomas Warton, George Saintsbury, C. S. Lewis, E. M. W. Tillyard. 1964

ROBERT HENRYSON POEMS. Selected and Edited with an Introduction, Notes, and Glossary by CHARLES ELLIOTT. Appreciations by Sir Francis Kinaston, G. Gregory Smith, Edwin Muir, and others. 1963

HENRY HOWARD, EARL OF SURREY, POEMS. With an Introduction, Notes, and Glossary by EMRYS JONES. Appreciations by Thomas Warton, G. F. Nott, C. S. Lewis, Maurice Evans. 1964

Woodcut by Sebastian Brant: from the edition of Virgil printed
at Strassburg 1502: Aen. IX

SELECTIONS FROM
GAVIN DOUGLAS

With an Introduction, Notes
and Glossary by
DAVID F. C. COLDWELL

———

Appreciations by

THOMAS WARTON · GEORGE SAINTSBURY
C. S. LEWIS · E. M. W. TILLYARD

OXFORD
AT THE CLARENDON PRESS
1964

Oxford University Press, Amen House, London E.C.4

GLASGOW NEW YORK TORONTO MELBOURNE WELLINGTON
BOMBAY CALCUTTA MADRAS KARACHI LAHORE DACCA
CAPE TOWN SALISBURY NAIROBI IBADAN ACCRA
KUALA LUMPUR HONG KONG

PRINTED IN GREAT BRITAIN

CONTENTS

CONTENTS

INTRODUCTION

SEBASTIAN BRANT, artist, scholar, and printer, in 1502 published his edition of the *Aeneid*. It is of a type common in the Renaissance, a block of Latin in the centre of the page, sometimes surmounted by a woodcut, and wreathed by the marginal commentaries of Servius and Jodocus Badius Ascensius. The woodcuts are instructive to the modern reader, who sees Virgil's heroes in the marmoreal attitudes of Neo-classicism; the readers of the sixteenth century saw Aeneas as much like themselves. Let us turn to the first plate in Book IX. In the upper left is New Troy, on the model of Wittenberg or Strassburg. The gate is machicolated and flanked by stone towers which are themselves surmounted by half-timbered structures. There are shot holes, and drains from which hot oil is pouring. In the background rise roofs and towers and the apse of a Gothic church. On the ramparts soldiers brandish partisans, aim cross-bows, throw stones, and manipulate a flaming catapult. In the top right Turnus kneels as Iris disappears into heaven on a rainbow. She is wearing court dress; he, doublet and hose, very long, loose sleeves, and a three-pointed crown. In the lower foreground Turnus appears again, leading his army. As principal knight, he wears a visored helmet surmounted by an immense boar's head. His cavalry are fully armed from helmet to spurs; they sit on high saddles; each horse has a spike on its forehead. Over the company floats a pennon bearing the heraldic device of three swans. Next to the cavalry a group of shepherds, clad in cloaks and hoods, rest and gesticulate. Finally, two double-tailed mermaids (they hold a tail in each hand) watch a furious fire consuming one of Aeneas' square-rigged high-sterned ships. The Romans are completely transformed into medieval Germans. Brant has only two devices to create an authentic atmosphere: his practice of inscribing on pagan altars letters roughly modelled on Hebrew, and his use of a star on naked pagan gods to avoid the fig-leaf drawn from Christian myth.

Gavin Douglas's attitude towards Virgil is much like that of Brant. He makes little attempt to have his characters act in foreign, ancient ways, or to make them stately. He is proud of his fidelity to the text: *he* did not mangle the text as the unconscionable Caxton did; but his characters speak and fight like knights of the late fifteenth century, and the action takes place in terms the fifteenth century would readily recognize. Hence 'Sir' Diomeid, or 'Dan' Virgil, or 'child' Cillenyus, or Neptune's 'mattock', or the somewhat implausible 'nuns of Bacchus'. For all the reverence accorded to Virgil, the *Aeneid* seemed far closer and more natural in 1500 than it did in 1700 or 1900; improved Latinity seems to have cut off the Latin classics from popular imagination. Douglas's anachronisms should not be objectionable. He had an authoritative model in Virgil himself, for Dryden remarks on the 'famous anachronism, in making Aeneas and Dido contemporaries. For it is certain that the Hero lived almost two hundred years before the building of Carthage. . . . Chronology at best is but a Cobweb-Law, and he broke through it with his weight.' Furthermore, one of the aims of the translator is to produce a poem that might have been written in his own time. It may be that anachronism shows a kind of cultural vitality, where a careful antiquarianism would suggest the undertaker laying out the corpse. Douglas saw far less difference between the lives of Scots and Romans than Dryden did: his descriptions of ships, battlefields, and ghosts are therefore so much the more lively than Dryden's, where the dignified and decorous Romans always seem to be on parade.

Dryden's purpose, determined by his view of the graces of epic poetry, was to make all things 'grave, majestical, and sublime'. He is, therefore, at his best, perhaps, in the formal, dignified speeches that make up much of the poem. It is fitting that Juno should speak with god-like decorum:

> 'O Eolus! for to thee the King of Heav'n
> The Pow'r of Tempests, and of Winds has giv'n:
> Thy Force alone their Fury can restrain,
> And smooth the Waves, or swell the troubl'd Main.
> A race of wand'ring Slaves, abhorr'd by me,
> With prosp'rous Passage cut the Thuscan Sea:

To fruitful Italy their Course they steer,
And for their vanquish'd God design new Temples there.
Raise all thy Winds, with Night involve the Skies;
Sink, or disperse my fatal Enemies.
Twice sev'n, the charming Daughters of the Main,
Around my Person wait, and bear my Train:
Succeed my Wish, and second my Design,
The fairest, Deiopeia, shall be thine;
And make thee Father of a happy Line.' (I. 97–111.)

For Douglas she is rather a sharp-tongued Scottish housewife:

'Eolus, a pepill onto me ennemy
Salis the sey Tuscane, cariand to Italy
Thar venquyst hamehald goddis and Ilion;
Bot sen the fader of goddis every one
And kyng of men gave the power,' quod sche,
'To meys the flude or rays with stormys hie,
Infors thi wyndis, synk all thar schippis infeir,
Or skattir widquhar into cuntreis seir,
Warp all thar bodeis in the deyp bedeyn.
I have,' quod sche, 'lusty ladeis fourteyn,
Of quham the farest, clepit Diope,
In ferm wedlok I sal conjure to the
For thi reward, that lilly quhite of swar,
With the forto remane for evermar,
Quhilk propir spous and eik thi lady myld
Sal mak the fader to mony fair child.' (I. ii. 25–40.)

Dryden's pace, though majestic, is slow, and has disadvantages when the speed of the original quickens:

Thus while the Pious Prince his Fate bewails,
Fierce Boreas drove against his flying Sails,
And rent the Sheets: The raging Billows rise,
And mount the tossing Vessel to the Skies:
Nor can the shiv'ring Oars sustain the Blow;
The Galley gives her side, and turns her Prow:
While those astern descending down the Steep,
Thro' gaping Waves behold the boiling deep.
Three Ships were hurry'd by the Southern Blast,
And on the secret Shelves with Fury cast.

> Those hidden Rocks, th' Ausonian Sailors knew,
> They call'd them Altars, when they rose in view,
> And show'd their spacious Backs above the Flood.
> Three more, fierce Eurus in his angry Mood,
> Dash'd on the Shallows of the moving Sand,
> And in mid Ocean left them moor'd a-land. (I. 146–61.)

'Moor'd a-land'! Douglas is able to summon to his translation more nautical energy, and to capture something of the thunder and confusion of the shipwreck:

> And al invane thus quhil Eneas carpit,
> A blastrand bub out from the north brayng
> Gan our the forschip in the baksaill dyng,
> And to the sternys up the flude gan cast.
> The aris, hechis and the takillis brast,
> The schippis stevin frawart hyr went gan wryth,
> And turnyt hir braid syde to the wallis swyth.
> Heich as a hill the jaw of watir brak
> And in ane hepe cam on thame with a swak.
> Some hesit hoverand on the wallis hycht,
> And sum the swowchand sey so law gart lycht
> Thame semyt the erd oppynnyt amyd the flude—
> The stour up bullyrrit sand as it war wode.
> The sowth wynd, Nothus, thre schippis draif away
> Amang blynd cragis, quhilk huge rolkis thai say
> Amyd the sey Italianys Altaris callis;
> And othir thre Eurus from the deip wallis
> Cachit amang the schald bankis of sand—
> Dolorus to se thame chop on grond, and stand
> Lyke as a wall with sand warpit about. (I. iii. 14–33.)

Dryden can be bad when his dignity becomes stilted and artificial:

> No Vessels were in view: But, on the Plain,
> Three beamy Stags command a Lordly Train
> Of branching Heads; the more ignoble Throng
> Attend their stately Steps, and slowly graze along. (I. 259–62.)

Douglas makes it simpler:

> Na schip he saw, bot sone he gat a syght
> Of thre hartis waverand by the cost syde,
> Quham at the bak, throu out the gravis wide,

> The mekil herdis followit in a rowt
> And pasturit all the large valle about. (I. iv. 48–52.)

The simpler version seems closer to Virgil's Latin:

> navem in conspectu nullam, tris litore cervos
> prospicit errantis; hos tota armenta sequuntur
> a tergo et longum per vallis pascitur agmen. (I. 184–6.)

Ignoring the enchantment of the rhythm, one can see in this a plain meaning: 'He observed no ship in sight, but three stags wandering on the shore; whole herds follow behind them and in a long line graze through the valley.' A reader unaccustomed to the statuesque treatment of Latin might find Dryden's version of the passage empty and insincere. And yet it must be admitted that on occasion Douglas's rough-hewn vigour may become incongruous:

> For to the madynnys of Tyre this is the gyis
> To beir a cays of arowis on this wys,
> With rede botynys on thar schankis hie. (I. vi. 55–58.)

This is not Douglas at his best; he succeeds in vigorous passages describing action, and in passages where there is more human warmth and emotion than Dryden's stately composure and dignity allow him to transmit.

Douglas is closer to the common reader than Dryden is. He was less of a Latinist. He translated from an inferior text, by modern standards; he had few technical aids; he had no models; he worked fast: it is not surprising that he sometimes made mistakes. Yet his methods were sound, for he depended heavily on a monument of contemporary scholarship, the commentary made about 1500 by the Dutch humanist Ascensius. Ascensius made a running prose commentary on the poem, identifying the mythological allusions, providing alternative, simpler wording, and explaining the metaphors. When Douglas borrowed from this somewhat pedantic paraphrase, he was making his poem translation and commentary at the same time. Thus where Virgil has simply 'sola', Douglas may expand to 'allane in wedowheid', because Ascensius had the explanatory note 'idest in viduitate'. Or Virgil's 'auditque videtque' can be combined with Ascensius's 'audit & videt. scilicet per fantasiam & imaginationem illum scilicet amatum absentem' to produce Douglas's version:

> And of him absent thinkis scho heris the soun,
> His voce scho heris, and him behaldis sche,
> Thocht he, God wait, fer from her presence be.

Or a line with no equivalent in Virgil,' And all that to the schippis langis of rychtis' (XI. vii. 80) can come wholly from Ascensius, 'Atque cetera ad constructionem navium necessaria'. When Virgil was obscure or allusive, Douglas examined Ascensius. Part of the diffuseness of the poem is due to his determination to embody explanatory material in the text—and this was appropriate, because he wished to make Virgil available to schoolboys, and because almost every English writer of the early Renaissance seems to have been haunted by a sense of the impermanence of language, and determined to lay synonyms as props against decay. One may suspect that Virgil without the commentary was not wholly available to Douglas, and that some of the explanatory expansions borrowed from Ascensius mark the places where his own classical scholarship was uncertain.

Why did Douglas undertake the translation of the *Aeneid*, beyond assenting to the proposal of his cousin Lord Sinclair? He was not influenced by the medieval transformation of Virgil into a necromancer addicted to clandestine meetings with women, to whose window he was hoisted in a basket; to this body of legend Douglas alludes but once, when he says that the power of love 'crelit up the flour of poetry' (Prol. I. 32). Nor was he affected by the medieval legend that Virgil was the unconscious prophet of Christianity; though he alludes to it in Prologue VI:

> Thus faithfully in his Buikolikis he saith,
> The maid comith bryngis new lynage fra hevin.

Rather he adopts the Renaissance attitude towards Virgil, reverence for the master-poet, humility before the master-achievement:

> Maist reverend Virgill, of Latyn poetis prynce,
> Gem of engyne and flude of eloquens,
> Thow peirless perle, patroun of poetry,
> Roys, regester, palm, lawrer and glory. . . . (Prologue I.)

The hie wysdome and maist profund engyne
Of myne author Virgile, poete dyvyne,
To comprehend, makis me almaist forvay,
So crafty wrocht his wark is, lyne by lyne.   (Prologue V.)

In face of such excellence, Douglas sinks into self-depreciation:

. . . set that empty be my brayn and dull,
I have translait a volum wondirfull:
So profund was this wark at I have said,
Me semyt oft throw the deip sey to waid;
And so mysty umquhile this poecy,
My spreit was reft half deill in extasy . . .
Not as I suld, I wrait, but as I couth. (S.T.S. Edition IV, p. 190.)

And yet on occasion, particularly on the occasion of completing
the work, he abandons his pose of ignorance and unlettered
stupidity, and praises himself for doing, rather well even, what
no one had attempted in Scots before.

Douglas has, then, a double attitude towards himself, on the
one hand a sense of insufficience before the masters of the past, on
the other a sense of supremacy over his contemporaries. As the
first translator of a major classical poem into English, he had no
immediate rivals. Surrey's less lively blank-verse version of
the *Aeneid* was in the future, as were the tongue-twisting hexa-
meters of Stanyhurst and the graceless septenaries of Phaer. It is
illuminating to compare Douglas's work with Caxton's translation, if that loose rendering can so be called. In Prologue I Douglas
attacks Caxton's shameful perversion of the story, and in Prologue V he remarks complacently on his own superiority:

Now harkis sportis, myrthis and myrry plays,
Ful gudly pastans on mony syndry ways,
Endyte by Virgil, and heir by me translate,
Quhilk William Caxton knew nevir al hys days,
For, as I sayd tofor, that man forvays;
Hys febil proys beyn mank and mutulate,
Bot my propyne com from the pres fute hait,
Onforlatit, not jawyn fra tun to tun,
In fresch sapour new from the berry run.

He offers the heady wine of scholarship, inebriating after the poor dregs set out by Caxton. Caxton went wrong in three fashions: he offended the exact scholar by his mistakes in names; the poet, by his mutilated, feeble prose; and the humanist, by his omissions and expansions that changed the harmonious structure of the original. Nor is this last charge unjustified, for Caxton made his *Eneydos* a romance on Dido, so much is the Fourth Book expanded; and in fact he did not translate Virgil, but a French version of an Italian version of some parts of the *Aeneid*. So passionately did Douglas revere the Virgilian text that he reproved even Chaucer, a master and lantern for poets, for impugning the moral integrity of Aeneas, and thus of Virgil too.

It may be objected that Douglas himself departed from the sacred text by including the Thirteenth Book, the sequel composed in 1428 by Mapheus Vegius. The inclusion of the supplement is not surprising. For a century and a half after Vegius wrote the Thirteenth Book it was considered an inseparable part of the poem, even enjoying the same sort of scholastic comment that Badius Ascensius lavished on the other twelve books. Nor was Vegius's the only attempted sequel: it was commonly felt that hero-worship of Aeneas was incomplete without his death and deification and some account of the realized glory of Rome. Vegius paid Virgil the compliment of close imitation, and his contemporaries called him 'doctissimus' and an 'alter Maro'. Douglas was not, therefore, taking the same startling liberties with the text that Caxton did, yet nevertheless, in the Thirteenth Prologue, he seems to have had doubts (as did the printer Aldus Manutius) of the decorum of including even this very respectable supplement.

It may also be objected that he almost doubled the number of lines in the original. The considerable expansion of Virgil's bulk is partly due to the form: while Douglas did not translate strictly line by line, the couplet is his unit of composition corresponding to the hexameter, so that he has twenty syllables for Virgil's fifteen or so. This in part accounts for the *extra* words, the makeweight phrases such as 'I wene', 'full weill I wait', 'quod he', 'as was the gys', and 'I wis', and the doublets so characteristic of the translation, such as 'clepe and call', 'braid and large', 'begynnyng and original', 'wyse and sage', and 'reuthfull and devote'.

These are minor verbal additions, and it is clear that within the limits of his powers Douglas aimed at equivalence, that is, capturing all the sense of the original and transferring it without distortion into Scottish verse. He sacrificed many of the levels of suggestion that make the Latin so haunting and evocative; he may not have known they were there. But he captured the clear sense of the poem, especially in passages that rush with energy and effort. At best many translations make the poem a *tableau vivant*, at worst a *tableau mort*. Douglas felt life in the original and infused it into his translation.

Douglas's greatest achievement was the translation of the *Aeneid*; he recognized the *magnitude* of the task when he challenged harsh critics to

> assay als lang labour agane,
> And translait Ovid, as I have Virgill.

But what of his original poetry? It is not strikingly original; Douglas was simply competent in the manipulation of the standard forms of the late fifteenth century. Students of literary theory find much of interest in the First, Third, Fifth, Sixth, Ninth, and Thirteenth prologues, and in the Conclusio, Direction, and Exclamation that follow Book XIII. In these poems Douglas developed his somewhat inchoate theories of translation and aesthetics, indicating that the translator must aim at a just rendering of the 'sentence', or significance, of the poem; that he so aimed; that nevertheless he translated 'al maste word by word'; that he would have done better if he had not been limited by the existing text; that the style should fit the subject; that Virgil's transcendent meaning escaped him; that he was too rudely ignorant to capture Virgil's music; that the poem is 'translatit rycht'; that Scots was a poverty-stricken language; that critics should not be censorious; and that composing a vernacular version of the *Aeneid* was an honourable and useful task. Another group of prologues develops various philosophic, theological, and ethical ideas. The Second, as an introduction to the fall of Troy, is a meditation on a common, melancholy, medieval theme, 'All erdly glaidnes fynysith with wo'. The Fourth attacks Venus and Cupid as fosterers of burning, carnal delight, and solemnly warns young and old, male and female, against the power of love. In the Fifth (as incidentally in the First) Douglas disposes of the pagan gods and their claims to divinity; in the Sixth he demonstrates that Virgil, although a pagan, had philosophic insights nearly Christian. The Eighth, interesting for its intimidating vocabulary and as the author's sole exercise in the alliterative form (which by 1513 had lost the freshness of its prime), is a fairly conventional attack on the society of the day, its irrationality, its dispirited materialism, its permissive surrender of old moral values; though Douglas perhaps evaded responsibility for the charges by placing them in the mouth of a disgruntled misanthrope in a dream. The Tenth runs through the principal points of theology, Creation, the Trinity, the Incarnation, the Atonement, Transubstantiation, the sovereignty of God, the insufficiency of human understanding, and universal order. The Eleventh describes Douglas's idea of moral chivalry, tying the theological Tenth to the *Aeneid* by citing the virtues and prowess of the Christian knight, the perfect theologian and yet, like Aeneas, the perfect soldier. Most modern readers will find these moralizings tedious and prolix. Finally, among the prologues there are the nature poems. The Seventh, the description of winter, is probably the best because it captures authentic experience, the chill of an Edinburgh December. In contrast the Twelfth, more conventional in response and subject than the Seventh, is ecstatically lyrical in praise of May, piling up the 'flowers white and red' that dot medieval tapestries and perfume medieval lyric verse, coming to life with the singing country girls and the leering young men, and achieving point when the generative processes of nature in springtime inspire Douglas to complete the task of translation. The Thirteenth Prologue begins with a June evening, and ends—delightfully—with the world's awakening the following morning; the middle narrates Douglas's dream in which Mapheus Vegius appears and compels the reluctant translator to add one more book to the tale, the Vegian supplement that carries Aeneas to heaven. Some of these poems were evidently inspired by and are intimately connected with the books they precede, others seem to be affixed for form's sake when critical inspiration failed.

The *Palice of Honour* is a good example of a common medieval
form, the dream allegory. It explores the various roads humanity
can follow to honour, the roads of wisdom, chivalric love,
chastity, poetry, valiant knighthood, and, the surest way, moral
virtue. It begins with a splendid aureate prologue, an invocation
of nature, not, one fancies, the real natural world around Edinburgh, but the stylized, half-imaginary world of medieval tapestries. Indeed, Douglas himself is at pains to remind the reader
that this is an artificial dream-world, a world '*depaint* as paradice
amiabill', 'powderit with mony a set Of ruby, topas, perle, and
emerant', a world in which the blooming flowers 'Ovirspred the
levis of *natures tapestreis*', and in which the umbrate trees 'War
portrait, and on the eirth yschappit Be goldin bemis vivificative'.
The poem must be admired for its exuberance and energy, and
for the sensuous pleasure of language-play, not for its evocation of
the real world. In the vision itself, the enchantment of this
tapestry May is abandoned for the horror appropriate to Cocytus,
'that uglie flude horribill, rinnand blude reid, and impossibill that
it had been a river naturall'. But along the river's braes passes the
first of the poem's pageants, the Queen of Sapience and her
retinue, those who like Achitophel and Sinon achieved fame by
their immoral misuse of wisdom, and also those who like Solo-
mon, Aristotle, Josephus, and Cicero were 'groundit in ferme
intelligence'. The court of Diana, which follows next, the court
of the chaste and virginal, is very, very small. The court of Venus,
on the other hand, is impressively large and for a moment decep-
tively celestial, but Douglas tactlessly sings the darker side of love,
the 'panefull cairis infinite' and the 'frail unsteidfastnes' of this
'fervent diseis dolorous'. Not unnaturally, this gives offence to
Venus, and Douglas is put on trial for his life (or for his shape: he
fears penal transformation into a bear, a boar, an owl, or an ape).
But the court of the Muses appears, and Calliope saves him from
the wrath of Venus on condition he compose some work in
praise of love. Entrusted to one of Calliope's nymphs, he is transported by a devious geographical route to the palace of Honour.
It is surrounded by noble knights and moral poets, and by the
pitiful wraiths of the tormented idle and faithless; within are the
patriarchs of the Old Testament and the heroes of Greek history

and legend. The keepers of the court are Charity, Constancy, Liberality, Innocence, Devotion, Discretion, Conscience, Justice, Prudence, Clean Living—enough disembodied abstractions to fill five stanzas. Peeping through a keyhole, Douglas has his vision of Honour, 'ane God omnipotent, On quhais glorious visage as I blent In extasie, be his brichtnes atanis He smote me doun, and brissit all my banis'. To Honour's palace there is but one perfect, sure way, the way of virtue; but off the last narrow bridge Douglas slips and falls; he wakes, and the vision ends.

The poem has more to offer than ornamental flourishes, though here, more than elsewhere, Douglas displays his facility with aureate diction, the dulce, mellifluate, flowered, redolent rhetoric that impedes so many readers of sixteenth-century Scottish poetry. Douglas speaks of his 'rurall termis rude', but he manipulates to his purpose a difficult stanza (nine lines with but two rimes, as in *skatterit, batterit, odious, swatterit, tatterit, vennemous, contagious, clatterit, sulphurious*), and can even marshal his vocabulary in complicated internal rime:

> Haill rois maist chois till clois thy fois greit micht,
> Haill stone quhilk schone upon the throne of licht,
> Vertew, quhais trew sweit dew ovirthrew al vice,
> Was ay ilk day gar say the way of licht;
> Amend, offend, and send our end ay richt.

The lists become oppressive: poets, virtuous Greeks, the terms of music, the terms of architecture are displayed with pointless erudition—or is it the author's pleasure to fit as many items as possible into his rimes to display his virtuosity? He is enchanted with his own skill, and his enthusiasm is enough to carry the reader through most of the poem. But beyond the decorative skill, the poet shows flashes of wit, and finally rises to modest heights of philosophic vision.

Douglas must be regarded, then, as a competent poet in his own right—beyond this as a great translator. He had doubts about Scots, for it had not been dignified by age and use as Latin had. But he faced the difficulty of language with individuality and vigour, asserting the rightness of Scots as it was right for Virgil to use Latin, and aiming at a vitality unrestrained by the stately decorum of Neo-classicism. History on the whole has been kind to his reputation, and it would be an error in taste to find now nothing in his work except an archaic level of sensibility. His *Aeneid* differs from Virgil's, being less sensuous and melodic, more spirited and lively, and, above all, more nautical. But if the reader can accustom himself to the curiosities of Scottish orthography, then he may find here the most satisfying translation of the Latin original.

BIOGRAPHICAL NOTE

NEITHER the place nor the date of Gavin Douglas's birth is certain, but he probably was born in the eastern Lowlands in 1474 or 1475. He was the third son of Archibald, fifth Earl of Angus, called 'Bell-the-Cat' because he, unlike the timid mice of the fable, was willing to take personal action against authority. Douglas entered St. Andrews University in 1490 and became Master of Arts in 1494; thereafter he probably studied in Paris; and he may have studied abroad from 1505 to 1509. From 1497 on his name appears frequently in the public records as a contender for the benefices and political power that befitted the younger son of a powerful family.

The battle of Flodden, in 1513, with its massive slaughter of the Scottish aristocracy, worked to Douglas's political advantage. On 6 August 1514 the widowed queen of James IV married Alexander, sixth Earl of Angus, Douglas's nephew. At the solicitation of her new husband, she advanced Douglas's interest, appealing unsuccessfully to Leo X for his appointment to the Archbishopric of St. Andrews in 1514, and contriving his elevation to the See of Dunkeld in 1515. In this same year, however, in the give and take of politics, the regent Albany won a temporary victory that forced the Queen to take refuge with her brother Henry VIII, and Douglas was vindictively imprisoned on the charge of unlicensed purchase of benefices at Rome. He was therefore not admitted to the temporalities of his diocese until September 1516. In 1521 the Queen fell out of love with her husband, who thereupon sent Douglas to plead his cause at the English court. Much in disfavour with the Queen, Douglas died an exile in England shortly before 19 September 1522.

The last quarter of his life was almost exclusively concerned with politics, secular and ecclesiastical. It appears that all of his poetry was written by 1513, at which time he says (in the 'Conclusio' to the *Aeneid*) he hung up his pen and ended youthful occupations. He completed his translation 'Apon the fest of Mary Magdalen', i.e. 22 July 1513, having worked on it for eighteen months. At the end of the Twelfth Book he mentions his other works: the *Palice of Honour* and something mysteriously called 'Of Lundeys Lufe the Remeid'. This has been taken as an error for 'Ovideis Lufe the Remeid', that is, Ovid's *Remedia Amoris*; but this seems most unlikely, for in the 'Direction of the Book' at the end of Book XIII Douglas challenges his critics to attempt a labour as long as his, 'And translait Ovid, as I have Virgill', which he would scarcely say if he had already translated Ovid himself. *King Hart* was probably not composed by Douglas.[1] He did write the short poem 'Conscience', a bad pun unworthy of much attention. In John Small's edition of his works a considerable part of his political correspondence is reproduced.

[1] Cf. Priscilla Preston in *Medium Ævum*, xxviii (1959), pp. 31–47, and Florence H. Ridley in *Speculum*, xxxiv (1959), pp. 402–12.

A NOTE ON THE TEXT

THE manuscripts and editions of the *Aeneid*, omitting incomplete texts, are as follows:

The Cambridge MS., the property of Trinity College, Cambridge, is probably the earliest, *c.* 1515, and is the copy 'nixt efter the translation', made by Douglas's secretary, and annotated, perhaps in Douglas's own hand.

The Elphinstoun MS., in the library of the University of Edinburgh, probably should be placed between 1515 and 1520.

The Ruthven MS., also in the Library of the University of Edinburgh, is probably contemporaneous with the Elphinstoun.

The Lambeth MS., in the library of Lambeth Palace, is dated in a colophon 1545.

The Bath MS., belonging to the Marquis of Bath, is dated 1547.

The 1553 black-letter edition was published at London by William Copland. It is remarkable for its inaccuracies and for its occasional Protestant revisions.

Thomas Ruddiman published the first modern edition in 1710. The first forty-five pages are based on the 1553 edition, the rest on the Ruthven MS.

In 1839 Andrew Rutherford and George Dundas presented their two-volume edition to the Bannatyne Club. It is an accurate copy of the Cambridge MS., without introduction or notes.

John Small prepared the first complete edition of Douglas's poetry, *The Poetical Works of Gavin Douglas, Bishop of Dunkeld, With Memoir, Notes and Glossary*, Edinburgh, 1874, in four volumes. His text of the *Aeneid* is based on the Elphinstoun MS.

The present text is based on the edition prepared for the Scottish Text Society. It is a copy of the Cambridge MS., with the following exceptions:

(1) punctuation and capitalization follow modern usage;
(2) obvious slips are corrected;

(3) abbreviations are expanded without comment;

(4) *v*'s, *u*'s, *w*'s, *i*'s, and *j*'s are ordinarily adjusted to modern spelling;

(5) ß is printed as *s*, and ȝ as *y*.

Of the *Palice of Honour*, several editions were published in the sixteenth century, although only a fragment survives of the earliest known—that printed by Thomas Davidson and usually dated *c.* 1540. Of the two sixteenth-century editions extant, the first, printed by William Copland *c.* 1553, is inferior to the later Scottish one, printed by John Ross in 1579. The text of the extracts is derived from the copy of the Ross edition now in the National Library of Scotland (R), but incorporates a number of readings from Copland (C), recorded in the Notes.

The selections from the *Palice of Honour* were prepared and annotated by Priscilla Preston. Part of the work on the *Aeneid* was done in the leisure of a research fellowship given by the Danforth Foundation.

D.F.C.C.

APPRECIATIONS

THE translation is executed with equal spirit and fidelity; and is a proof that the lowland Scotch and English languages were now nearly the same: I mean the style of composition; more especially in the glaring affectation of anglicising Latin words. The several books are introduced with metrical prologues, which are often highly poetical; and show that Douglas's proper walk was original poetry. In the prologue to the sixth book, he wishes for the Sybill's golden bough, to enable him to follow his master Virgil through the dark and dangerous labyrinth of the infernal regions. But the most conspicuous of these prologues is a description of May, the greater part of which I will insert. . . . [Prol. XII. 13–264]

The poetical beauties of this specimen will be relished by every reader who is fond of lively touches of fancy, and rural imagery. But the verses will have another merit with those critics who love to contemplate the progress of composition, and to mark the original workings of genuine nature; as they are the effusion of a mind not overlaid by the descriptions of other poets but operating, by its own force and bias, in the delineation of a vernal landscape, on such objects as really occurred.

THOMAS WARTON
The History of English Poetry (1774–81)

NOBODY can deny that the good Bishop of Dunkeld (uneasiest to him of bishop-stools!) not only would have liked to be a critic, but shows both his critical and his Renaissance sides in the well-known and violent onslaught on poor Caxton in the first of the very agreeable Prologues to his own translation of the *Æneid*. In fact, those to whom the woman who killed Abimelech with a stone or slate is the patron saint of criticism, must regard him as a very considerable critic. How Caxton's work and Virgil's are 'no more like than the Devil and Saint Austin'; how the author 'shamefully perverted' the story; how the critic read it 'with harms at his heart' that such a book 'without sentence or engine' should be entitled after so divine a bard; how such a wight never knew three words of what Virgil meant; how he, Gavin, is 'constrained to flyte',—all this is extremely familiar. We seem to hear the very voice of the modern 'jacket-duster', of the man who finds his pet task anticipated, his pet subject trespassed upon, and is determined to make the varlet pay for it. Douglas, to be sure, is not quite in the worst case of this class of critic. He can render some reasons, neither garbled nor forged, for his censure. He has (and this is a sign that criticism was stirring) lost taste for, lost even comprehension of, the full, guileless, innocent, medieval licence of suppression, suggestion, and digression. He protests (quite truly) that Neptune did not join with Æolus in causing the storm that endangered Æneas, but on the contrary stilled that storm. He is indignant at the extension given to the true romantic part of the poem, the Tragedy of Carthage in the Fourth Book, and only less indignant at the suppression of the 'lusty games' and plays palustral in the Fifth. Most of all does he tell us of that aggravation of the critical misuse of allegory which was to be one of the main Renaissance notes. The 'hidden meaning' of poetry is the great thing for Douglas, and he has much to say about it before he 'turns again' on Caxton. Will it be believed that Caxton wrote 'Touyr for Tiber'! Alas! alas!

> For Touyr divides Greece from Hungarie,
> And Tiber is chief fluide of Italy.

But all this, and a great deal more like it, as the setting up of the old Rhetoric-Poetic theory of a poem as the story of a perfectly noble character, and the rebuke even to Chaucer not merely for being too literal, just as Caxton was too loose, but for actually saying (the more Chaucer he!) that Æneas was *not* a perfectly noble character but a forsworn traitor,—all this argues no real relinquishment of the medieval ideal except in a special case. Douglas shows in his own work that he is after all a chip of the old block, and not fresh hewn from a virgin quarry.

GEORGE SAINTSBURY
A History of Criticism and Literary Taste in Europe (1900)

When Douglas speaks of the Salii 'hoppand and singand wonder merely' in their 'toppit hattis' it is easy to remember that 'top hats', in our sense, were unknown to him. But it is not so easy to see aright the real qualities of his Scots language in general. Since his time it has become a *patois*, redolent (for those reared in Scotland) of the nursery and the kaleyard, and (for the rest of us) recalling Burns and the dialectal parts of the Waverley novels. Hence the laughter to which some readers will be moved when Douglas calls Leucaspis a 'skippair', or Priam 'the auld gray', or Vulcan the 'gudeman' of Venus; when *comes* becomes 'trew marrow' and Styx, like Yarrow, has 'braes', when the Trojans 'kecklit all' (*risere*) at the man thrown overboard in the boat race, or, newly landed in Latium, regaled themselves with 'scones'. For we see the language that Douglas wrote 'through the wrong end of the long telescope of time'. We forget that in his day it was a courtly and literary language,

> not made for village churls
> But for high dames and mighty earls.

Until we have trained ourselves to feel that 'gudeman' is no more rustic or homely than 'husband' we are no judges of Douglas as a translator of Virgil. If we fail in the training, then it is we and not the poet who are provincials.

About this first mental adjustment there can be no dispute; but there is another adjustment which I think necessary and which may not be so easily agreed to. Virgil describes Aeneas, on hearing Turnus's challenge, as *laetitia exsultans*; Douglas says 'he hoppit up for joy, he was so glad'. To get over the low associations of the verb 'hop' in modern English is the first adjustment. But even when this has been done, there remains something—a certain cheerful briskness—in Douglas which may seem to us very un-Virgilian. Here is another example; Virgil writes:

> Quamvis increpitent socii et vi cursus in altum
> Vela vocet, possisque sinus implere secundos. (iii. 454.)

Douglas translates:

> Ya, thocht thi fallowis cry out, Hillir haill!
> On burd! ane fair wind blawis betwix twa schetis!

It is admirably vivid; but it sounds very unlike the Virgil we knew at school. Let us suspend judgement and try another passage.

lumenque juventae
Purpureum et laetos oculis adflarat honores. (i. 590.)

Douglas says that Aeneas' mother made him 'Lyk till ane yonkeir with twa lauchand ene'. The picture is fresh and attractive; yet somehow unlike the Aeneas of our imagination. But is that because Virgil has never said anything about the beauty of Aeneas, both here and in other places? On the contrary, Virgil quite clearly has told us that his hero was of godlike beauty. There has been something in our minds, but not in the mind of Douglas, which dimmed the picture; our idea of the great king and warrior and founder apparently shrinks (as Virgil's and Douglas's did not) from the delighted vision of male beauty. Douglas shocks us by being closer to Virgil than we. . . . Time after time Douglas is nearer to the original than any version could be which kept within the limits of later classicism. And that is almost another way of saying that the real Virgil is very much less 'classical' than we had supposed. To read the Latin again with Douglas's version fresh in our minds is like seeing a favourite picture after it has been cleaned. Half the 'richness' and 'sobriety' which we have been taught to admire turns out to have been only dirt; the 'brown trees' disappear and where the sponge has passed the glowing reds, the purples, and the transparent blues leap into life.

C. S. LEWIS
English Literature in the Sixteenth Century (1954)

THAT Douglas's *Aeneid* (finished in 1513) is one of the great translations is undoubted; but there may be now the danger of making too much of it. When Ezra Pound calls it better than its original,[*] we need not take him seriously. But when he couples Douglas with Chaucer as the two medieval poets writing in English who matter most and illustrates abundantly,[†] it is time to reflect and ask questions. There are splendid things in the passages

[*] *How to Read* (London 1931) 45.   [†] *ABC of Reading* (London 1934) 101 ff.

Pound quotes, and there are splendid things all through Douglas's *Aeneid*. But what of the whole poem? Many people have read the original *Aeneid* from beginning to end with pleasure. Some people may have read Douglas's *Aeneid* right through with pleasure in his own day. But how many of those who have praised it recently have read and enjoyed the whole? The knottiness of Douglas's language, admirably effective for certain passages and in small doses, does not make for intelligible narrative and wearies the reader after a few hundred lines. Douglas's prosody, admirably expressive in some passages, often collapses into incoherence; leaving the reader doubtful how to read lines, and having no particular point on any reading. One need go no further than one of the passages anthologised by Pound, for illustrations. It comes from the description of the storm at the opening of Book One.

> *With the cloudis hevynnys son and dayis lycht*
> *Hid and brest out of the Troianis sycht;*
> *Derknes as nycht beset the see about,*
> *The firmament gan rumyllyng rare and rout.*
> *The skyis oft lychtned with fyry leven;*
> *And schortlie baith are see and hevyn;*
> *And every thyng manissis the men to de*
> *Schewand the dede present before thare E.*

There is a good deal of noise and violence here, but it is not especially appropriate. The wrenched rhythm of 'Hid and brest' at the beginning of line two has no special point. The rumbling alliteration in the fourth line is crude and poetically elementary. How did Douglas mean us to read the fourth and fifth lines: do they form a decasyllabic or octosyllabic couplet? should we accent them thus.

> *The skýis óft lýchtned with fýry léven;*
> *And schórtlíe báith are* ★ *sée and hévyn,*

or thus,

> *The skýis oft lýchtned with fýry léven,*
> *And schórtlie báith are sée and hévyn?*

The first accentuation supplies an unpleasantly halting and quite inept rhythm; the second a lilt and a speed out of keeping with

★ [the 'ayr' of the Cambridge MS. seems to require an accent—D. F. C. C.]

APPRECIATIONS

the rest of the passage. I can only agree with Saintsbury's comment* on Douglas's Alexandrines: that they are entirely legitimate if he intended them as such; but that you cannot be certain that he did. Douglas's weakness is cruelly conspicuous if you set his lines against their Latin original:

> Eripiunt subito nubes caelumque diemque
> Teucrorum ex oculis; ponto nox incubat atra.
> intonuere poli et crebris micat ignibus aether,
> praesentemque viris intentant omnia mortem.†

Here rhythmically every detail stands out clear and startling; and with the terrifying clarity in which perilous things are seen by those who experience them. . . .

In spite of these weaknesses Douglas's *Aeneid* is a very distinguished work, probably the best translation of one of the great epics till Dryden and Pope. It is permeated throughout, even if spasmodically, with passion, and a passion which, different from the Virgilian, gives the work a character. Virgil can deal with quick and violent action surpassingly well, but it is not his special and central concern. Douglas has the keenest sense for close and rapid action. He pictures happenings so vividly that he constantly adds particular strokes that are missing in Virgil. Often when he appears to err by breaking the taut, packed, yet exquisite quality of his original, he compensates by infusing his own special vigour through greater amplitude and circumstantiation.

E. M. W. TILLYARD
The English Epic and its Background (1954)

* George Saintsbury, *A History of English Prosody* (London 1906), i. 275.
† *Aeneid*, i. 88–91. 'Suddenly the clouds snatch away sky and daylight from the Trojans' eyes; black night settles on the sea. The poles of heaven thunder and the upper air flashes with many fires. Everything threatens the men with instant death.'

THE AENEID
BOOK I

Incipit Prologus in Virgilii Eneados

LAWD, honour, praysyngis, thankis infynyte
To the and thy dulce ornat fresch endyte,
Maist reverend Virgill, of Latyn poetis prynce,
Gem of engyne and flude of eloquens,
Thow peirles perle, patroun of poetry,   5
Roys, regester, palm, lawrer and glory,
Chosyn charbukkill, cheif flour and cedyr tre,
Lantarn, laid stern, myrrour and A per se,
Maister of masteris, sweit sours and spryngand well
Wyde quhar our all rung is thyne hevynly bell—   10
I meyn thy crafty warkis curyus
Sa quyk, lusty and maist sentencyus,
Plesand, perfyte and feilabill in all degre,
As quha the mater beheld tofor thar e,
In every volume quhilk the lyst do wryte   15
Surmontyng fer all other maner endyte,
Lyke as the roys in June with hir sweit smell
The maryguld or dasy doith excell.
Quhy suld I than with dull forhed and vayn,
With rude engyne and barrand emptyve brayn,   20
With bad, harsk spech and lewit barbour tong
Presume to write quhar thy sweit bell is rung
Or contyrfate sa precyus wordys deir?
Na, na, noth swa, but kneill quhen I thame heir.
For quhat compair betwix mydday and nycht?   25
Or quhat compair betwix myrknes and lycht?
Or quhat compar is betwix blak and quhyte?
Far grettar difference betwix my blunt endyte
And thy scharp sugurate sang Virgiliane,
Sa wysly wrocht with nevir a word invane.   30

My waverand wyt, my cunnyng febill at all,
My mynd mysty, thir may nocht mys a fall—
Stra for thys ignorant blabryng imperfyte
Besyde thy polyst termys redymyte.
And netheles with support and correctioun,   35
For naturall lufe and frendely affectioun
Quhilkis I beir to thy warkis and endyte—
All thocht God wait tharin I knaw full lyte—
And that thy facund sentence mycht be song
In our langage alsweill as Latyn tong—   40
Alsweill? na, na, impossibill war, per de—
Yit with thy leif, Virgile, to follow the,
I wald into my rurall vulgar gros
Wryte sum savoryng of thyne Eneados.
But sair I dreid forto disteyn the quyte   45
Throu my corruppit cadens imperfyte—
Disteyn the? nay forsuyth, that may I nocht;
Weill may I schaw my burall bustuus thocht
Bot thy wark sall endur in lawd and glory
But spot or falt condyng etern memory.   50
Thocht I offend, onwemmyt is thy fame;
Thyne is the thank and myne salbe the schame.
Quha may thy versis follow in all degre
In bewtie, sentence and in gravite?
Nane is, nor was, ne yit salbe, trow I,   55
Had, has or sal have sic craft in poetry.
Of Helicon so drank thou dry the flude
That of thy copios fouth or plenitude
All mon purches drynk at thy sugurit tun;
So lamp of day thou art and schynand son   60
All otheris on fors mon thar lycht beg or borrow;
Thou art Vesper and the day stern at morow,
Thow Phebus lightnar of the planetis all—
I not quhat dewly I the clepe sall,
For thou art all and sum, quhat nedis more,   65
Of Latyn poetis that sens was, or befor.
Of the writis Macrobius sans faill
In hys gret volume clepit Saturnaill.

2

Thy sawys in sic eloquens doith fleit,
So inventive of rethorik flowris sweit   70
Thou art, and has so hie profund sentens
Tharto, perfyte but ony indigens,
That na lovyngis ma do incres thy fame,
Nor na reproche dymynew thy gud name.
Bot sen I am compellit the to translait,   75
And not only of my curage, God wait,
Durst interprys syk owtrageus foly,
Quhar I offend the les reprefe serve I;
And that ye knaw at quhais instans I tuke
Forto translait this maist excellent buke,   80
I meyn Virgillis volume maist excellent,
Set this my wark full febill be of rent,
At the request of a lord of renown
Of ancistry nobill and illustir baroun,
Fader of bukis, protectour to sciens and lair,   85
My speciall gud Lord Henry, Lord Sanct Clair,
Quhilk with gret instance divers tymys seir
Prayt me translait Virgill or Homeir,
Quhais plesour suythly as I undirstude
As neir conjunct to hys lordschip in blude   90
So that me thocht hys request ane command,
Half disparit this wark I tuke on hand
Nocht fully grantand nor anys sayand yee,
Bot only to assay quhou it mycht be.
Quha mycht gaynsay a lord so gentill and kynd   95
That ever had ony curtasy in thar mynd,
Quhilk besyde hys innatyve pollecy,
Humanyte, curage, fredome and chevalry,
Bukis to recollect, to reid and se,
Has gret delyte as ever had Ptholome?   100
Quharfor to hys nobilite and estait,
Quhat so it be, this buke I dedicait,
Writtin in the langage of Scottis natioun,
And thus I mak my protestatioun:
Fyrst I protest, beaw schirris, be your leif,   105
Beis weill avisit my wark or yhe repreif,

3

Consider it warly, reid oftar than anys;
Weill at a blenk sle poetry nocht tayn is,
And yit forsuyth I set my bissy pane
As that I couth to mak it braid and plane,   110
Kepand na sudron bot our awyn langage,
And spekis as I lernyt quhen I was page.
Nor yit sa cleyn all sudron I refus,
Bot sum word I pronunce as nyghtbouris doys:
Lyke as in Latyn beyn Grew termys sum,   115
So me behufyt quhilum or than be dum
Sum bastard Latyn, French or Inglys oys
Quhar scant was Scottis—I had nane other choys.
Nocht for our tong is in the selvyn skant
Bot for that I the fowth of langage want   120
Quhar as the cullour of his properte
To kepe the sentens tharto constrenyt me,
Or than to mak my sayng schort sum tyme,
Mair compendyus, or to lykly my ryme.
Tharfor, gude frendis, for a gymp or a bourd,   125
I pray you note me nocht at every word.
The worthy clerk hecht Lawrens of the Vaill,
Amang Latynys a gret patron sans faill,
Grantis quhen twelf yheris he had beyn diligent
To study Virgill, skant knew quhat he ment.   130
Than thou or I, my frend, quhen we best weyn
To have Virgile red, understand and seyn,
The rycht sentens perchance is fer to seik.
This wark twelf yheris first was in makyng eyk
And nocht correct quhen the poet gan deces;   135
Thus for small faltis, my wys frend, hald thy pes.
    Adherdand to my protestatioun,
Thocht Wilyame Caxtoun, of Inglis natioun,
In proys hes prent ane buke of Inglys gros,
Clepand it Virgill in Eneados,   140
Quhilk that he says of Franch he dyd translait,
It has na thing ado tharwith, God wait,
Ne na mair lyke than the devill and Sanct Austyne.
Have he na thank tharfor, bot loys hys pyne,

4

So schamefully that story dyd pervert.   145
I red his wark with harmys at my hart,
That syk a buke but sentens or engyne
Suldbe intitillit eftir the poet dyvyne;
Hys ornate goldyn versis mair than gilt
I spittit for dispyte to se swa spilt   150
With sych a wyght, quhilk trewly be myne entent
Knew never thre wordis at all quhat Virgill ment—
Sa fer he chowpis I am constrenyt to flyte.
The thre first bukis he has ourhippyt quyte
Salfand a litill twychyng Polidorus   155
And the tempest furth sent by Eolus,
And that full sempilly on hys awyn gys;
Virgill thame wrait all on ane other wys,
For Caxton puttis in hys buke owt of toyn
The storm furth sent by Eolus and Neptune,   160
Bot quha sa redis Virgill suythfastly
Sall fynd Neptune salf Eneas navy.
Me lyst nocht schaw quhou thystory of Dydo
Be this Caxtoun is haill pervertit so
That, besyde quhar he fenys to follow Bocas,   165
He rynnys sa fer from Virgill in mony place,
On sa prolixt and tedyus fasson,
So that the ferd buke of Eneadon,
Twichand the lufe and ded of Dido queyn,
The twa part of his volume doith conteyn   170
That in the text of Virgill, trastis me,
The twelt part scars contenys, as ye may se.
The fyfte buke of the festis funerall,
The lusty gamys and plays palustrall,
That is ourhippit quyte and left behynd—   175
Na thing tharof yhe sall in Caxtoun fynd.
The saxt buke eyk, he grantis, that wantis haill,
And, for tharof he understude nocht the taill,
He callis it fenyeit and nocht forto beleif;
Sa is all Virgill perchans, for by hys leif   180
Juno nor Venus goddessis never wer,
Mercur, Neptune, Mars nor Jupiter;

5

Of Fortune eik nor hir necessite,
Sik thingis nocht attentik ar, wait we,
Nor yit admittis that quent philosophy   185
Haldis sawlys hoppys fra body to body,
And mony thingis quhilkis Virgill dyd rehers,
Thocht I thame write furthfollowand hys vers.
Nor Caxtoun schrynkis nocht siclyke thingis to tell
As nocht war fabill bot the passage to hell,   190
Bot trastis weill, quha that ilke saxt buke knew,
Virgill tharin ane hie philosophour hym schew,
And under the clowdis of dyrk poecy
Hyd lyis thar mony notabill history—
For so the poetis be the crafty curys   195
In similitudes and undir quent figuris
The suythfast materis to hyde and to constreyn;
All is nocht fals, traste weill, in cace thai feyn.
Thar art is so to mak thar warkis fair,
As in the end of Virgill I sall declair.   200
Was it nocht eik als possibill Eneas
As Hercules or Theseus tyll hell to pas,
Quhilk is na gabbyng suythly nor na lie,
As Jhone Bocas in the Genealogie
Of Goddys declarys, and lyke as yhe may reid   205
In the Recolles of Troy, quha lest tak hed.
Quha wait gyf he in visioun thydder went
By art magike, socery or enchantment,
And with hys fader sawle dyd speke and meyt,
Or in the lyknes with sum other spreit,   210
Lyke as the spreit of Samuell, I ges,
Raysit to Kyng Saul was by the Phitones?
I will nocht say all Virgill beyn als trew
Bot at syk thyngis ar possibill, this I schew.
Als in tha days war ma illusionys   215
By devillich warkis and conjurations
Than now thar beyn, so doith clerkis determ,
For, blissit be God, the faith is now mair ferm.
Enewch tharof; now will I na mor sayn
Bot onto Caxtoun thus I turn agane.   220

The namys of pepill or citeis beyn so bad
Put by this Caxtoun that, bot he had beyn mad,
The flude of Tovyr for Tibir he had nocht write:
All men may knaw thar he forvayt quyte.
Palente the cite of Evander kyng,   225
As Virgill playnly makis rehersyng,
Stude quhar in Rome now stant the cheif palyce;
This sam buke eyk in mair hepit malyce
On the self ryver of Tovyr says playnly
Eneas dyd hys cyte edify.   230
Thus ay for Tibir Tovyr puttis he,
Quhilk mony hundreth mylis syndry be,
For sykkyrly, les than wys authoris leyn,
Ene saw nevir Tovyr with hys eyn,
For Tovyr dividis Grece from Ungary   235
And Tibir is cheif flude of Italy,
Tovyr is kend a grayn of that ryver
In Latyn hecht Danubium or Hyster—
Or gyf it be Tanais he clepis sa,
That flude dividis Europ from Asia.   240
In lyke wys eik this Caxtoun all invane
Crispina clepis Sibilla Cumane,
That in the text of Virgill, trastis us,
Hait Deiphebe, douchtir of Glawcus,
Quhilk was Eneas convoyar to hell.   245
Quhat suld I langar on hys errouris dwell?
Thai beyn so playn and eik sa monyfald
The hundreth part tharof I leif ontald.
The last sax bukis of Virgill all inferis,
Quhilk contenys strang batalis and werys,   250
This ilk Caxtoun so blaitly lattis ourslip
I hald my tung for schame, bytand my lyp.
The gret afferis of athir host and array,
The armour of Eneas, fresch and gay,
The quent and curyus castis poeticall,   255
Perfyte symylitudis and exemplis all
Quharin Virgill beris the palm of lawd,
Caxtoun, for dreid thai suld hys lippis scald,

7

Durst nevir twich. Thus schortly for the nanys
A twenty devill way fall hys wark atanys,   260
Quhilk is na mair lyke Virgill, dar I lay,
Than the nycht owle resemblis the papyngay.
Quharfor, you gentill redaris, I besich
Traste on na wys at this my wark be sich,
Quhilk dyd my best, as the wyt mycht atteyn,   265
Virgillis versys to follow and no thing feyn.
Yhe worthy noblys, redis my wark for thy
And cast this other buke on syde far by,
Quhilk undir cullour of sum strange Franch wycht
So Franchly leys, oneith twa wordis gais rycht.   270
I nold yhe trast I said this for dispyte,
For me lyst with nane Inglis bukis flyte,
Na with na bogill nor browny to debait,
Nowder ald gaistis nor spretis ded of lait,
Nor na man will I lakkyn nor dispys   275
My warkis till authorys be sik wys;
Bot twichyng Virgillis honour and reverens,
Quha ever contrary, I mon stand at defens;
And bot my buke be fundyn worth sik thre
Quhen it is red, do warp it in the see,   280
Thraw it in the fyre or rent it every crum.
Twichand that part, lo, heir is all and sum.
    Syne I defend and forbiddis every wight
That can nocht spell thar Pater Noster rycht
Fortill correct or yit amend Virgill,   285
Or the translatar blame in hys vulgar stile;
I knaw quhat payn was to follow hym fut hait
Albeit thou think my sayng intricate.
Traste weill to follow a fixt sentens or mater
Is mair practike, deficill and far strater,   290
Thocht thyne engyne beyn elevate and hie,
Than forto write all ways at liberte.
Gif I had nocht be to a boundis constrenyt,
Of my bad wyt perchance I couth have fenyt
In ryme a ragment twys als curyus,   295
Bot nocht be twenty part so sentencyus.

Quha is attachit ontill a staik, we se,
May go na ferthir bot wreil about that tre:
Rycht so am I to Virgillis text ybund,
I may nocht fle les than my falt be fund,   300
For thocht I wald transcend and go besyde,
Hys wark remanys, my schame I may nocht hyde.
And thus I am constrenyt als neir I may
To hald hys vers and go nane other way,
Les sum history, subtell word or the ryme   305
Causith me mak digressioun sum tyme.
So thocht in my translatioun eloquens skant is,
Na lusty cast of oratry Virgill wantis;
My studyus brayn to comprehend his sentens
Leit me nevir taist hys flude of eloquens.   310
And thus forsuyth becaus I was nocht fre,
My werk is mair obscur and gros, per de,
Quharof, God wait, Virgill has na wyte—
Thocht myne be blunt, hys text is maist perfyte.
And yit persave I weill, be my consait   315
The kyng of poetis ganys nocht for rurall estait
Nor hys fresch memor for bowbardis; he or scho
Quha takis me nocht, go quhar thai have ado—
The sonnys lycht is never the wers, traste me,
All thocht the bak hys brycht bemys doith fle.   320
Greyn gentill ingynys and breistis curageus,
Sik ar the pepill at ganys best for us;
Our werk desiris na lewyt rebalddaill,
Full of nobilite is thistory all haill.
For every vertu belangand a nobill man   325
This ornate poet bettir than ony can
Payntand discryvis in person of Eneas—
Not forto say sikane Eneas was,
Yit than by hym perfytely blasons he
All wirschip, manhed and nobilite,   330
With every bonte belangand a gentill wycht,
Ane prynce, ane conquerour or a valyeand knycht.
In luffis cuyr eneuch heir sall yhe fynd,
And schortly, Virgill left na thing behynd

9

That mycht hys volume illummyn or crafty mak.   335
Reid quha hym knawys, I dar this undertak,
Als oft as ye hym reid, full weill I wait,
Yhe fynd ilke tyme sum mery new consait.
   Thoght venerabill Chauser, principal poet but peir,
Hevynly trumpat, orlege and reguler,   340
In eloquens balmy, cundyt and dyall,
Mylky fontane, cleir strand and roys ryall,
Of fresch endyte, throu Albion iland braid,
In hys legend of notabill ladeis said
That he couth follow word by word Virgill,   345
Wisar than I may faill in lakar stile.
Sum tyme the text mon have ane expositioun,
Sum tyme the collour will caus a litill additioun,
And sum tyme of a word I mon mak thre,
In witnes of this term 'oppetere'.   350
Eik weill I wait syndry expositouris seir
Makis on a text sentens divers to heir,
As thame apperis, accordyng thar entent,
And for thar part schawis ressonys evident.
All this is ganand, I will weill it swa be,   355
Bot a sentens to follow may suffice me.
Sum tyme I follow the text als neir I may,
Sum tyme I am constrenyt ane other way.
Besyde Latyn our langage is imperfite
Quhilk in sum part is the caus and the wyte   360
Quhy that of Virgillis vers the ornate bewte
Intill our tung may nocht observyt be,
For thar be Latyn wordis mony ane
That in our leyd ganand translatioun has nane
Less than we mynys thar sentens and gravyte   365
And yit scant weill exponyt. Quha trewys nocht me,
Lat thame interprit 'animal' and 'homo'
With many hundreth other termys mo
Quhilkis in our langage suythly as I weyn
Few men can tell me cleirly quhat thai meyn.   370
Betweyn 'genus', 'sexus' and 'species'
Diversyte in our leid to seik I ces.

For 'objectum' or 'subjectum' alsswa
He war expert couth fynd me termys twa,
Quhilkis ar als ryfe amangis clerkis in scuyll   375
As evir fowlis plungit in laik or puyll.
Logicianys knawys heirin myne entent,
Undir quhais boundis lurkis mony strange went
Quharof the proces as now we mon lat be.
Bot yit twychyng our tungis penuryte,   380
I meyn into compar of fair Latyn
That knawyn is maste perfite langage fyne,
I mycht also percace cum lyddir speid
For 'arbor' and 'lignum' intill our leid
To fynd different proper termys twane   385
And tharto put circumlocutioun nane.
Richt so by aboutspech oftyn tymys
And semabill wordis we compile our rymys.
God wait, in Virgill ar termys mony a hundir
Fortill expone maid me a felloun blundir.   390
To follow alanerly Virgilis wordis, I weyn,
Thar suld few undirstand me quhat thai meyn.
The bewte of his ornate eloquens
May nocht al tyme be kepit with the sentens.
Sanct Gregor eik forbyddis us to translait   395
Word eftir word bot sentence follow algait:
'Quha haldis,' quod he, 'of wordis the properteis
Full oft the verite of the sentens fleys.'
And to the sammyn purpos we may apply
Horatius in hys Art of Poetry: 400
'Pres nocht,' says he, 'thou traste interpreter,
Word eftir word to translait thi mater.'
Lo, he reprevis and haldis myssemyng
Ay word by word to reduce ony thing.
I say nocht this of Chauser for offens,   405
Bot till excus my lewyt insufficiens,
For as he standis beneth Virgill in gre,
Undir hym alsfer I grant my self to be.
And netheles into sum place, quha kend it,
My mastir Chauser gretly Virgill offendit.   410

II

All thoch I be tobald hym to repreif,
He was fer baldar, certis, by hys leif,
Sayand he followit Virgillis lantern toforn,
Quhou Eneas to Dydo was forsworn.
Was he forsworn? Than Eneas was fals—   415
That he admittis and callys hym traytour als.
Thus, wenyng allane Ene to have reprevit,
He has gretly the prynce of poetis grevit,
For, as said is, Virgill dyd diligens
But spot of cryme, reproch or ony offens   420
Eneas for to loif and magnyfy,
And gif he grantis hym maynsworn fowlely,
Than all hys cuyr and crafty engyne gais quyte,
Hys twelf yheris laubouris war nocht worth a myte.
Certis Virgill schawys Ene dyd na thing   425
From Dydo of Cartage at hys departyng
Bot quhilk the goddis commandit hym beforn,
And gif that thar command maid hym maynsworn,
That war repreif to thar divinyte
And na reproch onto the said Enee.   430
Als in the first, quhar Ilioneus
Spekis to the queyn Dido, says he nocht thus,
Thar curs by fait was set tyll Italy?
Thus mycht scho not pretend na just caus quhy
Thocht Trojanys eftir departis of Cartage,   435
Sen thai befor declaryt hir thar vayage.
Reid the ferd buke quhar Queyn Dido is wraith,
Thar sal yhe fynd Ene maid nevir aith,
Promyt nor band with hir fortill abyde:
Thus hym tobe maynsworn may nevir betyde,   440
Nor nane onkyndnes schew forto depart
At the bydding of Jove with reuthfull hart,
Sen the command of God obey suld all
And undir his charge na wrangwys deid may fall.
    Bot sikkyrly of resson me behufis   445
Excus Chauser fra all maner repruffis:
In lovyng of thir ladeis lylly quhite
He set on Virgill and Eneas this wyte,

                        12

For he was evir (God wait) all womanis frend.
I say na mair, but, gentil redaris heynd,   450
Lat all my faltis with this offens pas by.
Thou prynce of poetis, I the mercy cry,
I meyn thou Kyng of Kyngis, Lord Etern,
Thou be my muse, my gydar and laid stern,
Remittyng my trespas and every mys   455
Throu prayer of thy Moder, Queyn of Blys.
Afald godhed, ay lestyng but discrepans,
In personys thre, equale, of a substans,
On the I call, and Mary Virgyn myld—
Calliope nor payane goddis wild   460
May do to me na thing bot harm, I weyn:
In Criste is all my traste, and hevynnys queyn.
Thou, Virgyn Moder and Madyn, be my muse,
That nevir yit na synfull lyst refus
Quhilk the besocht devotly for supple.   465
Albeit my sang to thy hie majeste
Accordis nocht, yit condiscend to my write,
For the sweit liqour of thy pappis quhite
Fosterit that Prynce, that hevynly Orpheus,
Grond of all gude, our Salvyour Jhesus.   470
Bot forthirmor, and lawar to discend,
Forgeif me, Virgill, gif I the offend.
Pardon thy scolar, suffir hym to ryme
Sen thou was bot ane mortal man sum tyme.
In cace I faill, have me not at disdenye,   475
Thocht I be lewit, my leill hart can nocht fenye,
I sall the follow; suld I tharfor have blame,
Quha can do bettir, sa furth in Goddis name.
I schrynk nocht anys correkkit for tobe
With ony wight grundit on cherite,   480
And glaidly wald I baith inquire and leir
And till ilke cunnand wight la to myne eyr.
But laith me war but owther offens or cryme
Ane brimell body suld intertrike my ryme.
Thocht sum wald swer that I the text have vareit,   485
Or that I have this volume quyte myscareit,

13

Or threpe playnly that I come nevir neir hand it,
Or at the wark is wers than evir I fand it,
Or yit argue Virgill stude weill befor,
As now war tyme to schift the werst our scor;   490
Ellis have I said thar may be na compar
Betwix his versis and my stile vulgar.
All thocht he stant in Latyn maist perfyte,
Yit stude he nevir weill in our tung endyte
Les than it be by me now at this tyme.   495
Gyf I have falyeit, baldly reprufe my ryme.
Bot first, I pray you, grape the mater cleyn,
Reproche me nocht quhill the wark be ourseyn.
Beis not ourstudyus to spy a moyt in myne e,
That in your awyn a ferry boyt can nocht se,   500
And do to me as yhe wald be done to.
Now hark, schirris, thar is na mair ado;
Quha list attend, gevis audiens and draw neir,
Me thocht Virgill begouth on this maner: . . .

The poet first proponyng hys entent
Declaris Junois wreth and mailtalent.   c. i

THE batalis and the man I wil discrive
Fra Troyis boundis first that fugitive
By fait to Ytail come and cost Lavyne,
Our land and sey katchit with mekil pyne
By fors of goddis abufe, from every steid,   5
Of cruell Juno throu ald remembrit fede.
Gret pane in batail sufferit he alsso
Or he his goddis brocht in Latio
And belt the cite fra quham, of nobill fame,
The Latyne pepill takyn heth thar name,   10
And eik the faderis, princis of Alba,
Cam, and the wallaris of gret Rome alswa.
O thou my muse, declare the causis quhy,
Quhat majeste offendit schaw quham by,
Or yit quharfor of goddis the drery queyn   15
Sa feil dangeris, sik travell maid susteyn

14

A worthy man fulfillit of piete:
Is thare sik greif in hevynly myndis on hie?
   Thare was ane ancyant cite hecht Cartage,
Quham hynys of Tyre held intill heritage,   20
Ennymy to Itail, standand fair and plane
The mouth of lang Tibir our forgane,
Myghty of moblys, full of sculys seyr,
And maist expert in crafty fait of weir,
Of quhilk a land Juno, as it is said,   25
As to hir special abuf al otheris maid;
Hir native land for it postponyt sche
Callit Same—in Cartage sett hir see;
Thar war hir armys and here stude eik hir chair.
This goddes ettillit, gif werdis war nocht contrar,   30
This realme tobe superior and mastres
To all landis, bot certis netheles
The fatale sisteris revolve and schaw, scho kend,
Of Trojane blude a pepill suld discend,
Vailliant in weir, to ryng wydquhar, and syne   35
Cartage suld bryng ontill finale rewyne,
And clene distroy the realme of Lybia.
This dredand Juno, and forthirmor alswa
Remembring on the ancyant mortell weir
That for the Grekis, to hir leif and deir,   40
At Troy lang tyme scho led befor that day
(For yit the causys of wreth war nocht away
Nor cruell harm foryet ne out of mynd—
Ful deip engravyn in hir breist onkynd
The jugement of Parys, quhou that he   45
Preferrit Venus, dispisyng hir bewte;
Als Trojane blude till hir was odyus,
For Jupiter engendrit Dardanus
Fra quham the Trojanys cam in adultry,
And Ganymedes revist abuf the sky,   50
Maid him his butler, quhilk was hir douchteris office),
Juno inflambit, musyng on thir casis nyce
The quhile our sey that salit the Trojanys
Quhilkis had the ded eschapit and remanys

Onslane of Grekis or of the fers Achill,   55
Scho thame fordryvis and causys oft ga will
Frawart Latium, quhilk now is Italy,
By fremmyt werd ful mony yeris tharby
Cachit and blaw wydquhar all seys about.
Lo quhou gret cure, quhat travell, pane and dowt   60
Was to begyn the worthy Romanys blude!

Quhou that Ene was with the tempest schaik
And quhou Neptune his navy salvyt fra wraik.   c. iii

BELIVE Eneas membris schuk for cald,
And murnand baith his handis up did hald
Towart the sternys, with petuus voce thus gan say:
'O sevin tymys quhou happy and blissit war thai
Under hie wallis of Troy, by dynt of swerd,   5
Deit in thar faderis syght, bytand the erd!
O thou of Grekis mast forcy, Diomed,
Quhy mycht I not on feldis of Troy have deit
And by thi rycht hand yaldin forth my sprete
Quhar that the valiant Hectour losit the swete   10
On Achillis speir, and grisly Sarpedon,
And ondyr flude Symois mony one
With scheld and helm stalwart bodeis lyis warpit?'
And al invane thus quhil Eneas carpit,
A blastrand bub out from the north brayng   15
Gan our the forschip in the baksaill dyng,
And to the sternys up the flude gan cast.
The aris, hechis and the takillis brast,
The shippis stevin frawart hyr went gan wryth,
And turnyt hir braid syde to the wallis swyth.   20
Heich as a hill the jaw of watir brak
And in ane hepe cam on thame with a swak.
Sum hesit hoverand on the wallis hycht,
And sum the swowchand sey so law gart lycht
Thame semyt the erd oppynnyt amyd the flude—   25
The stour up bullyrrit sand as it war wode.

16

The sowth wynd, Nothus, thre schippis draif away
Amang blynd cragis, quhilk huge rolkis thai say
Amyd the sey Italianys Altaris callis;
And othir thre Eurus from the deip wallis   30
Cachit amang the schald bankis of sand—
Dolorus to se thame chop on grond, and stand
Lyke as a wall with sand warpit about.
Ane othir, in quham salit the Lycianys stowt,
Quhilum fallowis to Kyng Pandor in weir,   35
And Orontes, Eneas fallow deir,
Befor his eyn from the north wynd
Ane hydduus sey schippit at hir stern behynd,
Smate furth the skippar clepit Lewcaspis,
His hed doune warpit, and the schip with this   40
Thrys thar the flude quhirlit about round,
The swokand swelth sank under sey and drond.
On the huge deip quhoyn salaris dyd appeir;
The Trojanys armour, takillis and othir geir
Flet on the wallis; and the strang barge tho   45
Bair Ilioneus, and scho that bair also
Forcy Achates, and scho that bair Abas,
And scho quharin ancyant Alethes was,
The storm ourset, raif rovis and syde semmys—
Thai all lekkit, the salt watir stremmys   50
Fast bullerand in at every ryft and boyr.

[*Aeneas introduces himself to Dido*]   c. ix

'Hүм quham ye seik behald now present heir,   27
Enee the Trojan, delyverit from danger
Of storm and wallys of the Libiane see.
O thou only, quhilk rewth hes and piete   30
On the ontellabill pyne of the Trojanys,
Quhilk us, the Grekis levyngis and remanys,
Ourset with all maner necessiteis
And every perrell baith be landis and seis,
Within thy cyte ressavys till herbry   35
And to famyliar frendschip and ally;

To quyte the, rendring ganand thankis rycht,
That lyis nocht, Dido, intill our mycht,
Nor all the laif of the Trojan menye,
Throw out this warld skatterit quhar ever thai be,   40
Bot the hie goddis, gif ony deite takis tent
To thame at petuus beyn and pacient,
For justice eik gif ever reward beis get,
And rychtwys myndis ramembrit and nocht foryet,
Thai ilke goddis mot dewly reward the   45
Accordyng thy desert in all degre.
Quhou happy and joyus was that tyme serene
That the producit hes, sa nobill a queyn!
Quhou wirschipfull eik war thai parentis of mycht
Quhilk the engendrit hes, sa worthy a wight!   50
Quhill fludis rynnys in the sey but dowt,
Quhil sonnys schaddow circlys hillis about,
And the firmament starris doith conteyn,
Thy honour and thy fame sall evir be grene,
And thy renown remane perpetualy,   55
Throu all realmys quharto that drevyn am I.'

BOOK II

'THE Grekis chiftanys, irkit of the weir
Bypast or than samony langsum yeir,
And oft rebutyt by fatale destany,
Ane huge hors, lyke ane gret hil, in hy
Craftely thai wrocht in wirschip of Pallas   5
(Of sawyn beche the ribbis forgyt was)
Fenyeand ane oblacioune, as it had be
For prosper returnyng hame in thar cuntre—
The voce this wys throu owt the cite woyk.
Of choys men syne, walit by cut, thai tuke   10

18

A gret numbyr, and hyd in bylgis dern
Within that best, in mony huge cavern;
Schortly, the belly was stuffit every deill
Ful of knychtis armyt in plait of steill.
Thair standis into the sycht of Troy ane ile   15
Weil knawin by name, hecht Tenedos, umquhile
Myghty of gudis quhil Priamus ryng sa stude;
Now it is bot a fyrth in the sey flude,
A raid onsikkyr for schip or ballyngare.
In desert costis of this iland thar   20
The Grekis thame ful secretly withdrew,
We wenyng thame hame passit and adew,
And, with gude wynd, of Myce the realm had socht.
Quharfor al thai of Troy, blyth as thai mocht,
Thair langsum duyl and murnyng dyd away,   25
Kest up the portis and yschit furth to play,
The Grekis tentis desyrus forto se
And voyd placis quhar thai war wont tobe,
The cost and strandis left desert al cleyn.
"Heir stude the army of Dolopeis," sum wald meyn,   30
"Cruel Achil heir stentit his pailyeon;
Quhar stude the navy, lo the place yonder down;
Heir the ostis war wont to joyn in feild."
And sum wondring the scaithfull gyft beheld
Suldbe offerit to the onweddit Pallas;   35
Thai mervellit fast the hors samekill was.
Bot Tymetes exortis first of all
It forto leid and draw within the wall
And forto set it in the cheif palyce—
Quhidder for dissait I not, or for malyce,   40
Or destany of Troy wald sa suldbe.
Bot Capis than, with ane othir menye
Quhilk bettir avys thar myndis set apon,
Bad cast or drown into the sey onone
That suspek presand of the Grekis dissait,   45
Or kyndill tharundir flambe of fyris hait,
Or forto rype that holkit hug belly,
And the hyd hyrnys to sers and weil espy.

19

Quhat nedis mair? The onstabill common voce
Dividit was in mony seir purpos,   50
Quhen thidder come befor thame al onone,
Followand a gret rowt, the prest Laocon
From the cheif tempil rynnand in ful gret hy.
On far, "O wrachit pepil," gan he cry,
"Quhou gret wodnes is this at ye now meyn,   55
Your ennymyis away salit gif ye weyn,
Or gif ye traist ony Grekis gyftis be
Withowt dissait, falshed and subtelte.
Knaw ye na bettir the quent Ulixes slycht?
Owder in this tre ar Grekis closit ful rycht,   60
Or this engyne is byggit to our skaith,
To wach our wallis and our byggyngys bath,
Or to confound and ourquhelm our cite.
Thar lurkis sum falshed tharin, trastis me.
Lippyn nocht, Trojanys, I pray you, in this hors: 65
Quhow ever it be, I dreid the Grekis fors,
And thame that sendis this gyft always I feir."
Thus sayand, with al his strenth a gret speir
At the syde of that bysnyng best threw he,
And in jonyngis of the thrawyn wame of tre   70
Festynnyt the lance, that trymlyng gan to schaik;
The braid belly schudderit, and with the straik
The boys cavys sowndit and maid a dyn.
And had nocht beyn that owder his wit was thyn,
Or than the fatis of goddis war contrary,   75
He had assayt, but ony langar tary,
Hyd Grekis covert with irne to have rent owt;
Than suld thou, Troy, have standyn yit, but dowt,
And the prowd palyce of Kyng Priamus
Suld have remanyt yit ful gloryus.'   80

Quhou stranglit was the prest hecht Laocon
And how the hors clam our the wallis of stone.   c. iv

'BETYD, the ilke tyde, a fer grettar woundir
And mair dreidful to catyvis be sik hunder,

20

Quhilk of Trojanys trublit mony onwarnyt breste.
As Laocon, that was Neptunus prest
And chosyn by kavill onto that ilk office,   5
A fair gret bull offerit in sacrifyce
Solemnytly befor the haly alteir,
Throw the styl sey from Tenedos infeir,
Lo, twa gret lowpit edderis, with mony thraw,
Fast throu the flude towart the land gan draw.   10
My spreit abhorris this mater to declare:
Abufe the watir thar hals stude evermare,
With bludy crestis owtwith the wallis hie;
The remanent swam always under see,
With grysly bodeis lynkit mony fald;   15
The salt fame stowris from the fard thai hald.
Onto the grund thai glaid with glowand eyn
Stuffit ful of vennom, fyre and fellon teyn,
Wyth tongis quhislyng in thar mowthis rede
Thai lyk the twynkland stangis in thar hed.   20
We fled away al bludeles for affeir,
Bot, wyth a braid, to Laocon infeir
Thai stert atanys, and hys twa sonnys ying
First athir serpent lappit lyke a ryng,
And, with thar cruell byt and stangis fell,   25
Of tendir membris tuke mony sary morcell.
Syne thai the prest invadit, baith twane,
Quhilk with hys wapynnys dyd hys byssy pane
His childryng forto helpyn and reskew.
Bot thai about hym lowpit in wympillis threw   30
And twys cyrkyllit his myddil rownd about
And twys faldis thar sprutlit skynnys but dowt
About hys hals—bath nek and hede thai schent.
As he etlys thar hankis to have rent
Of with his handis, and thame away have draw,   35
Hys hed bendis and garlandis all war blaw
Ful of vennom and rank poyson atanys,
Quhilk infekkis the flesch, blude and banys.
And tharwith eik sa horribilly schowtis he,
His cryis dynnyt to the sternys on hie;   40

Lyke as a bull doith rummysing and rayr
Quhen he eschapis hurt from the altair,
And charris by the ax with his nek wight,
Gif on his forhed the dynt hyttis nocht rycht.
Syne thir twa serpentis hastely glaid away,   45
Onto the cheif tempil fled ar thai
Of stern Pallas to the hallowit place
And crap in under the feit of the goddes,
Hyd thame behynd the boys of hir bukleir.
Than trymlit thar mony stowt hart for feir,   50
The onkowth dreid into thar brestis crap.
All said, "Laocon justly, sik was his hap,
Has deir ybocht his wikkit and schrewit deid,
For he the haly hors or stalwart steid
With violente strake presumyt forto deir   55
And tharintil to fessyn his cursit speir.
Onto the hallowit sted bryng in," thai cry,
"The gret fygur! And lat us sacryfy
The haly goddes, and magnyfy hyr mycht
With orysonys and offerandis day and nycht!"   60
Quhat will ye mair? The barmkyn down we rent,
And wallis of our cite we maid patent.
Onto that wark al sped thame bissely;
Turnand quhelis thai set in by and by
Undir the feit of this ilke bysnyng jaip,   65
Abowt the nek knyt mony bassyn raip.
This fatale monstre clam our the wallis then,
Gret wamyt and stuffit ful of armyt men,
And tharabout ran childer and madis ying
Syngand karrellis and dansand in a ryng—   70
Ful weil war thame, and glaid was every wight
That with thar hand anys twich the cordis mycht.
Furth drawyn haldis this suttell hors of tre
And mannysand slydis throu the myd cite.
O natyve cuntre and rial realm of Troy!   75
O goddis hows, Ilion ful of joy!
O worthy Trojane wallis chevalrus!
Four tymys stoppyt that monstre peralus,

22

Evin at the entre of the portis wyde,
And four sys the armour, that ilk tyde,   80
Clynkit and rang amyd the large belly;
Bot netheles, intil our blynd fury
Foryetting this, instantly we wirk
And forto drug and draw wald never irk,
Quhil that myschancy monstre, quently bet,   85
Amyd the hallowit tempill up was set.
Cassandra than the fatis tocum tald plane,
Bot, by command of Phebus, al was invane,
For thocht scho spayit the suthe and maid na bowrd,
Quhat ever scho said Trojanys trowit nocht a word.   90
The tempillis of goddis and sanctuaryis all
We fey pepill—allace, quhat say I sall?—
Quhamtill this was the duylfull lattir day,
With festuale flowris and bewys, as in May,
Dyd weil anorn, and fest and ryot maid   95
Throu owt the town, and for myscheif was glaid.'

Grekis entrys by trayson in the cite,
And how Hector apperis till Ene.   c. v

'WYTH this the hevyn sa quhyrlit about his speir
Out of the sey the dym nycht gan appeir,
With hir dyrk weid bath erth and firmament
Involvyng, by hir secret schaddowis quent
Covering Gregion and Myrmydonys slyght;   5
Within the wallis to bed went evere wyght;
Still war in all, and soft vapour of sleip
Apon thar wery lymmys fast doith creip.
Be than the army of mony a Gregioun,
Stuffit in schippis, come fra Tenedon,   10
Stil under frendly sylens of the moyn,
To the kend costis speding thame ful soyn;
And quhen the takynnyng or the bail of fyre
Rays from the kyngis schip, up byrnand schyre,
Of the goddis be frawart destany   15
Synon preservit couth this syng aspy,

23

The fyrryn closeris oppynnys, but noys or dyn,
And Grekis hyd the horssis cost within
Patent war maid to sight and to the ayr.
Joyfull and blyth from that boys statu thar   20
Discending, thai downlat by cordis atanys
Thersander and Sthenelus, twa capitanys,
The dowr Ulixes als, and Athamas,
Pelyus nevo Pyrrus, and Kyng Thoas,
The first Machaon, and Menelaus,   25
And the engyne forgyar hait Epeus.
The cite thai invaid and fast infest,
With wyne and sleip yberyit and at rest.
Slane ar the wachis liggyng on the wall,
Opnyt the portis, leyt in thar feris all,   30
Togidder jonyt every cumpany:
Throu the cite sone rays the noys and scry.
Thys was that tyme quhen the fyrst quyete
Of naturale sleip, to quham na gyft mair swete,
Stelis on fordoverit mortale creaturis,   35
And in thar swevynnys metis quent figuris.
Lo, in my sleip I se stand me befor
(As to my syght) maist lamentabil Hector
Wyth large flude of teris, and al besprent,
As he umquhile eftyr the cart was rent,   40
With barknyt blude and powder. O God, quhat skath!
Boldynnyt ful gret war feit and lymmys baith
By bandis of the cordis quhilk thame drewch.
Ha, walloway, quhat harm and wo eneuch!
Quhat ane was he, how far changit from joy   45
Of that Hector, quhilum returnyt to Troy
Cled with the spulye of hym Achillys,
Or quhen the Trojane fyry blesis, I wys,
On Grekis schippis thyk fald he slang that day
Quhen that he slew the duke Prothesylay!   50
Hys fax and berd was fadyt quhar he stude
And all hys hayr was glotnyt ful of blude.
Full mony woundis on his body bayr he,
Quhilk in defens of hys natyve cuntre

24

About the wallys of Troy ressavyt he had.   55
Me thocht I first wepyng and na thing glaid
Rycht reverently begouth to clepe this man,
And with sik dolorus wordis thus began:
"O thou, of Troy the lemand lamp of lycht,
O Trojane hope, maist ferm defens in fyght,   60
Quhat has the tareit? Quhy maid thou this delay,
Hector, quham we desyrit mony a day?
From quhat cuntre this wys cummyn art thou?
That eftir feil slauchter of thi frendis now
And of thi folkis and cite efter huge payn,   65
Quhen we beyn irkit, we se the heir agayn!
Quhat hard myschance fylyt so thi plesand face?
Or quhy se I tha feil woundis, allace?"
Onto thir wordis he nane answer maid,
Nor to my voyd demandis na thyng said,   70
Bot with ane hevy murmour, as it war draw
Furth of the boddum of his breste weil law,
"Allace, allace, thou goddes son," quod he,
"Salf thi self from this fyre and fast thou fle.
Our ennemys has thir worthy wallys tane;   75
Troy from the top down fallys, and all is gane.
Enewch has lestit of Priamus the ryng,
The fatis wil na mair it induryng.
Gif Pergama, the Trojane wallys wyght,
Mycht langar have beyn fendit into fyght,   80
With this rycht hand thai suld have be defendit.
Adew, fair weil, for ever it is endit.
In thi keping committis Troy but les
Hir kyndly goddis clepit Penates;
Tak thir in falloschip of thi fatis all,   85
And large wallis for thame seik thou sall,
Quhilk at the last thi self sall beld up hie
Eftir lang wandryng and errour our the see."
Thus said Hectour, and schew furth in his handis
The dreidfull valis, wymplis and garlandis   90
Of Vesta, goddes of the erth and fyre,
Quhilk in hir tempil eternaly byrnys schyre.'

25

Into this nixt cheptour ye may attend
Of Priam, kyng of Troy, the fatale end.

'PERAVENTUR of Priamus wald ye speir
Quhou tyd the chance. Hys fait, gif ye lyst, heir:
Quhen he the cite saw takyn and downbet,
And of his palyce brokyn every yet,
Amyd the secret closettis eik hys fays,   5
The auld grayth, al for nocht, to hym tays
Hys hawbryk quhilk was lang furth of usage,
Set on his schulderis trymlyng than for age;
A sword but help about hym beltis he
And ran towart hys fays, reddy to de.   10
Amyd the clos, under the hevyn al bayr,
Stude thar that tyme a mekil fair altare,
Neyr quham thar grew a rycht ald lawrer tre
Bowand towart the altare a litill wie,
That with his schaddow the goddis dyd ourheld.   15
Hecuba thyddir with hir childer for beild
Ran al invane and about the altare swarmys,
Brasand the godlyke ymage in thar armys,
As for the storm dowis flokkis togidder ilkane.
Bot quhen scho saw how Priamus has tane   20
His armour, so as thocht he had beyn ying:
"Quhat fulych thocht, my wrachit spows and kyng,
Movis the now syk wapynnys forto weld?
Quhidder hastis thou?" quod sche. "Of na sik beld
Have we now mystir, nor syk diffendouris as the, 25
The tyme is nocht ganand tharto we se,
In cace Hectour war present heir, my son,
He mycht nocht succur Troy, for it is won.
Quharfor I pray the syt doune and cum hydder
And lat this altare salve us al togidder,   30
Or than atanys al heir lat us de."
Thus said scho and with sik sembland as mycht be
Hym towart hir has brocht, but ony threte,
And set the auld doune on the haly sete.

Bot lo, Polytes, ane of Priamus sonnys   35
Quhilk from the slauchter of Pyrrus away run is,
Throw wapynnys fleyng and his ennemys all,
Be lang throwgangis and mony voyd hall;
Woundit he was, and come to seik reskew.
Ardently Pyrrus gan him fast persew,   40
With grondyn lance at hand so neir furthstrekit,
Almaist the hed hym twichit and arekit,
Quhil at the last, quhen he is cummyn, I weyn,
Befor his faderis and his moderis eyn,
Smate hym down ded in thar sycht quhar he stude,   45
The gaist he yald with habundans of blude.
Priamus than, thocht he was halfdeill ded,
Mycht nocht conteyn his ire nor wordis of fed,
Bot cryis furth: "For that cruell offens
And owtragyus fuyl hardy violens,   50
Gif thar be piete in the hevin abone
Quhilk takis heid to this at thou has done,
The goddis mot condyngly the foryeld,
Eftir thi desert rendring sik gaynyeld,
Causit me behald myne awyn child slane, allace,   55
And with hys blude fylit the faderis face.
Bot he quhamby thou fenys thi self byget,
Achil, was not to Priam sa hard set,
For he, of rycht and faith eschamyt eik,
Quhen that I come hym lawly tobeseik,   60
The ded body of Hector rendrit me,
And me convoyit hame to my cite."
Thus sayand the ald waykly, but fors or dynt,
A dart dyd cast, quhilk with a pyk gan stynt
On his harnes, and in the scheild dyd hyng   65
But ony harm or other dammagyng.
Quod Pyrrus, "Sen always thou saist swa,
To Pellyus son, my fadir, thou most ga.
Beir hym this message, ramembir weil thou tell
Him al my warkis and dedis sa cruell—   70
Schaw Neoptolemus is degenerit cleyn.
Now salt thou de." And with that word in teyn

27

The ald trymlyng towart the altare he drew,
That in the hait blude of his son, sched new,
Fundrit; and Pyrrus grippis hym by the hayr   75
With his left hand, and with the tother albayr
Drew furth his schynand swerd, quhilk in his syde
Festynnyt, and onto the hyltis dyd he hyde.
Of Priamus thus was the finale fait—
Fortone heir endit his gloryus estait,   80
Seand Ilion albyrn in fyris brown
And Troys wallis fall and tumlyt down.
That ryal prince, umquhile our Asya
Apon sa feil pepil and realmys alswa
Ryngnyt in welth, now by the cost lyis ded   85
Bot as a stok and of hakkit his hed,
A corps but lyfe, renown or other fame,
Onknawyn of ony wight quhat was his name.'

             Quhou Eneas hys fader bayr away,
             And how he lost Creusa by the way.   c. xi

'WYTH skyrlys and with scrykis thus sche beris,
Fillyng the hows with murnyng and salt teris,
Quhen suddanly, a wonder thing to tell,
A feirful takyn betyd of gret marvell.
For lo! the top of litill Ascanyus hed,   5
Amang the duylfull armys wil of red
Of his parentis, from the sched of his crown,
Schane al of lycht onto the grond adown.
The leym of fyre and flambe, but ony skath,
In his haris, about his halffettis baith,   10
Kyndyllis up brycht, and we than, al in weir,
Abasit, trymlyng for the dreidfull feir,
The blesand haris bet furth at brynt sa schyre,
And schupe with watir to sloyk the haly fyre.
Bot Anchises, my fader, blyth and glaid   15
Lyft eyn and handis to hevyn, and thusgatis said:
"O thou almychty Jupiter," quod he,
"With ony prayeris inclynyt gif thou may be,

28

Tak heid to us, and gif we have deservyt
For our piete and rewth tobe conservyt,   20
Haly fader, send us thi help als yoir,
And conferm al thir takynnys seyn befor."
Scarsly the auld thir wordis had warpit owt,
Quhen sone the ayr begouth to rumbill and rowt
On our left hand, towart the north ful rycht,   25
And from the hevin fell, in the dyrk nycht,
A fayr brycht starn, rynnand with bemys cleir,
Quhilk on the top of our lugyng, but weir,
First saw we lycht, syne schynyng went awa
And hyd it in the forest of Ida,   30
Markand the way quhidder at we suld spur;
Thar followis a streym of fyre, or a lang fur,
Castand gret lycht about quhar that it schane,
Quhil al enveron rekit lyke bryntstane.
With that my fader venquyst start on fute,   35
And to the goddis carpis tobe our bute,
The haly starn adornyt he rycht thar:
"Now, now," quod he, "I tary na langar;
I follow, and quhidder ye gyde me sal I wend.
O natyve goddis, your awyn kynrent defend,   40
Salve your nevo; youris is this oracle,
In your protectioun is Troy, for this myracle
I wil obey, and grantis onto your will:
My deir son, quhidder ever thou wend will,
I sal na mair reffus tobe thi feyr."   45
Thus sayd he, and be than, thar and heir,
Throw out the wallis the rerd of fyris grew
Ay mair and mair, and the heit nerrar drew.
"Have done," quod I, "fader, clym up onone
And set the evyn abuf my nek bone;   50
Apon my schuldris I sal the beir, but weyr,
Nor this lawbour saldo to me na deir:
Quhat ever betyde, a weilfair and a skaith
Salbe common and equale to us baith.
Lytil Julus salbeir me cumpany,   55
My spows ondreich eftyr our trays sal hy.

29

And ye, my servandis, tak heid quhat I say:
As ye pas furth of the cite this ilk way,
Thar is a mote, quhar ane ald tempil, but les,
Now standis desert of the goddes Ceres,   60
Besyde quham growis a sypir tre full auld,
With forfaderis feil yeris in wirschip hald;
In that place lat us meit on athir syde.
Fader, sen that we may na langar byde,
Tak up tha haly rellykis in thi hand,   65
And our penates or goddis of this land—
It war onleifful and wykkitnes to me
From sa gret slauchter, blude schedding and melle
Newly departit, to twich thame, for the blude,
Quhil I be weschyn into sum rynnand flude."   70
And sayng thus, I spred my schulderis brayd,
Syne our my nek, abuf the wedis, laid
A yallow skyn was of a fers lyoun,
And tharapon gart set my fader down;
Lytil Julus grippis me by the hand,   75
With onmeit pays his fader fast followand;
Neir at our bak Creuse my spows ensewys:
We pas by secret wentis and quyet rewys.
And me, quham laitly na wapyn, nor dartis kast,
Nor pres of Grekis rowtis maid agast,   80
Ilke swowch of wynd and every quhispir now
And alkyn sterage affrayt, and causyt grow,
Baith for my byrdyng and my litil mait.
Quhen we war cummyn almaist to the yet,
And al danger we thocht eschapit neyr,   85
A fellon dyn belyve of feit we heir;
My fader than lukand furth throw the sky,
Cryis on me fast, "Fle, son! fle, son, in hy,
Thai cum at hand! Behynd me I gat a sycht
Of lemand armour and schynand scheildis brycht."   90
Thar knaw I nocht quhat fremmyt god onkynd
So me astonyst, and reft fra me my mynd,
For throu the secrete stretis fast I ran
Befor the laif, as weil bekend man.

Allace to me catyve! I wait never quhydder   95
My spows Creuse remanyt or we come thydder,
Or by sum fait of goddis was reft away,
Or gif scho errit, or irkit by the way,
For nevir syne with eyn saw I hyr eft,
Nor never abak, fra scho was lost or reft,   100
Blent I agane, nor perfyte mynd has nummyn,
Quhil to the mote of Ceres war we cummyn.
And fynaly, quhen we beyn gadderit thidder,
Fast by the haly tempil al togydder,
Scho was away, and betrumpit suythly   105
Hyr spows, hir son and all the cumpany.
Than wod for wo, so was I quyte myscaryit
That nowder god nor man I left onwaryit:
For quhat mair hard myschance, quhen Troy down fell,
Apperit to me as that, or sa cruell?   110
Ascanyus tho and my fader Anchises,
And eik our Trojane goddis penates,
Onto my feris betauch I for to keip
And hyd thame darn within a valy deip.
To town agane I sped with al my mycht,   115
Claspit ful meit into fyne armour brycht,
Wilful al aventuris newlyngis to assay,
And forto sers Troy, every streit and way,
And eik my hed agane in perrell set.
Bot first the wallis, the darn entre and yet,   120
Quharat we yschit furth, I seik agane,
Haldyng bakwart ilk futstep we had gane,
Lukand and sersand about me as I myght.
The ugsumnes and silens of the nycht
In every place my spreit maid sayr agast.   125
Fra thyne ontil our lugyng hame I past
To spy perchance gif scho had thidder returnyt;
It was with Grekis beset and hail ourturnyt,
Alhail the hows with thame sa occupyit;
Belyve the fyre al waistand I espyit   130
Bles with the wynd; our the rufe, heir and thar,
The flambe upsprang and hait low in the ayr.'

31

'To Priamus palyce eftyr socht I than,
And syne onto the tempil fast I ran,
Quhar at the porchis or clostir of Juno,
Than al bot waist, thocht it was gyrth, stude tho
Phenix and dowr Ulixes, wardanys tway,   5
Forto observe and keip the spreth or pray.
Thydder in a hepe was gadderit precyus geir,
Riches of Troy, and other jowellis seyr
Reft from all partis; and of tempillis brynt
Of massy gold the veschel war furth hynt   10
From the goddis, and goldyn tabillis all,
With precyus vestmentis of spulye triumphall;
The ying childring, effrayt matronys eik,
Stude al on raw, with mony petuus screik
Abowt the tresour quhymperand wondir sayr.   15
And I alsso my self sa bald wolx thair
That I durst schaw my voce in the dyrk nycht,
And clepe and cry fast throu the stretis on hycht
Ful dolorusly, "Creusa! Creusa!"
Agane, feil sys, invane I callit swa   20
Throu howsys and the cite quhar I yoyd,
But owder rest or resson, as I war woyd;
Quhil that the figur of Creusa and gost,
Of far mair statur than ayr quhen scho was lost,
Befor me, catyve, hyr sekand, apperit thar.   25
Abasyt I wolx, and widdyrsyns start my hayr;
Speke mycht I not, the voce in my hals swa stak.
Than scho, belyfe, on this wys to me spak,
With sik wordis my thochtis to asswage:
"O my sweit spows, into sa furyus rage   30
Quhat helpis thus thi selvyn to torment?
This chance is not but goddis willis went;
Nor it is nocht leifful thing," quod sche,
"Fra hyne Creuse thou turs away with the,

32

Nor the hie governour of the hevin abufe is   35
Wil suffir it so tobe; bot the behuffis
From hens to wend ful far into exile
And our the braid sey sail furth mony a myle
Or thou cum to the land Hesperya,
Quhar wyth soft cowrs Tybris of Lydya   40
Rynnys throu the rych feldis of pepil stowt;
Thar is gret substans ordanyt the but dowt,
Thar salt thou have a realm, thar salt thou ryng
And wed to spows the douchtir of a kyng.
Thy wepyng and thi teris do away   45
Quhilk thou makis for thi luffyt Creusay,
For I, the neyce of mychty Dardanus
And gude douchtyr onto the blyssit Venus,
Of Myrmydonys the realm sal nevir behald
Nor yit the land of Dolopeis so bald,   50
Nor go to serve na matron Gregion,
Bot the gret modir of the goddis ilkon
In thir cuntreis withhaldis me for evyr.
Adew, fayr weil, for ay we mon dissevir.
Thou be gude frend, lufe weil and keip fra skath   55
Our a yong son is common til us baith."
Quhen this was spokkyn, fra me away scho glaid,
Left me wepyng and feil wordis wald have said,
For sche sa lychtly vanysyt in the ayr
That with myne armys thrys I presyt thar   60
About the hals hir fortil have belappit,
And thrys, al waist, my handis togiddir clappit:
The figur fled as lycht wynd or the son beym,
Or maist lykly a waverand swevyn or dreym.
Thus finaly, the nycht al passit and gane,   65
Onto my falloschip I return agane,
Quhar that I fand assemlyt al newly
So huge a rowt of our folkis that I
Wondryt the nowmyr, thai so mony weir
Of men and women gadderit al infeir   70
And yong pepil to pas in exile abill
And of commonys a sort sa miserabill

Fra every part that flokkyng fast about,
Baith with gude wil and thar moblis, but dout,
Reddy to wend in quhat cost or cuntre   75
That evir me list to cary thame our see.
Wyth this the day starn, Lucifer the brycht,
Abuf the top of Ida rays on hycht,
Gydand the day hard at his bak followyng:
The Grekis than we se in the mornyng   80
Stand forto kepe the entreis of the portis,
And thus quhen na hope of reskew at schort is
My purpos I left, obeyand destanye,
And careit my fader to Ida hyll on hie.'

BOOK IV

From the Prologue

THOU cheyn of luf, ha benedicite,   36
Quhou hard strenys thi bandis every wyght!
The God abuf, from his hie majeste,
With the ybond, law in a maid dyd lycht:
Thou venquyst the strang gyant of gret mycht;   40
Thou art mair forcy than the ded sa fell;
Thou plenyst paradyce and thou heryit hell.

Thou makist febill wight and lawyst the hie;
Thou knyttis frendschyp quhar thar beyn na parage;
Thou Jonathas confederat with Davy,   45
Thou dantyt Alexander for al his vassalage,
Thou festnyt Jacob fourteyn yheir in bondage,
Thou techit Hercules go lern to spyn,
Reke Dyomeir hys mays and lyoun skyn.

   .   .   .   .   .   .

Lust is na lufe, thocht ledis lyke it weill;   107
This furyus flambe of sensualite
Ar nane amouris bot fantasy ye feill;
Carnale plesance, but syght of honeste,   110

34

Hatis hym self forsuyth, and luffis nocht the.
Thare beyn twa luffis, perfyte and imperfyte,
That ane leful, the tother fowle delyte.

Lufe is a kyndly passioun, engendryt of heyt
Kyndlyt in the hart, ourspredyng al the cors,   115
And, as thou seys sum person waik in spreyt,
Sum hait byrnyng as ane onbridillyt hors—
Lyke as the pacient hes heyt of our gret fors,
And in yong babbys warmnes insufficient,
And into agyt failyeis, and is out quent,   120

Rycht so in lufe thou may be excessyve,
Inordinatly luffand ony creature;
Thi luf alsso it may be defectyve,
To lufe thine awin and geif of otheris na cure.
But quhar that lufe is rewlyt by messure,   125
It may be lyknyt to ane hail manis estait,
In temperat warmnes, nowthir to cald nor hait.

Than is thi lufe inordinat, say I,
Quhen ony creatur mair than God thou luffis,
Or yit luffis ony to that fyne, quharby   130
Thi self or thame thou frawartis God remufis:
Fortil attempir thine amouris the behuffis.
Lufe every wyght for God, and to gude end,
Thame be na wys to harm, bot to amend.

That is to knaw, lufe God for his gudnes,   135
With hart, hail mynde, trew servyce, day and nycht;
Nixt luf thi self, eschewand wykkytnes;
Luf syne thi nychtburris, and wyrk thame nane onrycht,
Willyng at thou and thai may have the sycht
Of hevynnys blys, and tyste thame not tharfra,   .   140
For, and thou do, syk luf dowe nocht a stra.

. . . . . .

The thochtfull queyn, with mony amorus claws,
Till hir systir complenys in luffis caws.

BE this the queyn, throw hevy thochtis onsound,
In every vayn nurysys the greyn wound,
Smytyn so deip with the blynd fyre of lufe
Hir trublyt mynd gan fra all rest remufe.
Compasing the gret prowes of Ene,   5
The large wirschip feill sys remembris sche
Of his lynnage and folkis; for ay present
Deip in hir breist so was hys figur prent
And all hys wordis fixt, that, for bissy thocht,
Noyn eys hir membris nor quyet suffir mocht.   10
The nyxt day following, with hys lamp brycht
As Phebus dyd the grund or erth alycht,
Eftir the dawing heth the donk nychtis clowd
Chasyt from the sky and the ayr new schrowd,
Ful evil at eys Queyn Dido on this kynd   15
Spak to hir systir, wes of the sammyn mynd:
'My sistir An, quhat swevynnys beyn thir,' quod sche,
'Quhilk me affrays in sik proplexite?
Quhat be he, this gret new gest or stranger,
Onto our realm laitly is drevyn heir?   20
Quhou wys in speche and in his commonyng
He schawys hym self! O God, quhat wondir thing!
Quhou stout in curage, in weir quhou vailyeand!
I trow, sistir, and, as I undirstand,
Myne opinion is nane oncertane thing,   25
Thai beyn sum lynnage of verray goddis ofspring,
For dreid always and schaymful kowardys
Degeneryt wightis and bowbartis notyfys.
Allace, quhat wondir fatale aventuris
Hes hym bywaif! quhat travel, pane and curis,   30
How huge batellis, be hym eschevit, tald he!
Now certis, war it not determyt with me
And fixit in my mynd onmovabilly
That to no wyght in wedlok me list I

Cuppil nor knyt, sen my first luf is gane,   35
By deth dissoverit, and left me alane;
War not alsso to me is displesant
Genyus chalmyr or matrymone to hant;
Perchans I mycht be venquist in this rage,
Throu this a cryme of secund mariage.   40
Annes, I grant to the, sen the deces
Of my sory husband Syche, but les,
Quhar that our hows with brodyrris ded wes sprent,
Only this man hes movit myne entent,
And heth my mynd inducyt to forvay: 45
I knaw and felis the wemmys and the way
Of the ald fyre and flambe of luffis heit.
Bot rather I desyre baith cors and spreit
Of me the erth swelly law adown,
Or than almychty Jove with thundris soun   50
Me smyte ful deip onto the schaddoys dern,
Amang pail gastis of hellis holl cavern,
In the profond pot of deth and dyrk nycht,
Or I becum so schamful wrachit wyght
That I myne honeste fyle or womanhed,   55
Or brek your lawis—na, quhil I be ded!
He that me first to hym in wedlok knyt
My first flowr of amouris tuke, and yit
For evermair with hym he sal thame have,
And he most keip thame with hym in his grave.'   60
Thus sayand, the brycht teris onon owtbrist
And fillyt all hir bosum or scho wist.
Annes answerd: 'O thou, sa mot I thryve,
To thi systir derrar than hir awyn lyve,
Quhiddir gif thou wilt alane, in wedowhed,   65
Evir murnand thus waist away thy yowthed,
Nowthir yit the comfort of sweit childring thou knawis,
Nor the plesour felis of Venus lawys?
Quhat, wenys thou assys cald and gastis in grave
Of al syk walyng ony fest sal have?   70
In cays that in thi duyll afor thir days,
Thy lord new ded, the list inclyne na ways

37

Nowthir prynce nor duke to tak as for husband;
Suppos thou lychtlyit than, of Lyby land,
Hyarbas kyng, and othir heris all,   75
Quhilkis in the rich sulye triumphall
Of Aufrik boundis dwelling wydequhar;
Quhat, wilt thou als debatyng ever mar
Agane this lykand lufe, cummys of plesance?
Consideris thou not, and hes in remembrance,   80
Amyddis quhays grond heir thou remanys?
On this hand, citeis of Getulyanys,
A kynd of pepill invincibill in batell;
Heir the ondantit folk of Numyda dwell,
And on that other part ombyset, I wys,   85
We ar with bustuus onfrendly Syrtis;
And yondir the desert region alsswa,
Ay ful of thyrst, in barrand Libya;
And wydquhar thens the wild pepil of Barchay.
The weris moving from Tyre quhat sal I say,   90
And the gret brag and mannans of our brothir?
Be dispositioun of goddis, I weyn, nane othir,
And by the purvyans of Juno, to our supple,
Thir Trojane schippis by prospir wynd our see
Heth hyddir set thar coursys fortunate.   95
O systir myne, considir in quhat estait
Thys cite, quhilk thou beildis, sal uprys!
Persave quhou that this realm may, on syk wys,
Beyn upheyt throu sa nobil a mariage!
Behald quhou mekill the glory of Cartage   100
Salbe extollyt, and encres in every thyng,
Throu help in armys of the Trojanys ofspryng!
Quharfor the nedis beseik goddis of thar grace,
With sacrifyce, tobe favorabil in this cace.
Do set alhaill thi cure and diligence   105
To causyng hym mak with the residence,
And fenye causys to tary hym and wythhall,
So lang as thus, duryng the wyntir cald,
The sey ragis throu watry Orion,
And quhil the stormys be al our blawyn and gon;   110

And quhil hys schippis, with the tempest schaik,
Be bet, byd spair nowthir fyr, elm nor aik.'

Dido enflambyt in the lusty heyt,
With amorus thochtis trublys al hir spreit.   c. ii

WYTH thir wordys the spreit of Dido queyn,
The quhilk tofor in lufe wes kyndlyt grene,
Now al in fyre the flambe of lufe furth blesys;
Hir doutsum mynd with gude hope so scho esys
That al the schame and dreid wes blaw away;   5
And to the tempill furth held tha baith tway.
Eftir the serymonys of thar payane gys,
Benevolence and gude luk, syndry wys,
Thai sekyng and thai sers at ilke altar;
And twyntris, walit for sacrifyce, heir and thar   10
Thai brytnyt; and sum in honour dyd addres
Of the law ledar Ceres, the goddes,
To Phebus, and to Bachus part alsso,
Bot principaly onto the queyn Juno,
Quhilk heth in cuyr the band of mariage.   15
Hir self, most gudly Queyn Dido of Cartage,
Held in hir richt hand a cowp full of wyne;
Betwix the hornys twa furthyet it syne
Of ane ontamyt yong quy, quhite as snaw;
And othir quhilis wald scho raik on raw   20
Or pays tofor the altaris, wyth fat offerandis
Ay chargyt full, and oft with hir awyn handis
Renew and beyt the sacrifyce all day;
And rich gyftis geif Trojanys; and wald ay
The beistis costis, as thai debowellit wer,   25
And thar entralis behald flekkyr and steir,
Accordyng the auld usans to that effect,
Sum augury to persave or gude aspect.
O wallaway! of spamen and dyvynys
The blynd myndis, quhilkis na way diffynys   30
The fors ne strenth of luf with hys hard bandis!
Quhat avalyt thir sacrifice and offerandis?

39

Quhat helpis to vyssy tempillis in luffis rage?
Behald onhappy Dido of Cartage
In this meyn sesson byrnyng hait as gleyd: 35
The secrete wound deip in hir mynd gan spreyd,
And of hoyt amouris the subtell quent fyre
Waistis and consumys merch, banys and lyre.
Our all the cite enragyt scho heir and thar
Wandris, as ane strykkyn hynd, quhom the stalkar,   40
Or scho persave, from far betis with hys flane
Amyd the woddis of Creyt, and lattis remane
The braid hed, onknaw the beste was hyt;
Scho skypping furth, as to eschew the byt,
Gan throu the forest fast and gravys glyde,   45
Bot evir the dedly schaft stykkis in hir syde.
Sum tyme the queyn Ene with hir dyd leid
Throu owt the wallys onto every steid,
The tresour al and riches of Sydony
Schawyng to hym, and offerit al reddy   50
The cite of Cartage at hys commandment:
Begyn scho wald to tell furth hir entent,
And in the myd word stop and hald hir styll.
And quhen the evyn come, it wes hir will
To seik ways hym to feste, as scho dyd ayr;   55
And, half myndles, agane scho langis sayr
For tyll enquyre and heir the sege of Troy,
And in a stair behaldis hym for joy.
Eftir all wes voydyt, and the licht of day
Ay mair and mair the moyn quynchit away,   60
And the declynyng of the starris brycht
To sleip and rest persuadis every wight,
Within hir chalmyr alane scho langis sayr,
And thocht al waist for lak of hir luffar.
Amyd a voyd bed scho hir laid adoun,   65
And of hym absent thinkis scho heris the sown;
Hys voce scho heris, and hym behaldis sche,
Thocht he, God wait, far from hir presens be:
And sum tyme wald scho Ascanyus, the page,
Caucht in the figur of hys faderis ymage,   70

And in hir bosum brace, gif scho tharby
The lufe ontellabill mycht swik or satisfy.
The wark and wallys begun ar not upbrocht,
The yonkeris dedis of armys excersis nocht,
Nothir fortres nor turettis suyr of weir   75
Now graith tha mair, for al the wark, but weir,
Cessis and is stoppyt, baith of pynnakillis hie,
And byg towris, semyt to rys in the skie.

Tyl Venus carpys Juno the goddes,
And of thar spech and sermond, mar and les.   c. iii

ALSSWYTH as Juno, with syk maleys ourtane,
Persavyt hir deir frend that remeid was nane,
Nothir fame ne honour the rage resyst mycht,
Saturnus douchtir with syk wordis on hyght
Begouth to carp onto Venus, I wys: 5
'A huge honour and lawd ye sal of this
Raport, and richt large spulye beir away,
Thou and thi child forsuyth,' quod scho, 'bath tway:
O Lord, quhou gret power and notabil mycht,
Gif that, of twa hie goddis throu the slycht,   10
A sylly woman sal ourcummyn be!
Not so, I wys, hes thou dissavyt me,
Bot that I knaw thou had in feir and dreid
Our cite, and held the lugyng suspek in deid
Of our renownyt hie burgh of Cartage.   15
Bot on quhat wys sall sesyng al this rage?
Or now quhat nedis sa gret stryfe and contak?
Far rather perpetuell pes lat us mak,
And knyt up band of mariage thartill,
Sen thou hes gottin al thyne hartis will;   20
For Dido byrnys in hait lufe al atanys,
The brym fury glydis throu owt hir banys.
Lat us thir pepill to us common, for thy,
Be frendly favouris govern equaly;
So that it lesum be Dido remane   25
In spousage bund, and serve a lord Trojane,

41

And suffir Tirreanys, and al Lyby land,
Be geif in dowry to thi son in hand.'
Than Venus (knawing hir spech of fenyeit mynd,
To that effect scho mycht the Trojane kynd,   30
And werys tocum furth of Itail alsswa,
With hald and kepe from boundis of Lybia)
Answerd and sayd: 'Quhat wikkyt wyght wald ever
Refuys syk proffyr, or yit with the had levir
Contend in bataill or stand at debait,   35
Gif that, as thou rehersis, the deid algait
Als sovirly mycht follow fortunabill?
Bot I affeir me les the fatis onstabill
Nor Jupiter consent not ne aggre
That bot a cite to Tyryanys suld be   40
And eik to folkis from Troy in vayage cummyn,
Or list appreif thai pepillis all and summyn
Togiddir myddill, or joyn in lyge or band.
Thou art hys spows; til the to tak on hand
Is lefull with request hys mynd to assay.   45
Pas on befor, I follow the perfay.'
Than Juno queyn syk answer maid agane:
'This laubour I tak on hand, al myne alane.
Bot on quhat wys, sen tyme is convenabill,
The fasson quhou this stant to do maist habill,   50
Hark, at schort wordys that poynt I sal you say.
Eneas and onsilly Dido, baith tway,
To forest grathis in huntyng furth to wend,
To morow, als fast as Titan doith ascend
And our the warld gan hys bemys spreid.   55
Quhen that the rangis and the faid on breid
Dynnys throu the gravys, sersyng the woddis wyde,
And setis set the glen on every syde,
I sal apon thame a myrk schour down skaill
Of weit and wynd, mydlit with fellon haill,   60
And al the hevyn with thundyrris blast sa steir
That all thar falloschip sall withdraw for feir
Enclosyt with a myst als dyrk as nycht.
Dido and eik the Trojane duke full rycht,

42

Alanerly, bot be thame selvyn twane,   65
Togiddir sal entir in a cave of stane:
Thar sal I be reddy, and, but delay,
Gif thi mynd be ferm tharto the ilk day,
In sovir wedlok I sal conjoyn hir thar,
Tobe his propir spous for evermair: 70
Apon this wys thar wedding salbe wrocht.'
Affermys all hir wil, contrarying nocht,
Of Cetheron Venus the goddes brycht,
Lauchyng scho fund had so controvit a slycht.

Quhou that the queyn to huntyng raid at morow,
And of the first day of hir joy and sorow.   c. iv

FURTH of the sey, with this, the dawyng spryngis.
As Phebus rays, fast to the yettis thringis
The chos gallandis, and huntmen thame besyde,
With ralys and with nettys strang and wyde,
And huntyng sperys styf with hedis braid;   5
From Massilyne horsmen thik thiddir raid,
With rynnyng hundis, a full huge sort.
Nobillys of Cartage, hovand at the port,
The queyn awatys that lang in chawmyr dwellys;
Hyr fers steyd stude stampyng, reddy ellys,   10
Rungeand the fomy goldyn byt gynglyng;
Of gold and pal wrocht hys rych harnasyng.
And scho at last of palyce yschit owt,
With huge menye walking hir abowt,
Lappyt in a brusyt mantill of Sydony,   15
With gold and perle the bordour al bewry,
Hyngand by hir syde the cays with arowis grund;
Hir bricht tressis envolupyt war and wond
Intil a quayf of fyne gold wyrin threid;
The goldyn button claspyt hir purpour weid—   20
And furth scho passyt with all hir cumpany.
The Trojane pepill forgaderit by and by,
Joly and glaid the fresch Ascanyus ying,
Bot first of all, maist gudly, hym self thar kyng

43

Enee gan entir in falloschip, but dout,   25
And onto thame adjonyt hys large rowt,
Lyke quhen Apollo list depart or ga
Furth of hys wyntring realm of Lysya,
And leif the flude Exanthus for a quhile,
To vissy Delos, his moderis land and ile,   30
Renewand ryngis and dansys, mony a rowt;
Mixt togiddir, hys altaris standing about,
The pepil of Creit, and thame of Driopes,
And eik the payntit folkis Agathirces,
Schowtand on thar gys with clamour and vocis hie: 35
Apon thi top, mont Cynthus, walkis he,
Hys wavand haris, sum tyme, doyng doun thryng
With a soft garland of lawrer sweit smellyng,
And umquhile thame gan balmyng and enoynt
And into gold addres at full gude poynt,   40
Hys grundyn dartis clattering by hys syde—
Als fresch, als lusty dyd Eneas ryde,
With als gret bewte in hys lordly face.
And eftyr thai ar cummyn to the chace,
Amang the montanys in the wild forest,   45
The rynnyng hundis of cuppillys sone thai kest,
And our the clewys and the holtis, belyve,
The wild beistis doun to the dail thai dryve.
Lo! thar the rays, rynnyng swyft as fyre,
Drevyn from the hyghtis, brekkis out at the swyre;   50
Ane othir part, syne yondyr mycht thou se
The herd of hartis with thar hedis hie,
Ourspynnerand with swyft cours the plane vaill,
The hepe of duste upstowryng at thar taill,
Fleand the hundis, levand the hie montanys.   55
And Ascanyus, the child, amyd the planys,
Joyus and blith hys startling steid to assay,
Now makis hys rynk yondir, and now this way
Now prekis furth by thir and now by thame,
Langyng, amang faynt frayt beistis ontame,   60
The fomy bair, doun from the hyllis hycht,
Or the dun lyoun discend, recontyr he mycht.

44

In the meyn quhile, the hevynnys al about
With fellon noys gan to rummyll and rowt.
A bub of weddir followyt in the tayll,   65
Thik schour of rayn myddillit ful of haill.
The Tyriane menye skalis wydequhar,
And al the gallandis of Troy fled heir and thar,
And eik with thame the yong Ascanyus,
Nevo to Kyng Dardan and to Venus.   70
For feir, to divers stedis throu the feildis,
Thai seik to haldis, howsis, hyrnys and beildis:
The ryveris rudly ruschit our hillis bedene.
Within a cave is entrit Dido queyn,
And eik the Trojane duke, al thame alane,   75
By aventur, as thai eschewyt the rane.
Erth, the first moder, maid a takyn of wo,
And eik of wedlok the pronuba Juno,
And of thar cuplyng wittering schew the ayr:
The flambe of fyreslaucht lychtnyt heir and thar   80
And on the hillys hie toppis, but les,
Sat murnand nymphis, hait Oreades.
This wes the formaste day of hir glaidnes
And first morrow of hir wofull distres.
For nother the fasson nor the maner sche   85
Attendis now, nor fame ne honeste,
Ne from thens furthwart Dido ony mor
Musis on lufe secrete, as of befor,
But clepis it spousage, and with that fayr name
Clokyt and hyd hir cryme of oppyn schame.   90

Of Fame that monstre, and Kyng Hyarbas fury
And how fra Jove wes send the god Mercury.   c. v

THE fame heirof, belyve, gan walx and spreid
Throu cheif citeis of all Affrik on breid:
Fame is myscheif, quham na harm undyr the lyft
In motioun nor sterage is mair swyft.
Movand scho growis, and, passand our alquhar,   5
Hir strenth encressis and walxis mair and mayr.

45

Lytil, for feir, the fyrst tyme semys sche,
Sone eftir rysys to the starnys on hie;
Apon the grond scho walkis fra sted to sted,
And up amang the clowdis hydis hyr hed.   10
Throu greif of goddis commovyt, and nocht glaid,
Erth, the gret moder, bayr this child, as is said,
Last systir to Ceyos and Enchelades,
Ane huge, horribill and strange monstre, but les,
Spedy of fut, and on weyngis swyft as wynd.   15
Quhou mony fedderis bene on hir body fynd,
Als mony walkryfe eyn lurkis thar undir,
Als feil tongis, that for totell is wondir,
With als feil mouthis carpis sche and beris,
Als mony hes scho prik upstandand eris.   20
By nycht scho fleys amyd the hevyn throu owt,
Circuland the schaddow of the erth about
With huge fard, nother cuyr gevand nor keip
Hir eyn anys to rest nor tak a sleip;
Al day scho syttis, wachand byssely,   25
Apon the top of nobillis howsis, to spy,
Or on thir princis palyce with towris hie,
And with hir noys gret citeis affrays sche—
Als weil ramembring fenyeit and schrewit sawys
As scho the treuth and verite furth schawis.   30
Thys ilke wensch, that tyme, with mony a taill,
Glaidly this rumour gan throu the pepill skaill,
Telland the thing wrocht, and not wrocht, togiddir;
Quhou of the Trojane blude wes cummyn thiddir
Ene, with quham the fair Dido be wed   35
Dedenyt, and as husband go to bed;
And how the wyntir sesson betwix thame tway
Thai spend in lang reffell, lust and play,
Of thar realmys na thing remembring,
In fowle delyte ybond by Cupyd kyng.   40
Thys menskles goddes in every mannys mouth
Skalys thir newis est, west, north and sowth.
Hir cours, onon, but langar tarying,
Addressys scho ontill Hyarbas kyng,

46

With hir sawis his mynd inflambyng as fyre,   45
Provokand hym to wreth and fellon ire.
To Amon he wes son, beget alswa
Apon the maid revist Garamantida;
Within his large realmys huge braid
Ane hundreth tempillis to Jupiter he maid,   50
Ane hundreth altaris, quharon the walkryfe fyre
He dedicate, altymys byrnand schyre,
Set wachis in honour of goddis perpetuelly
Of beistis blude the fat grond nevir dry,
Strowit with garlandis and flowris of divers kynd.   55
This ilke kyng, wod wroith, half owt of mynd,
And for thir schrewyt rumouris sor ammovit,
In presens of the goddis quhilk he luffit,
Befor the altar, to Jupiter, as thai say,
Hevand up handis, devotly thus gan pray: 60
'Almychty Jove,' quod he, 'quhamto, feill sys,
On brusyt beddis hie fest and sacryfys
Of Mawrusya the pepill hantis thus,
Offeryng to the the honour of Bachus,
Consideris thou this? or quhidder, fader, gif we   65
For nocht the dredis, quhen thou lattis thundir fle?
Or gif thi fyreslauch, the blynd clowdis within,
To fley our myndis, invane makis noys and dyn?
Yone woman, lait exile and vagabund
Com to our boundis, that by pryce bocht the grund   70
A litil village to byg, and quhamto we
For to manuyr gave the strand of the see,
Quhamto our lawis and statutis we gart mak,
Our mariage gan lychtly and forsaik,
And in hir ryng hes tane Ene for lord.   75
And now that secund Parys, of ane accord
With his onworthy sort, skant half men beyn,
Abufe his hed and halffettis, weil beseyn,
Set lyke a mytir the Trojane foly hat,
Hys hair enoynt weil prunyeit undir that,   80
By reif mantemys hir suld owris be—
Becaus onto thi templis dayly we

Bryngis offerand and invane hallowis thi name.'
With syk wordis Kyng Hyarbas at hame
Makyng hys prayeris, and grippand the altar,   85
Him hard onon almychty Jupiter,
And hys eyn turnys towart the riall wallis
Of Cartage, and thir luffaris (quhilkis so fallis
At thai thar fame and gude renown foryet),
Syne thus said to Mercuryus, but let,   90
And with sik maner charge gan hym direk:
'Pas, son, inhaist, graith the wyndis in effek;
Slyde with thi feddyrame to yon Trojane prynce,
Quhilk now in Cartage makis residence,
Gevand no cuyr of citeis in Italy   95
To hym ygrant by fatale destany.
Do beir my message swyftly throw the skyis,
Sa to hym thus my wordis on syk wys:
His derrest moder promist us not that he
Of hys gydyng sa faynt a man suldbe,   100
Nor, for syk causys, hym delyverit twys
Furth of the Grekis handis, hys ennemys;
Bot at he suld have beyn wys, sage and grave,
Hie senyeoreis and gret empyre to have,
And Itale dant, quhilk brandysis in battell,   105
And, by his dedis, declair and cleyrly tell
Hym cummyn of Teuceris hie genealogy,
And to subdew the warldis monarchy.
Of sa gret thingis thocht na wirschip hym steris,
Nor for hys honour list not laubour as efferis,   110
Yit than, the fader aucht na wys to envy
That Ascanyus bruke Romys senyeory.
Speir quhat he beildis, or how that he dar dwell
Amang a pepill salbe hys ennemys fell.
Hys lynnage tocum in Itale foryettis he,   115
And gevis na compt of Lavyne the cuntre.
Byd hym mak saill. This is all in effek;
Thiddir on our message thus we the direk,'
Said Jupiter, and Mercur but arest
Dressyt to obey hys gret faderis behest;   120

And first ontill hys feyt fast buklyt he
Hys goldyn weyngis, quharwith he doith fle,
Quhen so hym lyst, abuf the fludis on hyght,
Or on the erth, with great fard and swyft flycht;
Syne tuke his wand, quharwith, as that thai tell,   125
The pail sawlis he cachis furth of hell,
And other sum tharwith gan schet full hoyt
Deip in the sorofull grisly hellys pote—
Quharwith he makis folk sleip, magre thar hed,
And revis fra othir al sleip, and to the ded   130
Closis thar eyn, and brekis the stryngis tway—
Throu help tharof he chasys the wyndis away,
And trubly clowdis dyvidis in a thraw.
Tho furth he fleys, till at the last he saw
The heich top and sydis braid onevyn   135
Of hard Atlas, baryng on his crown the hevyn,
The mysty clowdis cirkilland his hed about
(Quharon of fyrryn treis stant mony rowt,
With wynd and storm full oft to schaik and blaw),
Hys schulderis heildit with new fallyn snaw;   140
Furth of the chyn of this ilk hasard auld
Gret fludis ischis, and styf ise schokyllis cauld
Doun from his stern and grysly berd hyngis.
Heir first Mercur, with evynly schynand weyngis,
Gan hym arest, and with hail fard fra thens   145
Unto the sey fludis maid hys discens.
Lyke till a fowle that, endlang the cost syde,
About the strandis, of fysch plentuus, and wyde,
Fleys by the watyr, skummand the fludis law;
Betwix the hevyn and erth, the sam wys, flaw   150
Mercury, clepit the child Cyllenyus,
Discendyng from hys moder granscher thus,
The sandy costis and desertis of Lyby,
And eik the wyndis, persyng by and by.
And, with the weyngit solys of hys feyt,   155
As he of Cartage fyrst tred on the streyt,
Eneas foundand towris he gan aspy,
And garrand beild new lugyngis byssyly:

Belt he wes with a swerd of mettale brycht
Of quham the scawbart with brown jasp wes pight;   160
His rych array dyd our hys schuldris hyng,
Bet of a purpour claith of Tyre glittering,
Fettysly stykkit with prynnyt goldyn thredis;
Of mychty Didois gift wrocht all his wedis.
Mercur recontris hym and said onon: 165
'Of Cartage now the prowd wallis of stone
Thou foundis,' quod he, 'and biggis at al devyce
A cite, excersyt intill a wyfis servyce,
Thyne awyn materis and realm foryetting, allace!
Hiddir onto the, from his bricht hevynly place,   170
The governour of goddis heth me sent,
Quhilk rewlys at will erd, hevyn and elyment;
He bad me throw the skyis bair this charge:
Quhat beildis thou heir in Lyby or Cartage?
Or to quhat fyne or beleif takis on hand   175
To waist thi tyme into this fremmyt land?
Gif that na laud ne honour move the list
Of sa hie thingis as ar to the promyst,
Nor thi selvyn thou wil not occupy
To purches thine awyn renown ne glory,   180
Yit than behald Ascanyus upwalxing,
And the gret hope of his seid and ofspring,
Quhamtil the realm and kynryk of Itaill,
With Romys boundis, beyn destinate, sans faill.'
On syk wys thus carpys Mercuryus,   185
And in the myddis of his sermond, thus,
He vanyst far away, I wait nevir quhar,
Furth of this mortale syght, in the schyre ayr.

Quhou Eneas hym grathys to depart
To quhom Dido heir carpys with sayr hart.   c. vi

BOT than Ene half mad and dum stude als,
Upstart his hair, the voce stak in his hals.
Sayr he langis to fle and to depart;
And that sweit cuntre, on the tother part,

50

To leif ful laith wes hym, or go at large.   5
Astonyst he wes to syt sa hie a charge—
Or dysobey the gret godis beheste
(Allace! quhat suld he do? oneth he wist);
Or with quhat wordis suld he now assay
The amorus queyn forto requir and pray;   10
Or on quhat wys hys taill he mycht begyn;
Baith to and fra compasyng, hys breist within,
Feill purpossys for every part about.
And, at the last, thus as he stude in dout,
Thys resson hym semyt fynaly the best: 15
He callys to hym Mynestheus and Sergest
And strang Cloanthus, and bad thai suld in hy
Do graith hys schyppys and navyn secretly,
And gaddir hys folkis towart the cost togydder,
Armour and al thyng necessar bring thyddir,   20
And to dissymyll, gif ony axit quhy
Thai thus addressyt thar geyr sa suddanly,
Hym self, he said, the meyn quhile, suld assay
To purches leif to pas and go away,
And wait hys tyme to speke tharof maist habill, 25
Quhen that the queyn Dido, maist honorabil,
Suld not beleif sa sone he kouth depart,
Nor sa gret luf dissyvir mycht be na art.
At hys command thai al glaidly furth w
And bissely begouth speid hys entent.   30
Bot sone the queyn persavyt al the slycht—
Quhay may begile a luffer, day or nycht?
Thar departing at hand fyrst scho aspyis,
Dredyng all sovir thing, as is the gys
Of every luffar altyme to stand in feir.   35
This ilke cursyt Fame we spak of eyr
Bair to the amorus queyn noys and gan rown,
'The schippis ar grathand, to pas thai mak thaim boun.'
Quharfor, inpacient and myndles in hir rage,
Scho wyskis wild throu the town of Cartage,   40
Syk wys as quhen thir nunnys of Bachus
Ruschis and relis our bankis, brays and bus,

Quhen, every thryd yeir, on thar payane gys,
Thar goddis feist thai hallow with lowd cryis,
That, al the nycht, the mont of Cytheron   45
Resoundis of thar clamour, quhar thai gone.
And at the last, yit thus, of hir fre will,
Eftir lang musyng, scho spak Eneas tyll:
'With dissymulance wenyt thou, onfaithfull wight,
Thou mycht have hyd fra me sa fals a slycht,   50
And, myne onwyttyng, steill furth of my land?
That nothir our gret lufe, promys, nor rycht hand
Gevyn me umquhile, may the heir withhald,
Nor cruel deth of Didois cors so cald!
Gif thou depart (and forthir quhat wald thou do,   55
In wyntir sesson pres graith thi navy, lo!)
And the addres to pas throu the wod see,
Myd tyme quhen stormys and wyndis blaw maist hie—
Art thou sa cruel? I put the cace, alsso,
That to nane onkouth landis the list go   60
Nother to fremmyt place, nor stedis will,
Bot that auld Troy war yit upstandand still;
Aucht thou, yit than, leif this weilfair and joy,
And in sik perrell seik throu the sey to Troy?
Quhat! wilt thou fle from me? allace! allace!   65
Be all thir teris trygland our my face,
And be that rycht hand umquhile thou me gave
(Sen to my self nocht ellis left I have,
Now wrachit catyve), be our treuth plychting eyk,
And be our spowsage begunnyn, I the beseik,   70
Gif ever ony thank I deservit towart the,
Or ocht of myne to the wes leif,' quod sche,
'Have mercy of our lynnage reddy to spill;
Gif tyme remanys yit thou heir prayeris will,
This fremmyt mynd, I pray you, do away.   75
For the I have beyn hatyt, this mony a day,
With all the pepill of Affrik, and with the kyng
That rewlys the land of Numyda and ryng;
For the myne awyn Tyrianys ar with me wraith;
For the is womanheid went and wirschip baith,   80

52

And my first fame, laud and renownye,
Quharby I wes rasyt to the starnys hie.
Reddy to de and my selvyn to spill,
My sweit gest, quhamto thou me leif will?
My gest, ha God! quhou al thyng now invane is,   85
Quhen of my spows nane othir name remanys!
Bot quharto suld I my ded langar delay?
Sal I abyde quhile thou be went away,
And quhil myne awyn brothir, Pigmaleon,
Bet down the wallis of my cite onon,   90
Or stern Hyarbas, kyng of Getule,
Led me away into captivite?
Bot, at the leist, tofor thi wayfleyng,
Had I a child consavyt of thyne ofspryng,
Gif I had ony yong Eneas small,   95
Befor me forto play within my hall,
Quhilk representit by symylitude thi face,
Than semyt I nocht, thus wys, allace! allace!
Aluterly dissavyt nor dissolate.'
Thus said the queyn Dido, in febil estate.   100
Bot, apon Jovis message fermly he
Stude musyng so, he movit nocht ane e,
Refrenyt his will, hydand in hart his thocht,
And, at the last, thir few wordis hes furth brocht:
'O gentil queyn, that sall I nevir deny,   105
Thy gude deid and desart is mair worthy
Than thou with wordis or tong may expreme;
Nor it sal nevir me irk, na yit mysseym,
The worthy Dido to hald in fresch memory,
So lang as that my self remembir may I,   110
Or quhil the spreit of lyfe this body steris.
As the mater requiris, a litil heris:
I purposyt nocht forto hyde thyftuusly
My vayage, nor, as ye weyn, secretly
Away to steil; quhat nedis you sa tofeyn?   115
For I pretendit nevir, be na meyn,
With you to mak the band of mariage,
Nor in that yok, ne frendschip in Cartage,

Yit come I nevir: bot gif the fatis, but pled,
At my plesour sufferit me lyfe to led,   120
At my fre wil my warkis to modyfy,
The cite of Troy than first agane suld I
Restore, and of our deir frendis remanys
Gaddir togiddir, and to the venquist Trojanys
Raparal with my handis agane thar wallis,   125
And beild up Priamus palyce at now fallis.
Bot sen Appollo, clepit Gryneus,
Gret Italy to seik commandis us,
To Itale eik oraclys of Lycia
Admonyst us, but mair delay, to ga;   130
Thar is my lust now and delyte at hand,
Thar is my cuntre and my natyve land.
Gif the, of Cartage the burgh and towris swa,
Quhilk art a woman of Phenycia,
And the aspect of citeis Affricane   135
Delytis, and withhaldis heir toremane,
Quhat wrang is it, caus of envy or schame,
Thocht Trojanys seik to Itale for thar hame?
Or is it nocht als lesum and ganand
That fynaly we seik to onkouth land?   140
Als oft as day is gone, and the dyrk nycht
With hir donk schaddow hydis of the erth the sycht,
Als oft as schynyng starnys doith uprys,
My faderis gost, Anchises, als feil sys
Into my sleip mannasis me tharto fast,   145
And oft his feirfull ymage doith me agast;
And in lyke wys the child Ascanyus,
Quhais deir hed suffir injurys is hard to us,
Quham of the realm of Itail I defraud,
And fra the grond to hym promyst withhawd.   150
Be athir of our hedis this I sweir;
Now laitly eik of goddis the messynger,
From hie Jupiter in hasty message sent,
Down throu the ayr brocht the ilk commandment:
On fair day lycht, myne awyn self dyd I se   155
Mercur the god entyr in this cite,

And his wordis with thir sam eris hard I.
With thy complayntis ony langar, forthy,
Lat be to vex me, or thy self to spyll,
Sen I seik nocht to Itale with fre will.'   160

Of the scharp wordys Queyn Dydo dyd say,
And how Eneas bownys fast away.   c. vii

DYDO, aggrevit ay quhil he his tayl tald,
With acquart luke gan towart hym behald,
Rollyng umquhile hir eyn, now heir, now thar,
With syght onstabil waverand our alquhar
And all enragyt thir wordis gan furth braid: 5
'Nothir wes a goddes thy moder, as is sayd,
Nor yit Kyng Dardanus cheif stok of thi kyn,
Thou treuthles wyght, bot of a cald, hard quhyn
The clekkyt that horribill mont, Cawcasus hait—
Thou sowkyt nevir womanis breist, weil I wait,   10
Bot of sum cruel tygir of Araby
The pappis the fosterit in the wod Hyrcany.
To quhat effect suld I hym langar perswaid,
Or quhat bettir may beleve than he hes said?
Quhiddir gif he murnyt quhen we wepit and walyt?   15
Quhiddir gif he steryt his eyn, as ocht hym alyt?
Quhidder gif for rewth he furth yet anys a teyr
Or of hys lufe had piete? Na, not to yeir.
Quhou sal I begyn, quhat first, quhat last to say?
Now, now, nothir gretast Juno, wallaway,   20
Nor Saturnys son, hie Jupiter, with just eyn
Hes our querrell considerit, na ourseyn;
For no quhar now faith nor lawte is fund.
I ressavyt hym schypbrokkyn fra the sey grund,
Wilsum, and mystyrfull of al warldis thyng,   25
Syne, myndles, maid hym my fallow in this ryng:
Hys navy lost reparalyt I, but faill,
And hys feris fred from the deth alhaill.
Allace! enragyt or enchantit am I;
Quhen now Appollo, with hys sossery,   30

55

And quhilis, he says, the kavillys of Lycia,
And quhilis, fra Jupiter down sent alsswa,
The messynger of goddis bryngis throu the skyis
Sa feirful charge and command on this wys:
Lyke as the goddis abufe nocht ellys rocht,   35
Bot on thi passage war al thar cuyr and thocht.
Nothir wil I hald the, nor thi wordis contrar:
Pas on thi way, towart Itale thou fair;
Seik throu the fludis with wyndis to that ryng.
Forsuyth, gif reuthfull goddis may ony thing,   40
Amyd thi way, I traist on rolkis blak
Thou sal deir by thy treuth thou to me brak,
And clep oft my richt name, "Dido, Dido!"
With fyre infernale, in thine absens alsso,
I sal the follow; and, fra the cald ded   45
Reif from my membris this sawle, in every sted
My gost salbe present the to agrys:
Thou salt, onworthy wyght, apon this wys
Be punyst weil; and tharof wald I heyr—
The fame tharof sal cum onto myne eyr,   50
Undir the erth, amang the schaddowys law.'
And this spokkyn, hir sermond with the ilk saw
Brak scho in twanc, ful dolorus in hir thocht:
The lycht scho fled, and als fast as scho mocht
Turnys frawart hym, and wyskyt of hys sycht,   55
On seir materis leifand hym pensyve wight,
And purposyng to have said mony thyngis.
The damycellis fast to thar lady thryngis,
That was in dedly swoun plat for dispar:
Up thai hyr hynt, and to hyr chawmyr bayr,   60
Quhilk was of marbill wrocht, and in hir bed
Laid softly down apon rych carpettis spred.
Bot yit, althocht the reuthful Eneas
The dolorus queyn to meys ful bissy was,
To do hir comfort, and hir dyseys asswage,   65
And with hys wordis return hir sad curage,
Bewalyng mekill hyr sorow and distres,
Proplexte in mynd by gret lufe; netheles,

The command of the goddis, by and by,
He execut, and vysseys hys navy.   70
Than byssely the Trojanys fell to wark,
And mony gret schyp, ballyngar and bark
Langis the cost brocht in and bet full weill.
Now fletis the mekil holk with tallonyt keyll.
The burgionyt treys on burd thai bring for aris,   75
Weltis down in woddis gret mastis, and na thing sparis,
Saysyng half onwrocht, so ithand thair war fair bown.
Rynnand heir and thar and wendyng fast of town,
Yhe mycht have seyn thame haist, lyke emmotis grete
Quhen thai depulye the mekill byng of quhete,   80
And in thar byke it careis, all and sum,
Providing for the cald wyntir tocum:
The blak swarm our the feildis walkis yarn,
Tursand throu the gers thar pray to hydlys darn:
Sum on thar nek the gret cornys upwrelis,   85
And our the furris bissely tharwith spelys;
Sum constrenyng the otheris fast to wirk,
And sum the sleuthful chasteis, that thocht irk
Of thar labour; quhil every rod and went
Wolx of that ithand wark hait, quhar thai went.   90

Quhou Dydo send hir systir Ene to pray,
And of the grysly syngnys dyd hir affray.   c. viii

QUHAT thocht thou now, Dydo, seand thir thingis?
Quhou mony sobbys gave thou and womentyngis
Quhen thou, out of thi castell from the hycht,
The large costis beheld thus at a sycht
Ourspred with Trojanys, in fervent bissynes   5
Gan spedely for thar vayage addres,
And of thar clamour befor thine eyn dyd se
Dyn and resoundyng al the large see?
O wytles lufe! quhat may be thocht or do,
At thou constrenys nocht mortell myndis tharto?   10
Scho is compellit to fal agane to teris
And Eneas assay with new prayeris,

57

And condiscendyt hir proud hart to submyt
Onto the strenth of lufe thus anys yit:
Les scho onwar, but caus, hir deth purvayt,   15
Hir list na thyng behynd leif onassayt.
Till hir scho gan hir systir call inhy:
'Annes,' quod scho, 'thou seys how byssely,
Our al the cost, for this vayage haist thai,
And now the wynd blawis weil to sail away: 20
The maryneris glaid lays thar schippis undyr croys.
O systir! in tyme kouth I have trowyt this loys
And sa gret dolour, I had providyt, but weir,
That this displesour suld have beyn eith to beir.
And netheles, for me, onhappy wight,   25
Do this a thing, Annes, with al thi mycht,
Sen yon ilk faithles man, deir systir, the
Was wont to cherys and hald in gret dante
And als hys secretis onto the reveill—
Hys sweit entres sum tyme thou knew ful weill,   30
Nane bot thou only the tyme of hys cummyng.
Pas on, systir, in my name this a thyng
Say lawly to my proud fa and declair
That in the port Aulyda I never swair
With the Grekis the Trojanys to distroy,   35
Nor I non navy send to sege Troy,
Nor yit his fader Anchises graf schent—
I nothir the muldis nor banys tharof rent.
Quhy doith he reffus my wordis and prayeris
To lat entir in his dul ontretabill eris?   40
Quhidder haistis he sa fast from hys behufe?
Beseik hym grant ontil his wrachyt lufe
This lattir reward, sen algatis he wil fle:
Tary quhil wynd blaw soft, and stabill see.
His ald promys na mair wil I hym crave,   45
Nor band of wedlok, quhilk he hes dissave,
Nor yit him pray go not to Italy,
Ne leif fair realmys onto him destany:
A litil delay I ask, but othir eys,
A space my furour to asswage and meys,   50

58

Quhill that my frawart forton and estait
Of my beleve schaw me I am frustrait,
And tech me for to murn mair paciently.
This lattir gift only at hym ask I.
Have mercy, systir, of thy systir deyr—   55
Quhilk servyce quhen thou done hes, without weir,
I sal the recompens weil twentyfald,
And quhil my ded the sam in memor hald.'
With syklyke wordis hir request scho maid,
Hir supplicatioun, with teris ful onglaid,   60
Reportis hir systir, and answer brocht agane
Quhou al hir prayeris and desyre was invane,
For al thar wepyng mycht not him anys steir;
Nane of thar wordis lykis hym to heir,
Thocht he of natur was tretabill and curtas.   65
The fatis war contrar thar desyre netheles,
And hys benyng eris the goddis dyttit,
That of thar askyng thar was nocht admittit.
And lyke as quhen the ancyant aik tre,
With hys byg schank, by north wynd oft we se   70
Is ombeset, to bet hym down and ourthraw,
Now heir, now thar, with the fell blastis blaw,
The swouchand byr quhisland amang the granys,
So that the hyast branchys, al atanys,
Thar croppys bowis towart the erth als tyte,   75
Quhen with the dynt the maister schank is smyte;
And, netheles, the ilk tre, fixit fast,
Stikkis to the rochis, not doun bet with the blast:
For quhy? als far as his crop heich on breid
Strekis in the ayr, als far hys rute doith spreid   80
Deip undir erth, towart the hell adoun—
The sammyn wys was this gentil baroun,
Now heir, now thar, with wordis ombeset,
And in his stout breist, ful of thochtis het,
Of reuth and amouris felt the perturbance.   85
Bot ever his mynd stude ferm, for ony chance
Onmovyt, quhar hys fyrst purpos was set,
That al for nocht the teris war furthyet.

Than suythly, the fey Dydo, al affrayt,
Seand fatis contrar, eftir deth prayt: 90
Scho irkit of hir lyfe, or to tak tent
Forto behald the hevynnys firmament.
Tharfor, in takyn hir purpos to fulfill,
And leif the lycht of lyfe, as was hyr will,
As on the altaris byrnand ful of sens   95
The sacrifyce scho offerit, in hir presence,
A grisly thyng to tell, scho gan behald
In blak adyll the hallowyt watir cald
Changyt and altyr, and furthyet wynys gude
Onon returnyt into laithly blude.   100
This visioun sche to nane reveil wald,
Nor yit to An, hir deir systir, it tald.
In wirschip eik, within hir palyce yet,
Of hir first husband, was a tempil bet
Of marbill, and hald in ful gret reverens,   105
With snaw quhite bendis, carpettis and ensens,
And festuale burgeonys arrayt, on thar gys;
Tharin was hard vocis, spech and cryis
Of hir said spous, clepand hir ful lowd,
Evir quhen the dyrk nycht dyd the erth schrowd.   110
And oft with wild scryke the nycht owle,
Heich on the rufe, alane, was hard yowle
With langsum voce and a ful petuus beir.
And eik bygane the feirful sawis seyr
Of the dyvynys, with terribil monysyngis,   115
Affrayt hir by mony grysly syngis.
And in hir sleip, wod wroth, in every place
Hir semyt cruel Eneas gan hir chace;
And evir, hir thocht, scho was left al alane,
And, but cumpany, mony far way had gane,   120
To seik hir folkis in a wilsum land—
Lyke Kyng Pentheus, in his wod rage dotand,
Thocht he beheld gret rowtis stand in staill
Of the Eumenydes, fureys infernale,
And in the lyft twa sonnys schynand cleir,   125
The cite of Thebes gan dowbil to hym appeir;

Or lyke Orestes, son of Agamenon,
On theatreis, in farcis mony one,
Rowpyt and sung how he his moder fled,
With fyre brondis and blak serpentis ourcled,   130
And saw the furyis, and grisly goddis fed,
Sittand in the tempill port to wrek hir ded.

Quhou Dydo queyn, hir purpos to covert,
Of enchantment dyd contyrfait the art.   c. ix

THUS quhen Dydo had caucht this frenasy,
Ourset with sorow and syk fantasy,
And determyt fermly that scho wald de,
The tyme quhen and maner quhou it suld be
Compasyng in hir breist, but mair abaid   5
Onto hir dolorus systir thus scho sayd,
Hir purpos by hir vissage dissymuland,
Schawand by hir cheir gude hope and glad sembland:
'Systir germane,' quod scho, 'away your smart;
Beys of your systeris weilfar glaid in hart.   10
I have the way fundyn, quharby yone syre,
Salbe to me rendryt at my desyre,
Or me delyvir from hys lufe al fre.
Neyr by the end of the gret occiane see,
Thar as the son declynys and goys doun,   15
At the far syde of Ethiope regioun,
A place thar is, quhar that the huge Atlas
On schuldyr rollys the round speir in cumpas,
Full of thir lemand starnys, as we se:
Thar dwellys, systir, as it is schaw to me,   20
Ane haly nun, a ful gret prophetes,
Born of the pepill of Massylyne, I ges,
And wardane of the ryal tempil, thai sa,
Set in the gardyngis hecht Hesperida,
And to the walkryfe dragon mete gave sche,   25
That kepyt the goldyn apyllis in the tre,
Strynkland to hym the wak hunny sweit,
And sleipryfe chesbow seyd, to quykkyn his spreit.

61

This woman hechtis, with hir enchantmentis,
From luffis bandis to lows al thar ententis   30
Quham so hir lyst, and bynd other sum alsso
In langsum amouris vehement payn and wo.
The rynnand fludis thar watir stop kan scho mak,
And eik the starnys turn thar cours abak,
And on the nycht the ded gastis assemmyll: 35
Undir thi feyt the erd rayr and trymmyll
Thou most se, throw hir incantatioun,
And from the hillys treys discendyng down.
To wytnes the gret goddis draw I heyr,
And thy sweit hed, myne awyn systir deir,   40
Agane my wil, ful sayr constrenyt am I
Art magyk to excers or sossary.
Richt secretly intil our innar clos,
Undir the oppyn sky, to this purpos
Pas on, and of treys thou byg a byng   45
Tobe a fyre, and tharapon thou hyng
Yon mannys sword, quhilk that wikkyt wight
Left stykand in our chawmyr this hyndir nyght,
Hys cote armour, and othir clethyng all,
And eik that maist wrachit bed conjugall,   50
Quharin I perychit and wes schent, allace!
For so the religyus commandyt has,
To omdo and distroy al maner thyng
Quhilk may yon wareit man to memor bring.'
This sayd, scho held hir tong; and tharwithall   55
Hir vissage wolx als pail as ony wall.
Thocht Annes wenyt not hir systir wald
Graith sacryfice for hir ded body cald,
Nor that syk fury was in hyr breist consavyt;
For by na resson dred sche, nor persavyt   60
Now mor displesour or harmys apperand
Than for Sycheus ded, hir first husband:
Quharfor, scho hes hir command done ilk deill.
Bot quhen the gret byng was upbeildit weill
Of ayk treys and fyrryn schydis dry,   65
Within the secrete clos, undyr the sky,

The place with flowris and garlandis stentis the queyn,
And crownys about with funerale bewis greyn.
Abuf the mowe the forsaid bed was maid,
Quharin the figur of Ene scho layd,   70
Hys clethyng and hys sword at he had left,
Ramembring weill the thyng that followyt eft.
Feill altaris stude about the fyre funerale,
And the religyus nun, with hair down skaill,
Thre hundreth goddis with hir mouth rowpyt sche—   75
Herebus, the grysly of the deyp hellys see,
Chaos, confoundar of elymentis, alssua,
And the thrynfald goddes Proserpina,
The thre figuris of the virgyn Dyan.
And evir the watir strynklis scho onan,   80
Contyrfait tobe of Avernus the well,
Quhilk lowch is situate at the mouth of hell.
Spryngand herbys eftir the cours of the moyn
War socht, and with brasyn hukis cuttit soyn,
To get thar mylky sap and vennom blak.   85
Thai seik alsso, and owt gan rent and tak
The lump betwix the new born folys eyn,
And fra the moder byreft the lufe sa greyn.
The queyn hir self fast by the altar standis,
Haldand the meldyr in hir devote handis,   90
Hir ta fute bayr, and the bandis of threyd
Nocht festynnyt, bot hung by hyr lowys weyd;
And, remembring scho was in poynt to de,
The goddis all onto wytnes drew sche,
The starnys and planetis, gydaris of fatis,   95
And gif thar ony deite be, that watis
Or persavys luffaris inequale of behest,
To have in memor hir just caus and request.

Quhat sorow dreys Queyn Dydo all the nycht,
And how Mercur bad Ene tak the flycht.   c. x

THE nycht followys, and every wery wight
Throu owt the erth hath caucht, onon rycht,

63

The sownd plesand sleip thame lykit best.
Woddis and rageand seys war at rest;
As the starnys thar myd cours rollys doun,   5
All feildis still, but othir noys or sown,
All beistis and byrdis of divers cullouris seir,
And quhatsumever in the braid lowys weir,
Or, amang buskis harsk, leyndis undir the spray,
Throu nychtis sylence slepit quhar thai lay,   10
Mesyng thar bissy thocht and curis smart,
All irksum laubour foryet and owt of hart.
Bot the onrestles fey spreit dyd not so
Of this onhappy Phenyssane Dydo,
For never mair may scho sleip a wynk,   15
Nor nychtis rest in eyn or breist lat synk.
The hevy thochtis multipleis ever on ane;
Strang luf begynnys to rage and rys agane
And fellon stormys of ire gan hir to schaik.
Thus fynaly scho owt bradis, allaik!   20
Rollyng alane seir thyngis in hir thocht:
'Ha! quhat do I?' quod scho, 'all is for nocht.
Sall I thus mokkit, and to hething dryve,
My fyrst luffaris agane assay belyve?
Or sal I lawly sum lord Numydane   25
Pray and beseik of mariage now agane,
Quhom I sa oft lychtlyit to spows or this?
Na, wyll I not! Quhat, sal I than, I wys,
Follow the Trojane navy in strange landis,
And reddely obey al thar commandis?   30
I hope it sal profyte, na litill thyng,
My gret help done thame and suppowellyng;
For amang kynd folkis this is na dreid,
Weil is remembrit the ald thankful deid.
Bot thocht in cace to do this war my will,   35
Quha wald me suffir my purpos to fulfyll,
Or in thar prowd schippis me ressave?
Thus drevyn to hethyng, and al thi grace bywave,
Tynt woman, allace! baris thou not yit in mynd
The maynsweryng of fals Laomedonis kynd?   40

64

And maratour, quhat ettill I for todo?
A queyn alane to steil away thus, lo!
Accumpanyit bot with mery maryneris?
Or than with all my Tyrianys, as efferis,
And all my power assemblit me about,   45
On schipburd entyr with al that huge rowt
Quhilk furth of Sydon scarsly draw I mycht,
Sal I thame cach agane our seys lycht?
Byd thame mak saill onon, and a new rays?
Na, rather de, as thou deservyt has,   50
And with a swerd mak of this duyl ane end.
O systir germane, thou me fyrst taucht and kend,
Allace the quhile! and offerit me to my fo;
Thou with thir harmys ourchargit me alsso,
Quhen I fell fyrst into this rage,' quod sche,   55
'Bot so to do my teris constreynt the.
Was it not lefull, allace! but cumpany,
To me but cryme in chawmyr alane to ly,
Or led my lyfe lyke to thir beistis wild,
And not beyn thus with thocht nor harmys fild?   60
Allace! onkepit is the trew cunnand
Hecht to Sycheus assys, my first husband.'
Syk gret complayntis from hir breist bryst kan.
Bot Eneas, sovir to depart or than,
And al hys neidful thyngis grathit, by and by,   65
Heich in hys eft schyp sownd slepand kan ly;
Quhamto in visioun the sam god dyd appeir,
In syklyke figur as that he dyd eyr,
Onto Mercuryus lyke, in al fasson,
Baith cullour of vissage and of vocis sown,   70
In form of a yongker with membris fair,
Plesand of cheir, and yallow glitterand hair.
Hym thocht agane he monyst on this wys:
'Son of the goddes, quhou is this heir thou lyis?
Quhat, may thou undir sa gret danger sleip,   75
And al forvayit takis nothir cuyr nor keyp
For tobehald quhat perrellys about the standis
Nor harknys the fair wynd blawys of landis?

Scho quham thou knawys, within hir breist ful hait
Sorowfull vengeans compasis and dissait,   80
And certanly determyt forto de,
In divers stowris of ire brandysys sche.
Quhy wilt thou not fle spedely be nycht,
Quhen forto haist thou hes laser and mycht?
Thou salt, onon, behald the seys large   85
All ombeset with toppyt schyp and barge,
The feirful brandis and blesys of hait fyre,
Reddy to byrn thi schippys, lemand schyre,
And al the cost belyve of flambys scald,
Gyf, quhil to morow, tary in this land thou wald.   90
Have done, speid hand, and mak na mair delay,
Variabill and changeand thyngis beyn wemen ay.'
And sayand this, into the dyrk nyght
He gan hym hyde, and vanyst out of sycht.
Eneas, of this hasty visioun affrayit,   95
Gan start on fut, and fast his feris assayit:
'Awalk onon, get up, my men, inhy,
Tyte to your wardis, span aris bissely,
Schaik down the salys sone and lat us wend.
From the hie hevyn the god agane is send,   100
Lo! spurrand us to haist and fle away,
And byddis smyte the twyne cabyll in tway.
O blissyt wyght! quhat god at evir thou be,
We sal obey thi charge and follow the,
And thy command fulfyll agane blithly,   105
Besekyng the assist to us frendly
Help and support, with prospir influens
The hevyn and starris dres our vayage hens.'
And with that word, hys scherand sword als tyte
Hynt owt of scheith, the cabil in twa gan smyte.   110
The sam maner of haist caucht al the lave;
Thai hurl away, ankyrris uphynt and rave,
Left the costis desert on athir sydis.
The stabil sey undir the schippis slydis;
The stour of fame upwelt thai egyrly,   115
And swepis our the haw fludis inhy.

BE this Aurora, leifand the purpour bed
Of hir lord Titan, heth the erd ourspred
With new days licht, and quhen the queyn
The first grekyng of the day hes seyn
And fra hir hie wyndoys gan espy,   5
With bent sail furth caryand, the navy,
The costis and the schor al desolate
Behaldis eik but owthir schip or bate,
Hir fayr quhite breist, thar as scho dyd stand,
Feil tymys smate scho with hir awyn hand,   10
And ryvand hir bricht haris petuusly,
'Jupiter,' quod scho, 'sal he depart, ha, fy!
And leful tyll a vavengeour stranger
Me and my realm betrump on this maner?
Sal not my menye to harnes ryn in hy   15
Our al the town, and follow bissely?
Speid, tak yon schippys! on burd fast to the raid!
Haist sone, and kast on thame fyre blesis braid!
Schute dartis thik, and quel thame with your glavys. . . .
Quhat said I or quhar am I? Now thou ravys;   20
Quhat wodnes, fey Dydo, movis thi mynd?
Now art thou hyt with frawart werdis onkynd?
Sa til have done than had bene mair ganand
Quhen thou hym gave the ceptour of thi land.
Ha! now behald hys gret prowes,' quod sche,   25
'Hys reuthful piete and faith! Is not yon he
Quham, as thai say, the goddis of hys land
In hys navy careis our sey and sand?
Is not yon he quhom on his schulderis, thai say,
For reuth his agit fader bair away?   30
Mycht I not caucht and rent in pecis his cors,
Syne swak the gobbettis in the sey by fors
Of hym and all hys fallowys? Weill I mocht!
And eik yone sam Ascanyus mycht I nocht

Have trynschit with a sword, and maid a meys   35
To his fader tharof to eyt at deys?
Forsuyth, in cace the aventur of bataill
Had beyn doutsum, wald God it war assaill!
Quham sall I dreid, now reddy forto de?
Wald God I mycht, in yon navy I se,   40
The hait fyre brandis set, and every boyr
Fyll all with flambys red, and forthirmor
Baith fader and son, with hail generacioun,
That I had brynt, distroyit and bryttnyt doun,
And thame abuf syne ded my self had laid!   45
O thou brycht son, that, with thi bemys glayd,
All erdly laubour clengis, circuland about;
And thou Juno, mediatrix, but dout,
Of al thir hevy thochtis, and weill thame knawis;
And thou Proserpyne, quhilk, by our gentile lawys,   50
Art rowpit hie and yellyt lowd by nyght,
In forkyt ways, with mony mudy wight;
And ye infernale fureys, that wrekis al wrang;
And ye goddis eik, quham now amang
Dido standis reddy tocum in poynt to de;   55
Ressave thir wordis quhilkis I sal say,' quod sche,
'Withdraw fra hyme your gret mychtis, quharby
Schrewis aucht be punyst for thar cryme, and not I;
And thir our prayeris accept, we you beseik.
Gyf it be necessar and determyt eik   60
Yon wikkit hed in portis of Itale
To entir and cum or to thai boundis saill,
And gyf the fatis and Jove wil it be so
And hes decreit he fynaly thyddir go,
Yit, at the lest, thar mot he be assail,   65
With hardy pepill ay trublyt in bataill,
By fors of armys expellyt hys boundis eik,
Far from Ascanyus help, constrenyt beseik
Ayd and supple, and als that he behald
Feil cayrfull corsys of hys folk ded and cald,   70
And quhen alsso hym self submyt hes he
Undir payce and lawis of iniquite,

That he bruke nowthir realm, nor gude lyfe led,
Bot fal fey or his day, and sone be ded,
And ly onerdyt in myddis of the sandis.   75
Thys I beseik you hevand up my handis;
Thys is my lattir word at I conclude,
Furthyettand it togiddir with my blude.
And forthirmor, O ye my Tyrianys,
Quhilk now in Affrik at Cartage remanys,   80
Yon clan, with thar successioun and kynrayd,
Persew with haitrent perpetual, and invaid;
Onto my assys grant this a gift,' quod sche.
'Nevir luf nor payce betwix thir pepill be.
Of our levingis sum revengar mot spryng,   85
With fyre and sword to persew and doun thryng
The lauboreris discend from Dardanus.
Now fra thyne furth, all that succedis til us,
Quhen ever thai may fynd tyme, with strenth and mycht
Batail to batail mot thai debait in fyght;   90
Thir costis mot be to tharis contrar ay,
And to thar stremys our seys frawart, I pray,
Thar ofspring eik amang thame self mot debate.'
Thus said scho, and with that word, God wate,
Hir faynt spreit in al partis writhis sche,   95
Sekand the way, alssone as it mycht be,
Forto bereif hir self the irksum lyve,
Tho callys scho to hyr Barcen belyve,
Nurys umquhile to Sychey hir husband,
For hir awyn nurys in hir native land   100
Was beryit in to assis broun or than.
'Deir nurys,' quod scho, 'fech my sister An;
Byd hir in haist with watir of a flude
Hir body strynkil; the bestis, and the blude,
And clengyng graith scho knawis, with hir bring.   105
Se on this wys scho cum, foryet na thyng;
And thou thy self thine halffettis als array
With haly garland. My will is to assay
And now perform the sacryfyce in hy
That onto Pluto dewly begun have I,   110

69

To mak end of my dolorus thochtis all,
And byrn yon Trojane statw in flamb funeral.'
Thus said Dido, and the tother, with that,
Hychit on furth with slaw pays lyke a trat.

Heir followys of the famus Queyn Dydo
The fatale dynt of deth and mortale wo.   c. xii

Bот now the hasty, egyr and wild Dydo,
Into hyr cruell purpos enragyt so,
The bludy eyn rollyng in hir hed,
Wan and ful paill for feir of the neir ded,
With chekis freklyt, and al of tychirris bysprent,   5
Quakyng throu dreid, ruschit furth, or scho wald stent,
Onto the innar wardis of hyr place,
As wod woman clam on the byng, allace!
And furth scho drew the Trojane swerd, fute hait,
A wapyn was never wrocht for syk a nate.   10
And sone as sche beheld Eneas clething,
And eik the bed bekend, a quhile wepyng,
Stude musyng in hir mynd, and syne, but baid,
Fel in the bed, and thir last wordis said:
'O sweit habyte, and lykand bed,' quod sche,   15
'So lang as God lyst suffir and destane,
Ressave my blude, and this sawle that on flocht is,
And me delyvir from thir hevy thochtis.
Thus lang I levyt have, and now is spent
The term of lyfe that forton heth me lent;   20
For now my gret gost undir erth mon go.
A richt fair cite have I beild alsso,
Myne awyn wark and wallys behald have I,
My spows wrokyn of my brothir ennemy,
Fra hym byreft hys tressour, and quyt hym weill.   25
Happy, allace! our happy, and ful of seyll,
Had I beyn, only gyf that never nane
At our cost had arryvit schip Trojane.'
And sayand this, hir mouth fast thristis sche
Doun in the bed: 'Onwrokyn sal we de?   30

70

'De us behufis,' scho said, 'and quhou behald!'
And gan the scharp sword to hir breist uphald;
'Ya, thus, thus lykis us starve and to depart!'
And with that word, rave hir self to the hart.
'Now lat yon cruel Trojane swelly and se   35
This our fyre funerale from the deip see,
And of our deth turs with hym fra Cartage
Thys takyn of myscheif in hys vayage,'
Quod scho; and tharwith gan hir servandis behald
Hir fallyn and stekit on the irne cald,   40
The blude outbullyrand on the nakyt swerd,
Hir handis furthsprent. The clamour than and rerd
Went to the toppys of the large hallys;
The noys ran wild out our the cite wallis,
Smate all the town with lamentabil murnyng.   45
Of greting, gowlyng and wyfly womentyng
The ruffis dyd resound, bray and rayr,
Quhil huge bewalyng al fordynnyt the air—
Nane other wys than thocht takyn and doun bet
War al Cartage, and with ennemys ourset,   50
Or than thar natyve cite the town of Tyre,
And furyus flambe, kendillit and byrnand schyre,
Spredyng fra thak to thak, baith but and ben,
Als weil our templis as howsis of othir men.
Hir systir An, spreitles almaist for dreid,   55
Herand sa feirful confluens thyddir speid,
With nalys ryvand reuthfully hir face,
And smytand with hir nevis hir breist, allace!
Fast ruschis throu the myddis of the rowt,
And on the throwand, with mony sprauch and schout, 60
Callys by name: 'Systir germane,' quod scho,
'Och! was this it thou fenyeit the to do?
Hes thou attempyt me with syk dissait?
This byng of treys, thir altaris and fyris hait,
Is this the thyng thai have onto me dycht?   65
Quhat sall I first compleyn, now dissolate wight?
O deir systir, quhen thou was reddy to de,
Ha! quhy hes thou sa far dyspysyt me

71

As to reffus thi systir with the to wend?
Thou suld have callyt me to the sammyn end,   70
That the ilk sorow, the sammyn swerd, bath tway,
And the self hour, mycht have tane hyne away.
Thys funeral fyre with thir handis biggyt I,
And with my voce dyd on our goddis heir cry,
To that effect as, cruel, tobe absent,   75
Thou beand thus sa duylfully heir schent!
Sistir, allace! with my counsell have I
The, and my self, and pepill of Sydony,
The heris all, and eik thi fayr cite,
Distroyt and ondoyn for ay,' quod sche.   80
'Fech hiddir sone the well watir lew warm,
To wesch hir woundis, and hald hir in myne arm;
Syne with my mowth at I may sowk, and se
Gyf spreit of lyve left in hir body be.'
This sayand, the hie byng ascendis onane,   85
And gan enbrays half ded hir systir germane,
Culyeand in hir bosum, and murnand ay,
And with hir wympil wipyt the blude away.
And scho agane, Dydo, the dedly queyn,
Pressyt fortil uplift hir hevy eyn,   90
Bot tharof falys; for the grysly wound
Deip in hir breist gapis wyde and onsound.
Thrys scho hir self raxit up to rys;
Thrys on hir elbok lenys; and als feill sys
Scho fallys bakwart in the bed agane.   95
With eyn rollyng, and twynkland up ful fane,
Assays scho to spy the hevynnys lyght,
Syne murmouris, quhen scho tharof gat a sycht.
Almychty Juno havand reuth, by this,
Of hir lang sorow and tarysum ded, I wys,   100
Hir mayd Irys from the hevyn hes send
The throwand sawle to lowys, and mak ane end
Of al the juncturis and lethis of hir cors;
Becaus that nothir of fatis throu the fors
Nor yit by natural ded peryschit sche,   105
Bot fey in hasty furour emflambyt hie

72

Befor hir day had hir self spilt,
Or that Proserpyne the yallow haris gilt
From hir fortop byreft, or dubbyt hir hed
Onto the Stygian hellis flude of ded.   110
Tharfor dewy Iris throu the hevyn
With hir safron weyngis flaw ful evin,
Drawand, quhar scho went, forgane the son cleir,
A thousand cullouris of divers hewys seir,
And abufe Dydoys hed arest kan: 115
'I am commandyt,' said scho, 'and I man
Omdo this hayr, to Pluto consecrate,
And lowis thi sawle out of this mortale stait.'
Thys sayand, with rycht hand hes scho hynt
The hair, and cuttis in twa, or that scho stynt;   120
And tharwithall the natural heyt outquent,
And, with a puft of aynd, the lyfe furthwent.

BOOK VI

Of Eneas sacrifyis be nycht,
And quhou to hel he tuk the way ful rycht.   c. iv

THIS beand done, Sibillais commandment
Ene addressis perform incontinent.
Thar stude a dirk and profound cave fast by,
A hidduus hoill, deip gapand and grisly,
All ful of cragis and of thir scharp flynt stanys,   5
Quhilk was weil dekkit and closit for the nanys
With a fowle layk, als blak as ony craw,
And skuggis dym of a ful dern wod schaw,
Abufe the quhilk na fowle may fle but skath.
Exalationys or vapouris blak and laith   10
Furth of that dedly golf thrawis in the air,
Sik wys na byrd may thiddir mak repair;
Quharfor Grekis Avernus clepis this sted,
The place bot fowlis to say, or pyt of ded.

73

Heir first Ene, at this ilk entre vyle,   15
Fowr yong stottis addressit, blak of pyle;
The nun Sibilla ressavys thame, and syne
Amyd thar forhedis quhelmyt on cowpis of wyne,
And of thar top, betwix the hornys twa,
The ovirmast haris has scho pullit awa,   20
And in the haly ingil, as was the gys,
Kest thame, in maner of the first sacrifice,
Apon Hecate cryand, with mony a yell,
Mychtful in hevin and dym dungeon of hell.
Sum slevit knyvis in the bestis throtis,   25
And otheris, quhilk war ordand for sik notis,
The warm new blude keppit in cowp and peys.
Ene him self a yow was blak of flece
Brittnnyt with hys sword, in sacrifice ful hie
Onto the moder of the fureys thre,   30
And hir gret systir; and to the, Proserpyne,
A yeld kow all to trynschit; and eftir syne
To the infernal kyng, quhilk Pluto hait,
Hys nycht altaris begouth to dedicate;
The hail bowkis of bestys, bayn and lyre,   35
Amyd the flambys kest and haly fyre;
The fat oly dyd he yet and peyr
Apon the entralys, to mak thame byrn cleir.
Bot lo, a litill befor the son rysyng,
The grond begouth to rummys, croyn and ryng,   40
Undir thar feyt, and woddy toppys hie
Of thir hillys begyn to move thai se;
Amang the schaddowys and the skuggis mark
The hell hundys hard thai yowl and bark,
At cummyng of the goddes Proserpyne.   45
Sibilla cryis, that prophetes dyvyne:
'All ye that bene prophane, away, away!
Swith, outwith al the sanctuar hy yow, hay!
And thou', quod sche, 'hald on thi way with me.
Draw furth thi swerd, for now is neid, Ene,   50
To schaw thi manheid, and be of ferm curage.'
Thus far scho said, smyte with the godly rage,

And tharwith entris in the oppynnyt cave;
Eneas onabasit, fra all the lave,
Followis his gide with equale pays ful rycht.   55
O yhe goddis, in quhais power and mycht
The sawlis beyn, and yhe dern skuggis dyrk,
Confusyt Chaos, quharof all thing beyn wirk,
Skaldand hellis flude, Flagiton, but lycht,
Placis of silence and perpetuall nycht: 60
Mot it be leful to me for to tell
Tha thyngis quhilkis I have hard said of hell,
And, by your myghtis, that I may furth schaw
Seir thingis drynchit in the erd ful law,
And deip envolvyt in myrknes and in myst!   65
Thai walking furth sa dyrk, oneth thai wyst
Quhidder thai went, amyd dym schaddowys thar,
Quhar evir is nycht, and nevir lyght dois repar,
Throwout the waist dongion of Pluto kyng,
Thai voyd boundis, and that gowsty ryng—   70
Siklyke as quha wald throw thik woddis wend
In obscure licht, quhen moyn may nocht be kend
As Jupiter, the kyng etheryall,
With erdis skugg hydis the hevynnys all,
And the myrk nycht, with hir vissage gray,   75
From every thing hes reft the hew away.
Befor the porch and fyrst jawys of hell,
Lamentatioun and wraikfull Thochtis fell
Thar lugyng had; and thar at dwellis eyk
Pail Maladeis that causys folk be seik,   80
The feirful Dreid, and als onweldy Age,
The fellon Hungir with hir ondantit rage;
Thar was alsso the laithly Indigence,
Terribill of port and schameful hir presence,
The grysly Ded at mony ane hes slane,   85
The hard Laubour, and diseysful Pane,
The slottry Sleip, Dedis cousyng of kynd,
Inordinat Blithnes of perversit mynd;
And in the yet forganyst thame dyd stand
The mortal Batall with hys dedly brand,   90

75

The irne chalmeris of hellys Fureys fell,
Witles Discord, that wondryng maist crewell,
Wymplit and buskit in a bludy bend,
With snakis hung at every harys end.
And in the myddis of the utyr ward,   95
With braid branschis spred our al the sward,
A rank elm tre stude, huge gret, and stok ald—
The vulgar pepil in that sammyn hald
Belevis thir vayn dremys makis thar duellyng;
Undir ilk leif ful thik thai stik and hyng.   100
Thar beyn eik monstreis of mony divers sort:
The Centawres war stablit at this port,
The dowbil porturat Scilla with thame infeir,
Bryareus with ane hundreth formys seyr,
The bysnyng best, the serpent of Lerna,   105
Horribilly quhysland, and quent Chymera
With fyre enarmyt on hir toppys hie,
The laithly Harpyes, and the Gorgones thre;
Of thrynfald bodeys gaistly formys dyd grone,
Baith of Erylus and of Geryon.   110
Eneas smartly, for the hasty dreid,
Hynt furth hys swerd in this place, and, gud speid,
The drawin blaid he profferis thar and heir
Onto tha monstreis, evir as thai drew neir;
And war not his expert mait Scybilla   115
Tawcht him thai war bot voyd gaistis all tha,
But ony bodeis, as wandrand wrechys waist,
He had apon thame ruschit in gret haist,
And with his bytand brycht brand, all invane,
The tume schaddowis smyttyn to have slane.   120

[*Æneas meets Dido in the Underworld*]   c. vii

AMANG otheris the Phenyssyane Dido   55
Within the gret wod walkis to and fro,
The greyn wound gapand in hir breist all new,
Quhom as the Trojane barroun nerrer drew,

76

And throw the dyrk schaddowis first dyd knaw—
Sikwys as quha throw clowdy skyis saw,   60
Or, at the leist, wenys he heth do se,
The new moyn quhen first upwalxis sche—
The terys leyt he fall, and tendyrly
With hartly lufe begrat hir thus in hy:
'O fey Dido, sen I persave the heyr,   65
A sovir warnyng, now I knaw ful cleir,
Was schawin me, at thou with swerd was slaw,
Byreft thi self the lyfe, and brocht of daw.
Allace, I was the causar of thy ded!
By al the starnys schynys abone our hed,   70
And be the goddis abone, to the I swer,
And be the faith and lawte, gif ony heir
Trewth may be fund deip undir erd,' quod he,
'Malgre my wyl, Pryncess, sa mot I the,
From thy costis depart I was constrenyt.   75
Bot the commandment of the goddis onfenyt,
Quhais gret mychtis hes me hyddir dryve,
To pas throwout thir dirk schaddowis belyve,
By gowsty placis, welch savorit, must and hair,
Quhar profund nycht perpetual doith repar,   80
Compellit me from the forto dissevir;
Nor in my mynde ymagyn mycht I nevir,
For my departing or absens, I wys,
Thou suldist kaucht sa gret dyseys as this.
Do stynt thy pays! Abide, thou gentil wight,   85
Withdraw the not sa sone furth of my sight!
Quham fleist thou? This is the lattir day,
By werdis schape, that with the speke I may.'
With sik wordis Eneas, full of wo,
Set him to meys the sprete of Queyn Dido,   90
Quhilk, all inflambit, ful of wreth and ire,
With acquart luke glowand hait as fyre,
Maid him to weip and sched furth teris wak.
All fremmytly frawart hym, as he spak,
Hir eyn fixit apon the grond held sche,   95
Moving na mair hir curage, face nor bre,

77

Than scho had bene a statu of marbil stane,
Or a ferm rolk of Mont Marpesyane.
Bot finaly, full swyft scho wiskis away,
Aggrevit fled in the darn woddis gray,   100
Quhar as Sycheus, hir first spows, ful suyr
Corespondis to hir desyre and cuyr,
Rendring in lufe amouris equivalent.
And, netheles, fast eftir hir furth sprent
Ene, perplexit of hir sory cace,   105
And weping gan hir follow a weil lang space,
Regratand in his mynd, and had piete
Of the distres that movit hir so to fle.

[*Anchises describes Æneas' posterity*]

'Now turnys hyddir, my sweit son, albedene,   71
The cirkillis and the sight of baith thy eyn—
Behald thir pepill and thy cheif Romanys.
Cesar Julyus, lo, in yonder planys,
And all the famyl of hym Julius,   75
Quhilk eftir thys ar tocum, trastis us,
Undre the gret hie hevynnys assiltre.
Yon man, yon man, my son, the sam is he
Quham thou so oft has hard promist or this,
Cesar August Octavyane, I wys,   80
Cum of the goddys geneology and kyn,
Quhilk sall agane the goldin warld begyn,
As umquhile was, in tyme of Saturn ald,
Throu Ital ryng baith be firth and fald;
And hys empire sal delait and wynde   85
Our Garamantas, and the forthar Inde;
The landis lyis without the starnys blenk,
Outwith the yheris cours and sonnys renk,
Quhar the upberar of the hevyn, Atlas,
On schuldir rollys the round speir in cumpas,   90
Ful of thir lemand starnys mony one.
Sall, at his hyddir cummyn, ror and grone

The realme of Caspys or of Assery,
All Scithya, Meothys land fast by,
Horribill answeris sall of goddis heir;   95
All trublit in affray, trymlyng for feir,
To quakyng sall sevyn mowthis of Nyle flude.
Nevir, forsuyth, strang Hercules the gude
Samekil space of erth or land ouryeid,
All thocht the wynd swift hart he schot to ded,   100
And stanchit Erymanthus forest roucht,
The serpent Lerna with hys bow persit throuch;
Nor Bachus, quhilk victor afor thir days
With wyne burgions the hillis top arays,
Dryvand the ferfull tygris fast away   105
Down fra the hyght of the gret mont Nysay.
And yit we dowt onto the forthir end
Hys gret vertu and dedys to extend!
Than quha suld dreid stop us to occupy
Or till inhabyt land of Italy?'   110

BOOK VII

The Prologue

As bryght Phebus, scheyn soverane hevynnys e,
The opposit held of hys chymmys hie,
Cleir schynand bemys, and goldyn symmyris hew,
In laton cullour alteryng haill of new,
Kythyng no syng of heyt be hys vissage,   5
So neir approchit he his wyntir stage;
Reddy he was to entyr the thrid morn
In clowdy skyis undre Capricorn;
All thocht he be the hart and lamp of hevyn,
Forfeblit wolx hys lemand gylty levyn,   10
Throu the declynyng of hys large round speir.
The frosty regioun ryngis of the yer,

The tyme and sesson bittir, cald and paill,
Tha schort days that clerkis clepe brumaill,
Quhen brym blastis of the northyn art   15
Ourquhelmyt had Neptunus in his cart,
And all to schaik the levis of the treis,
The rageand storm ourweltrand wally seys.
Ryveris ran reid on spait with watir browne,
And burnys hurlys all thar bankis downe,   20
And landbrist rumland rudely with sik beir,
So lowd ne rumyst wild lyoun or ber;
Fludis monstreis, sik as meirswyne or quhalis,
Fro the tempest law in the deip devalis.
Mars occident, retrograde in his speir,   25
Provocand stryfe, regnyt as lord that yer;
Rany Oryon with his stormy face
Bewavit oft the schipman by hys race;
Frawart Saturn, chill of complexioun,
Throu quhais aspect darth and infectioun   30
Beyn causyt oft, and mortal pestilens,
Went progressyve the greis of his ascens;
And lusty Hebe, Junoys douchtir gay,
Stude spulyeit of hir office and array.
The soyl ysowpit into watir wak,   35
The firmament ourcast with rokis blak,
The grond fadyt, and fawch wolx all the feildis,
Montane toppis slekit with snaw ourheildis;
On raggit rolkis of hard harsk quhyn stane
With frosyn frontis cauld clynty clewis schane.   40
Bewte was lost, and barrand schew the landis,
With frostis hair ourfret the feldis standis.
Seir bittir bubbis and the schowris snell
Semyt on the sward a symylitude of hell,
Reducyng to our mynd, in every sted,   45
Gousty schaddois of eild and grisly ded.
Thik drumly skuggis dyrknyt so the hevyn,
Dym skyis oft furth warpit feirfull levyn,
Flaggis of fire, and mony felloun flaw,
Scharpe soppys of sleit and of the snypand snaw.   50

The dolly dichis war all donk and wait,
The law valle flodderit all with spait,
The plane stretis and every hie way
Full of floschis, dubbis, myre and clay.
Laggerit leyis wallowit farnys schew,   55
Browne muris kythit thar wysnyt mossy hew,
Bank, bra and boddum blanchit wolx and bar.
For gurl weddir growit bestis hair.
The wynd maid waif the red wed on the dyke,
Bedowyn in donkis deip was every sike.   60
Our craggis and the front of rochis seir
Hang gret ische schouchlis lang as ony speir.
The grond stud barrant, widderit, dosk or gray,
Herbis, flowris and gersis wallowyt away.
Woddis, forrestis, with nakyt bewis blowt,   65
Stude stripyt of thar weid in every howt.
So bustuusly Boreas his bugill blew,
The deyr full dern doun in the dalis drew;
Smale byrdis, flokkand throu thik ronys thrang,
In chyrmyng and with cheping changit thar sang,   70
Sekand hidlis and hyrnys thame to hyde
Fra feirfull thuddis of the tempestuus tyde;
The watir lynnys rowtis, and every lynd
Quhislit and brayt of the swouchand wynd.
Puyr lauboraris and bissy husband men   75
Went wait and wery draglit in the fen.
The silly scheip and thar litil hyrd gromys
Lurkis undre le of bankis, woddis and bromys;
And other dantit grettar bestiall,
Within thar stabillis sesyt into stall,   80
Sik as mulis, horssis, oxin and ky,
Fed tuskyt barys and fat swyne in sty,
Sustenyt war by mannys governance
On hervist and on symmeris purvyance.
Wyde quhar with fors so Eolus schowtis schill   85
In this congelit sesson scharp and chill,
The callour ayr, penetratyve and puyr,
Dasyng the blude in every creatur,

Maid seik warm stovis and beyn fyris hoyt,
In dowbill garmont cled and wily coyt,   90
With mychty drink and metis confortyve,
Agane the stern wyntir forto stryve.
Repatyrrit weil, and by the chymnay bekyt,
At evin be tyme downe a bed I me strekyt,
Warpit my hed, kest on clathis thrynfald,   95
Fortil expell the peralus persand cald;
I crosyt me, syne bownyt forto sleip,
Quhar, lemand throu the glas, I dyd tak kepe
Latonya, the lang irksum nyght,
Hir subtell blenkis sched and watry lycht,   100
Full hie up quhirlyt in hir regioun,
Till Phebus ryght in oppositioun,
Into the Crab hir proper mansioun draw,
Haldand the hight all thocht the son went law.
Hornyt Hebowd, quhilk we clepe the nycht owle, 105
Within hir cavern hard I schowt and yowle,
Laithly of form, with crukyt camscho beke,
Ugsum to heir was hir wild elrich screke;
The wild geis claking eik by nyghtis tyde
Atour the cite fleand hard I glyde.   110
On slummyr I slaid full sad, and slepit sound
Quhil the oriyont upwart gan rebound.
Phebus crownyt byrd, the nyghtis orlager,
Clapping his weyngis thrys had crawin cleir;
Approching neir the greking of the day,   115
Within my bed I walkynnyt quhar I lay;
So fast declynys Synthea the moyn,
And kays keklis on the ruyf aboyn;
Palamedes byrdis crowpyng in the sky,
Fleand on randon, schapyn like ane Y,   120
And as a trumpat rang thar vocis soun,
Quhois cryis bene pronosticatioun
Of wyndy blastis and ventositeis;
Fast by my chalmyr, in heich wysnyt treis,
The soir gled quhislis lowd with mony a pew: 125
Quhar by the day was dawyn weil I knew,

82

Bad beit the fyre and the candill alyght,
Syne blissyt me, and in my wedis dyght,
A schot wyndo onschet a litill on char,
Persavyt the mornyng bla, wan and har,   130
With clowdy gum and rak ourquhelmyt the ayr,
The sulye stythly, hasart, rouch and hair,
Branchis bratlyng, and blaknyt schew the brays
With hirstis harsk of waggand wyndill strays,
The dew droppis congelit on stibbill and rynd,   135
And scharp hailstanys mortfundeit of kynd
Hoppand on the thak and on the causay by.
The schot I closit, and drew inwart in hy,
Chyvirrand for cald, the sesson was so snell,
Schupe with hayt flambe to fleym the fresyng fell.   140
And, as I bownyt me to the fyre me by,
Baith up and down the hows I dyd aspy,
And seand Virgill on a lettron stand,
To write onone I hynt a pen in hand,
Fortil perform the poet grave and sad,   145
Quham sa fer furth or than begun I had,
And wolx ennoyt sum deill in my hart
Thar restit oncompletit sa gret a part.
And to my self I said: 'In gud effect
Thou mon draw furth, the yok lyis on thy nek.'   150
Within my mynde compasyng thocht I so,
Na thing is done quhil ocht remanys ado;
For byssynes, quhilk occurrit on cace,
Ourvolvyt I this volume, lay a space;
And, thocht I wery was, me list not tyre,   155
Full laith to leif our wark swa in the myre,
Or yit to stynt for bitter storm or rane.
Heir I assayt to yok our pleuch agane,
And, as I couth, with afald diligens,
This nixt buke following of profond sentens   160
Has thus begun in the chil wyntir cald,
Quhen frostis doith ourfret baith firth and fald.

83

THO gan the sey of bemys walxin red,
And heich abuf, down from the hevinly sted,
Within hyr rosy cartis cleirly schane
Aurora vestit into brown sanguane.
Eftir the wyndys lownyt war at will,   5
And all the blastis pacefyit and still,
Out our the calm streym of marbill gray
With ayris palmys sweip thai furth thar way.
And suddanly heir from the stabillit see
A large semly schaw beheld Enee,   10
Amyddis quham the flude he gan aspy
Of Tybir flowand soft and esely,
With sworland welis, and mekill yallow sand,
Into the sey dyd entyr fast at hand.
The byrdis seir of mony divers hewis,   15
About the watir, abuf up in the clewis,
On bankis weilbyknaw and fludis bay,
Wyth wryblis sweit and myrthfull sangis gay
Gan meys and glaid the hevynnys and the ayr,
And throu the schaw went fleand our alquhar.   20
To turn thar cours he gan his feris command,
And stevin thar schippis to the sammyn land;
Joyfull and blith thai entring in the flude,
That dern about skuggyt with bewis stude.
Now, thou my muse, Erato, I the pray,   25
Do schaw me this, at I may scharply say
Quhatkynd proces of tyme was, and quhat kyngis
In ald Latium, and in quhat stait all thingis,
Quhen first this strange army or falloschip
In Italy gan arryvyn, every schip: 30
I sall declar all, and reduce fut hait,
From the begynnyng of the first debayt.
O thou sweit goddes, O thou haly wight,
Convoy and tech thy poet to say ryght!
I sall the horribill batellis schaw and tell,   35
The bludy ostis, and the feildis fell;

Quhou, throw thar curage, douchty kyngis seir
As ded corps becum war, and brocht on beir;
The power hale of all Tuscany,
And all the gret rowtis of Italy   40
Assemblit into armys on the land.
Per ordour now thar risis apon hand
Fer largear materis forto treit and write,
A grettar wark begyn we to endyte.

The portis of weir to twich the prynce refusis,
Quhilkis Juno brekis, syne al for batal musis.   c. x

THE maner than was, and the ald custum
Within the land of ancyent Latyum,
Quhilk blissit usance efter mony a day
The citeis and faderis of Alba kepit ay,
Now the gret master soverane cite dyng   5
Of Rome kepis and hantis the self thing;
That is to knaw, quhen first thai move or steir
The marciall ensenyeis for the wer,
Quhidder so thai list to set with ostis plane
On the Gethys, pepill Tartareane,   10
With dolorus and with ful lamentable wer
In Hyrcany or Araby to steir,
Or fortil ettill in to Inde furth eik,
Towart the dawyng and son rysyng to seik,
Or yit til ask and reduce hame agane   15
Thar standartis from the dowr pepill Persane.
Twa portis beyn of batale and debait,
So thai war clepit to thar name, and hait,
Haldyn in religioun of haly reverence
Of Martys cruel dreid and his offence;   20
A hundreth brasyn hespis thame claspit queym,
And strenthy irne slottis, that dyd seym
Tobe eternal and inconsumptive;
Nor Janus, kepar of this entre of strive,
Was no quhile furth of this ilk hallowit hald.   25
Bot quhen the ferm sentens of faderis ald

85

Was ony tyme determyt to move weir,
Than he that was cheif duke or consuler,
In rob ryall vestit, that hait Quyryne,
And rich purpour, eftir the gys Gabyne,   30
Gyrd in a garmont semly and fut syde,
Thir yettis suld up oppin and warp wyde;
Within that girgand hirst alsso suld he
Pronunce the new weir, batale and melle;
Quham all the fensabill men suld follow fast,   35
With plane assent and brasyn trumpis blast.
The kyng Latyn furthwith command thai than
On this maner, as prince and grettast man,
To proclame weir and decrete the melle
Agane Trojanys, thidder cum with Ene,   40
And warp tha sorofull yettis up on breid.
The prynce refusyt to do sa vile a deid,
Ne list not anys thame twich, nor brek his heist,
Sor agrevit planely ganestud thar requeste,
And in his secret closet hym withdrew.   45
Than from the hevin downe quhirland with a quhew
Come Queyn Juno, and with hir awin handis
Dang up the yettis, brak but delay the bandis:
This cruell douchter of the ald Saturn
The marbill hirst can weltir and ourturn,   50
And strang yet chekis of weirfar and batell
Strake down, and rent the gret irne postis fell.
Onsterit lang tyme, and onmovit, Ital
Now byrnys into fury bellicall.
Sum grathis thame on fut to go in feild;   55
Sum hie montit on horsbak under scheld
The dusty pulder updryvand with a stour,
And every man socht wapynnys and armour;
Thar schynand scheildis sum dyd burnys weill,
And sum polist scharp speir hedis of steill,   60
To mak thame brycht with fat creisch or same,
And on quhitstanys thar axis scharpis at hame;
To beir pynsellis it gladis thame up and downe,
And ar rejosyt to heir the trumpettis sowne.

86

Fyve the grettast and maist cheif citeis,   65
Thar wapynnys to renew in al degreis,
Set up forgis and steil styddeis fyne;
Rych Atyna, and the prowd Tyburyn,
Ardea the cite, and Crustumere,
And eik Antemne with strang towris he   70
And weirly wallis battellit about,
The sikkyr helmys penys and forgis owt;
Thar targettis bow thai of the lycht sauch tre,
And bos bukleris coverit with cuyrbulye;
Sum steil hawbrikis forgis furth of playt,   75
Burnyst flaukartis and leg harnes, fut hait,
With latit sowpill silver weill annelit;
All instrumentis of pleuch graith, irnyt or stelit,
As cultyris, sokkis and the somys gret,
With sythis and al hukis at scheris quhet,   80
War thidder brocht and tholis temper new.
The lust of all sik wark lomys was adew:
Thai dyd thame forge in swerdis of mettel brycht,
Forto defend thar cuntre and thar rycht.
Be this, thar armour grathit and thar geir,   85
The draucht trumpet blawis the brag of weir;
The sloggorn ensenye, or the wach cry,
Went for the batale all suldbe reddy.
He pullis down his sellet quhar it hang,
Sum deill effrayt of the noys and thrang;   90
He dryvis furth the stampand hors on raw
Onto the yok, the chareottis to draw;
He clethis hym with his scheld, and semys bald;
He claspis hys gilt habirgyon and thrynfald;
He, in his breistplait strang and his byrne,   95
A sover swerd beltis law down by his the.

BOOK VIII

From the Prologue

'Quhat wikkytnes, quhat wanthrift now in warld walkis!
Baill hes banyst blythnes, bost gret brag blawys,   80
Prattis ar reput polycy and peralus pawkis,
Dignyte is laid doun, darth to the dur drawis.
Of tratlys and tragedyis the text of all talk is:
Lordis ar left landles be onleill lawys,
Burgessis bryngis hame the bothe to breid in thar bawkis, 85
Knychtis ar kowhubeis and commonys plukkyt crawis,
Clerkis for oncunnandnes mysknawis ilk wight,
Wifis wald have all thar will,
Enewch is nocht halff fyll,
Is nowder resson nor skill   90
In erd haldin rycht.

'Sum latyt latton, but lay, lepys in lawyd lyt,
Sum penys furth a pan boddum to prent fals plakkis;
Sum gowkis quhill the glas pyg grow full of gold yit,
Throu cury of the quynt essens, thocht clay muggis crakkis; 95
Sum wernour for this warldis wrak wendis by hys wyt;
Sum crachour crynys the cunye, and kepys corn stakkis;
Sum prygpenny, sum pyke thank with prevy promyt,
Sum jarris with a jed staf to jag throu blak jakkis.
Quhat fenyeit fair, quhat flattry and quhat fals talys!   100
Quhat mysery is now in land!
Quhou mony crakkyt cunnand!
For nowther athis, nor band,
Nor selis avalis.

'Prestis, suldbe patterraris and for the pepill pray,   105
Tobe papis of patermon and prelaceis pretendis;

Ten tendis ar a trump, bot gif he tak ma
Ane kynryk of parroch kyrkis cuppillit with commendis!
Quha ar wyrkaris of this weir, quha walkynnaris of wa,
Bot incompetabill clergy, that Cristyndome offendis?   110
Quha revis, quha ar ryotus, quha rakles, bot tha?
Quha quellys the puyr commonys bot kyrkmen, weil kend is?
Thar is na stait of thar stile that standis content,
Knycht, clerk, nor common,
Burges, nor barroun—   115
All wald have up that is down,
Weltrit the went.'

.   .   .   .

BOOK IX

From the Prologue

THE ryall style, clepyt heroycall,   21
Full of wirschip and nobilnes our all,
Suldbe compilit but thewhes or voyd word,
Kepand honest wys sportis quhar thai bourd,
All lowus langage and lychtnes lattand be,   25
Observand bewte, sentens and gravyte.
The sayar eik suld weil considir thys,
Hys mater, and quhamto it entitilit is:
Eftir myne authouris wordis, we aucht tak tent
That baith accord, and bene convenient,   30
The man, the sentens, and the knychtlyke stile,
Sen we mon carp of vassalage a quhile.
'Gyf we discryve the woddis, the treis,' quod he,
'Suld conform to that manis dignyte
Quhamto our wark we direct and endyte.'   35
Quhat helpis it? Full litill it wald delyte
To write of scroggis, broym, haddir or rammale;
The lawrer, cedyr or the palm triumphale
Ar mar ganand for nobillis of estait:
The muse suld with the person aggre algait.   40

89

Stra forto spek of gayt to gentill wight;
A hund, a steid, mar langis for a knyght,
Quhamto efferis hant na rebald daill—
Thar suld na knycht reid bot a knychtly taill.
Quhat forsis hym the bussart on the brer,   45
Set weil hym semys the falcon heroner?
He comptis na mair the gled than the fewlume,
Thocht weil hym lykis the goshalk glaid of plume.
The cur, or mastys, he haldis at smal availl,
And culyeis spanyellis, to chace pertryk or quaill.   50
Ne byd I not into my stile for thy
To speke of trufis, nor nane harlotry;
Sen that myne author with sic eloquens
Hys buke illumnyt hes, and hie sentens,
Sa fresch endyte, and sang poeticall,   55
That it is clepyt the wark imperiall,
Endyt onto the gret Octavyane,
The emperour excellent and maste soverane;
By quham, the gospell makis mensioun,
The hail warld put was to discriptioun   60
To numbir all the pepill tharin suldbe,
So, but rebellioun, al quhar obeyit was he.
Bot, sen that Virgill standis but compar,
Thocht in our leid hys sayngis to declar
I have in ryme thus far furth tane the cur,   65
Now war me laith my lang laubour myssur:
All thocht my termys be nocht polist alway,
Hys sentence sall I hald, as that I may.
Guf ocht be weill, thank Virgil and nocht me;
Quhar ocht is bad, gays mys, or owt of gre,   70
My lewytnes, I grant, hes all the wyte,
Kouth not ensew hys ornat fresch endyte,
Bot, with fuylhardy curage malapert,
Schupe to enterprit, and dyd perchance pervert,
Thys maist renownyt prynce of poetry—   75
Quhar I sa dyd, *mea culpa* I cry.

· · · · · · ·

BOOK XII

From the Prologue

UNDER the bewys beyn in lusty valys,   175
Within fermans and parkis cloys of palys,
The bustuus bukkis rakis furth on raw;
Heyrdis of hertis throw the thyk wod schaw,
Baith the brokkettis, and with braid burnyst tyndis,
The sprutlyt calvys sowkand the red hyndis,   180
The yong fownys followand the dun days,
Kyddis skippand throw ronnys efter rays;
In lyssouris and on leys litill lammys
Full tayt and tryg socht bletand to thar dammys,
Tydy ky lowys, veilys by thame rynnys;   185
All snog and slekit worth their bestis skynnys.
On salt stremys wolx Doryda and Thetis,
By rynnand strandis Nymphes and Naedes,
Sik as we clepe wenschis and damysellis,
In gresy gravys wandrand by spryng wellis,   190
Of blomyt branchis and flowris quhite and red
Plettand thar lusty chaplettis for thar hed;
Sum sang ryng sangis, dansys ledys, and roundis,
With vocis schill, quhill all the dail resoundis;
Quharso thai walk into thar caralyng,   195
For amorus lays doith the rochys ryng:
Ane sang, 'The schyp salys our the salt faym,
Will bryng thir merchandis and my lemman haym';
Sum other syngis, 'I wilbe blyth and lycht,
Myne hart is lent apon sa gudly wight.'   200
And thochtfull luffaris rowmys to and fro,
To lys thar pane, and pleyn thar joly wo,
Eftir thar gys, now syngand, now in sorow,
With hartis pensyve, the lang symmyris morow:

Sum ballettis lyst endyte of hys lady,   205
Sum levis in hoip, and sum aluterly
Disparit is, and sa quyte owt of grace,
Hys purgatory he fyndis in every place.
To pleys his lufe sum thocht to flat and feyn,
Sum to hant bawdry and onlesum meyn;   210
Sum rownys to hys fallow, thame betwene,
Hys myrry stouth and pastans lait yisterevin:
Smyland says ane, 'I couth in previte
Schaw the a bourd.' 'Ha, quhat be that?' quod he,
'Quhat thyng?' 'That most be secrete,' said the tother.   215
'Gud Lord, mysbeleif ye your verray broder?'
'Na, never a deill, bot harkis quhat I wald;
Thou mon be prevy.' 'Lo, my hand uphald.'
'Than sal thou walk at evin.' Quod he, 'Quhidder?'
'In sik a place heir west, we baith togydder,   220
Quhar scho so freschly sang this hyndyr nycht;
Do choys the ane, and I sall quynch the lycht.'
'I salbe thar I hope,' quod he and lewch,
'Ya, now I knaw the mater weill eneuch.'
Thus oft dyvulgat is this schamefull play,   225
Na thyng accordyng to our hailsum May,
Bot rathar contagius and infective,
And repugnant that sesson nutrytyve,
Quhen new curage kytlys all gentill hartis,
Seand throu kynd ilk thyng spryngis and revertis.   230
Dame Naturis menstralis, on that other part,
Thar blysfull bay entonyng every art,
To beyt thir amorus of thar nychtis baill,
The merl, the mavys and the nychtyngale
With mery notis myrthfully furth brest,   235
Enforcyng thame quha mycht do clynk it best:
The cowschet crowdis and pyrkis on the rys,
The styrlyng changis divers stevynnys nys,
The sparrow chyrmys in the wallis clyft,
Goldspynk and lyntquhite fordynnand the lyft;   240
The gukgo galys, and so quytteris the quaill,
Quhill ryveris rerdit, schawis and every vaill,

And tender twystis trymlyt on the treis
For byrdis sang and bemyng of the beys;
In wrablis dulce of hevynly armonyis   245
The larkis, lowd releschand in the skyis,
Lovys thar lege with tonys curyus,
Baith to Dame Natur and the fresch Venus,
Rendryng hie lawdis in thar observance;
Quhais suguryt throtis maid glaid hartis dans,   250
And al smail fowlys syngis on the spray:
'Welcum the lord of lycht and lamp of day,
Welcum fostyr of tendir herbys grene,
Welcum quyknar of floryst flowris scheyn,
Welcum support of every rute and vayn,   255
Welcum confort of alkynd fruyt and grayn,
Welcum the byrdis beild apon the brer,
Welcum master and rewlar of the yer,
Welcum weilfar of husbandis at the plewys,
Welcum reparar of woddis, treis and bewys,   260
Welcum depayntar of the blomyt medis,
Welcum the lyfe of every thyng that spredis,
Welcum storour of alkynd bestiall,
Welcum be thy brycht bemys, gladyng all,
Welcum celestial myrrour and aspy,   265
Attechyng all that hantis sluggardy!'

.   .   .   .   .   .

[*The death of Turnus*]   c. xiv

AND as he stud on hovyr thus, Ene   80
The fatale dedly speir in hand gan tays,
And with hys eyn markit and walit has
Ane place be fortoun to smyte oportune,
And with the hail fors of hys body soyn
Furth from hys hand weil far the lance gan thraw.   85
Never sa swyftly quhidderand the stane flaw
Swakkit from the engyne onto the wall,
Nor fulderis dynt, that causis towris fall,
With sik a rummyll com bratland on sa fast.
Lyke the blak thud of awfull thundris blast   90

93

Furth flaw the schaft to smyte the dedly straik,
And with it brocht cruell myschevos wraik;
Quhilk throu the hawbrik skyrtis persyt has,
And the extreme bordour gan arras
Of hys strang scheild, cowchit of sevyn ply,   95
And quhirrand smait hym throw the thee in hy,
That with the dynt huge Turnus, full onsound,
With faldyn howchis duschit to the grund.
Upstart Rutilianys sammyn complenyng
With a yelloch and cairfull womentyng,   100
Quhill all the hillys rumysit thame abowt,
And far on breid thyk woddis gave a schowt.
And Turnus than, quhar he at erth dyd ly,
Addressis furth full humyll and lawly
Towart Ene hys syght and eyn tway,   105
And strekis eik hys rycht hand hym to pray,
And thus he said: 'Forsuyth I have deserve
The deth, I knaw, and of thy hand to sterve,
Ne wil I not beseik the me to spair.
Oys furth thy chance: quhat nedis proces mar?   110
Bot gif that ony cuyr or thocht,' quod he,
'Of ony wofull parent may twich the,
Have rewth and mercy of Kyng Dawnus the ald
(Thou had forsuyth, as I have hard betald,
Anchises, sik a fader as is he),   115
And me, or than, gif bettir lykis the,
My body, spulyeit and the life byreft,
Onto my folkis thou may rendir eft.
Thou hes me venquyst, I grant, and me ourcum.
Italian pepill present all and sum   120
Hes sene streke furth my handis humylly.
Lavinia is thy spows, I not deny:
Extend na forthir thy wraith and matalent.'
Eneas stern in armys tho present
Rolland hys eyn toward Turnus dyd stand,   125
And lyst nocht stryke, bot can withdraw hys hand,
And mor and mor thir wordis, by and by,
Begouth inclyne hym to reuth and mercy,

Abydand lang in hovir quhat he suld do,
Quhen, at the last, on Turnus schuldir, lo,   130
The fey gyrdill hie set dyd appeir,
With stuthis knaw and pendes schynand cleir,
The belt or tysche of the child Pallas,
Quhilk by this Turnus laitly venquyst was,
As we have said, and with a grevus wond   135
Slane in the feld, bet doun, and brocht to grund,
And Turnus, in remembrans of this thing,
Abowt his schuldris bair this onfrendly syng.
Bot eftir that Eneas with hys eyn
Sa cruell takynnys of dyseys hes seyn,   140
And can sik weid byreft thar aspy,
All full of furour kyndlys he inhy,
Full brym of ire and terribill thus can say:
'Sall thou eschape me of this sted away,
Cled with the spulye of my frendis deir?   145
Pallas, Pallas, with this wond rycht heir
Of the ane offerand to the goddys makkis,
And of thy wikkit blude punytioun takkis.'
And sayand thus, full fers, with all hys mayn,
Law in hys breist or cost, lay hym forgayn,   150
Hys swerd hes hyd full hait; and tharwithall
The cald of deth dissolvyt hys membris all.
The spreit of lyfe fled murnand with a grone,
And with disdeyn under dyrk erth is goyn.

BOOK XIII

*Heir begynnys the Proloug of the Threttene and last Buk of
Eneados ekit to Virgill be Mapheus Vegius*

TOWART the evyn, amyd the symmyris heit,
Quhen in the Crab Appollo held hys sete,
Duryng the joyus moneth tyme of June,
As gone neir was the day and supper doyn,

95

I walkyt furth abowt the feildis tyte,   5
Quhilkis tho replenyst stud full of delyte,
With herbys, cornys, catal, and frute treis,
Plente of stoir, byrdis and byssy beys,
In amerant medis fleand est and west,
Eftir laubour to tak the nychtis rest.   10
And as I lukit on the lift me by,
All byrnand red gan walxin the evyn sky:
The son enfyrit haill, as to my sight,
Quhirlit about hys ball with bemys brycht,
Declynand fast towart the north in deid,   15
And fyry Phegon, his dun nychtis steid,
Dowkit hys hed sa deip in fludis gray
That Phebus rollis doun undir hell away;
And Esperus in the west with bemys brycht
Upspryngis, as forrydar of the nycht.   20
Amyd the hawchis, and every lusty vaill,
The recent dew begynnys doun to scaill,
To meys the byrnyng quhar the son had schyne,
Quhilk tho was to the neddir warld declyne:
At every pilis poynt and cornys croppis   25
The techrys stude, as lemand beryall droppis,
And on the hailsum herbis, cleyn but wedis,
Lyke cristal knoppis or smal silver bedis.
The lyght begouth to quynchyng owt and faill,
The day to dyrkyn, declyne and devaill;   30
The gummys rysis, doun fallis the donk rym,
Baith heir and thar scuggis and schaddois dym.
Upgois the bak with hir pelit ledderyn flycht,
The lark discendis from the skyis hycht,
Syngand hir complyng sang, efter hir gys,   35
To tak hir rest, at matyn hour to rys.
Owt our the swyre swymmys the soppis of myst,
The nycht furthspred hir cloke with sabill lyst,
That all the bewte of the fructuus feld
Was with the erthis umbrage cleyn ourheld;   40
Baith man and beste, fyrth, flude and woddis wild
Involvyt in tha schaddois warryn syld.

Still war the fowlis fleis in the air,
All stoir and catall seysit in thar lair,
And every thing, quharso thame lykis best,   45
Bownys to tak the hailsum nychtis rest
Eftir the days laubour and the heyt.
Clos warryn all and at thar soft quyet,
But sterage or removing, he or sche,
Owder best, byrd, fysch, fowle, by land or sey.   50
And schortlie, every thing that doith repar
In firth or feild, flude, forest, erth or ayr,
Or in the scroggis, or the buskis ronk,
Lakis, marrasis, or thir pulys donk,
Astabillit lyggis still to slepe, and restis;   55
Be the smaill byrdis syttand on thar nestis,
The litill mygeis, and the vrusum fleys,
Laboryus emmotis, and the bissy beys;
Als weill the wild as the taym bestiall,
And every othir thingis gret and small,   60
Owtak the mery nychtgaill, Philomeyn,
That on the thorn sat syngand fra the spleyn;
Quhais myrthfull notis langyng fortil heir,
Ontill a garth undir a greyn lawrer
I walk onon, and in a sege down sat,   65
Now musyng apon this and now on that.
I se the poill, and eik the Ursis brycht,
And hornyt Lucyn castand bot dym lycht,
Becaus the symmyr skyis schayn sa cleir;
Goldyn Venus, the mastres of the yeir,   70
And gentill Jove, with hir participate,
Thar bewtuus bemys sched in blyth estait:
That schortly, thar as I was lenyt doun,
For nychtis silens, and this byrdis soun,
On sleip I slaid, quhar sone I saw appeir   75
Ane agit man, and said: 'Quhat dois thou heir
Undyr my tre, and willyst me na gude?'
Me thocht I lurkit up under my hude
To spy this ald, that was als stern of spech
As he had beyn ane medicyner or lech;   80

And weill persavit that hys weid was strange,
Tharto so ald, that it had not beyn change,
Be my consait, fully that fourty yeir,
For it was threidbair into placis seir;
Syde was this habyt, round, and closyng meit,   85
That strekit to the grund doun our his feit;
And on his hed of lawrer tre a crown,
Lyke to sum poet of the ald fasson.
Me thocht I said to hym with reverens:
'Fader, gif I have done you ony offens,   90
I sall amend, gif it lyis in my mycht:
Bot suythfastly, gyf I have perfyte sycht,
Onto my doym, I, saw you nevir ayr,
Fayn wald wyt quhen, on quhat wys, or quhar,
Aganyst you trespassit ocht have I.'   95
'Weill,' quod the tother, 'wald thou mercy cry
And mak amendis, I sal remyt this falt;
Bot, other ways, that sete salbe full salt.
Knawis thou not Mapheus Vegius, the poet,
That onto Virgillis lusty bukis sweit   100
The thretteyn buke ekit Eneadan?
I am the sammyn, and of the na thyng fayn,
That hes the tother twelf into thy tong
Translait of new, thai may be red and song
Our Albyon ile into your vulgar leid;   105
Bot to my buke yit lyst the tak na heid.'
'Mastir,' I said, 'I heir weill quhat yhe say,
And in this cace of perdon I you pray,
Not that I have you ony thing offendit,
Bot rathir that I have my tyme mysspendit,   110
So lang on Virgillis volume forto stair,
And laid on syde full mony grave mater,
That, wald I now write in that trety mor,
Quhat suld folk deym bot all my tyme forlor?
Als, syndry haldis, fader, trastis me,   115
Your buke ekit but ony necessite,
As to the text accordyng never a deill,
Mair than langis to the cart the fift quheill.

98

Thus, sen yhe beyn a Cristyn man, at large
Lay na sik thing, I pray you, to my charge;   120
It may suffys Virgill is at ane end.
I wait the story of Jherom is to you kend,
Quhou he was dung and beft intill hys sleip,
For he to gentilis bukis gaif sik keip.
Full scharp repreif to sum is write, ye wist,   125
In this sentens of the haly Psalmyst:
"Thai ar corruppit and maid abhominabill
In thar studeyng thyngis onprofitabill":
Thus sair me dredis I sal thoill a heit,
For the grave study I have so long forleit.'   130
'Ya, smy,' quod he, 'wald thou eschape me swa?
In faith we sall nocht thus part or we ga!
Quhou think we he essonyeis hym to astart,
As all for consciens and devoit hart,
Fenyeand hym Jherom forto contyrfeit,   135
Quhar as he lyggis bedovyn, lo, in sweit!
I lat the wyt I am nane hethyn wight,
And gif thou has afortyme gayn onrycht,
Followand sa lang Virgill, a gentile clerk,
Quhy schrynkis thou with my schort Cristyn wark?   140
For thocht it be bot poetry we say,
My buke and Virgillis morall beyn, bath tway:
Len me a fourteyn nycht, how evir it be,
Or, be the faderis sawle me gat,' quod he,
'Thou salt deir by that evir thou Virgill knew.'   145
And, with that word, doun of the sete me drew,
Syne to me with hys club he maid a braid,
And twenty rowtis apon my riggyng laid,
Quhill, 'Deo, Deo, mercy,' dyd I cry,
And, be my rycht hand strekit up inhy,   150
Hecht to translait his buke, in honour of God
And hys Apostolis twelf, in the numbir od.
He, glaid tharof, me by the hand uptuke,
Syne went away, and I for feir awoik,
And blent abowt to the north est weill far,   155
Saw gentill Jubar schynand, the day star,

And Chiron, clepit the syng of Sagittary,
That walkis the symmyrris nycht, to bed gan cary.
Yondyr doun dwynys the evyn sky away,
And upspryngis the brycht dawyng of day   160
Intill ane other place nocht far in sundir
That tobehald was plesans, and half wondir.
Furth quynchyng gan the starris, on be on,
That now is left bot Lucifer allon.
And forthirmor to blason this new day,   165
Quha mycht discryve the byrdis blisfull bay?
Belyve on weyng the bissy lark upsprang,
To salus the blyth morrow with hir sang;
Sone our the feildis schynys the lycht cleir,
Welcum to pilgrym baith and lauborer;   170
Tyte on hys hynys gaif the greif a cry,
'Awaik on fut, go till our husbandry.'
And the hyrd callis furth apon hys page,
'Do dryve the catall to thar pasturage.'
The hynys wife clepis up Katheryn and Gill;   175
'Ya, dame,' said thai, 'God wait, with a gude will.'
The dewy greyn, pulderit with daseis gay,
Schew on the sward a cullour dapill gray;
The mysty vapouris spryngand up full sweit,
Maist confortabill to glaid all manis spreit;   180
Tharto, thir byrdis syngis in the schawys,
As menstralis playng 'The joly day now dawys.'
Than thocht I thus: I will my cunnand kepe,
I will not be a daw, I will not slepe,
I wil compleit my promys schortly, thus   185
Maid to the poet master Mapheus,
And mak upwark heirof, and cloys our buke,
That I may syne bot on grave materis luke:
For, thocht hys stile be nocht to Virgill lyke,
Full weill I wayt my text sall mony like,   190
Sen eftir ane my tung is and my pen,
Quhilk may suffys as for our vulgar men.
Quha evir in Latyn hes the bruyt or glor,
I speke na wers than I have doyn befor:

Lat clerkis ken the poetis different,   195
And men onletterit to my wark tak tent;
Quhilk, as twiching this thretteynt buke infeir,
Begynnys thus, as furthwith followis heir.

Explicit prologus in decimumtertium librum Eneados

[*Æneas marries Lavinia*]

BE this the kyng Latyn, lord of that land,   37
With maste nobill Eneas hand in hand,
Within the cheif palys, baith he and he,
Ar entryt in the saill ryall on hie;   40
Quham followys nixt the ying Ascanyus fair,
That was hys faderis only child and ayr;
Syne folk of Itaill, mydlit with Trojanys,
Ar entrit in that riall hald attanys:
With pompos fest and joyus myrth our all   45
Resoundis tho baith palys, bowr and hall,
And all the chymmys riall rownd abowt
Was fyllyt with thar tryne and mekill rowt.
And tharwithall, of chalmyr by and by,
With sa gudly a sort and cumpany   50
Of ladeis fair and damysellys onwed,
Innumerabill almast, als furth was led
The fair fresch Lavinia the may,
Amyd thame schynand in hir ryall array;
The crystall bemys of hir eyn twane,   55
That as the brycht twynkland starnys schayn,
Sum deill eschamyt, towart the erth doith hald.
Quham as this Trojan prynce first gan behald,
Of bewte, schap and all afferys, perfay,
Sa excelland that wondir war to say,   60
At the first blenk astonyst half wolx he,
And musyng hovirris styll on hir to se,
And in hys mynd gan rew the hard myschans
Of Turnus, quham na litill apperans

Sa baldly movit to dereyn bargan,   65
To rays the weir and feght for sykkyn ane;
For weill, he thocht, the hope of syk a wight
To dedys of armys aucht constreyn ony knycht.
Syne, to abbryge our mater, hand in hand
Thai war conjunct intill eternall band   70
Of matrimonye, and tho at all devys
Thar wedlok with honour, as was the gys,
Be menstralys and herraldis of gret fame
Was playd and sung and throw the cowrt proclame.
Than joy and myrth, with dansyng and deray,   75
Full mery noys and soundis of gam and play
Abuf the bryght starnys hie upwent,
That semyt forto pers the firmament,
And joyus vocis ryngis furth alsso
Our all the palys ryall to and fro.   80
And syk ryot indurand amyd the pres,
Ene thus carpys to traste Achates,
And bad hym go belyve, but mair delay,
Do fech the rych robbys and array,
The fresch attyre and all the precyus wedis,   85
Wrocht craftely and weif of goldyn thredis
Quhilum be fair Andromachais hand,
By quham thai war hym gevyn in presand;
And eyk the collar of the fyne gold brycht,
With precyus stanys and with rubeys pight,   90
Quham scho also abowt hir hals quhyte
Was wont to weir in maste pompe and delyte,
Quhill that the Trojan weilfar stud abufe;
The gret cowpe eyk, the quhilk in syng of lufe
Quhilum Kyng Priam to hys fader gave,   95
Ald Anchises, of fyne gold and engrave.
Than, but delay, Achates at command
Brocht thir rych gyftis, a wonder fair presand;
Syne to hys fader in law, the kyng Latyn,
The precyus cowp gave he of brycht gold fyne,   100
And to hys spows, Lavinia the may,
The wedis ryall and the collar gay.

Than athir dyd thar dewly observans
With breistis blyth and plesand dalyans,
To festyng, entertenyr and cherys   105
Thar ferys abowt on the maist gudly wys:
With divers sermond carpyng all the day
Thai schort the howris and dryvis the tyme away.

Quhou Jupiter, for Venus caus and lufe,
Has set Eneas as god in hevyn abufe.   c. xi

VENUS with this, all glaid and full of joy,
Amyd the hevynly hald, rycht myld and moy,
Befor Jupiter down hir self set
And baith hir armys abowt hys feyt plet,
Enbrasand thame and kyssand reverently;   5
Syne thus with voce expres scho said inhy:
'Fader almychty, that from thy hevynly ryng
At thy plesour rewlys and sterys al thyng,
That manis dedys, thochtis and aventuris
Reknys and knawys, and therof hes the curis;   10
Weill I ramember, quhen that the pepill Trojan
With hard onfrendly forton was ourtane,
Thou promyst of thar laubouris and distres
Help and support, and efter dyseys soles.
Nowder thy promys, fader, nor sentens   15
Hes me dissavyt, for lo, with reverens
All the faderis of Italy hes se,
But discrepans, fully thir yheris thre,
In blyssyt peax my son enjoys that land;
Bot certis, fader, as I undirstand,   20
Onto the starnyt hevynly hald on hie
Thou promyst rays the maste douchty Enee,
And, for hys meryt, abufe thy schynand sky
Hym forto place in hevyn and deify.
Quhat thochtis now doith rollyng in thy mynd,   25
Sen, ellys, doith the vertuus thewys kynd
Of this reuthfull Eneas the requyr
Abuf the polys brycht to rays that syre?'

103

The fader tho of men and goddis all
Gan kys Venus hys child, and tharwithall   30
Thir profund wordis from hys breist furth braid:
'My deir douchtir Citherea,' he said,
'Thow knawys quhou strangly the mychty Ene
And the Eneadanys all of hys menye
Ithandly and onyrkyt luffyt have I,   35
On se and landis catchit by and by
In perrellis seir, and quhou that ofttyme eik,
Havand piete of the my douchtir meik,
For lufe of the, for thar dyseys was wo;
And now I have, lo, finaly alsso   40
All thar harmys and ennoy brocht till end,
And maid Juno, as that full weill is kend,
Fortobecum frendly and favorabill:
Now lykis me, forsuyth, all ferm and stabill
My sentens promyst to compleit,' quod he,   45
'Quhen that the riall Trojan duke Ene
Amang the hevynnys institut I sall,
And hym to numbyr of the goddis call:
All this I grant with gud willis pcr fay.
Tharfor, se that thou clenge and do away,   50
Gif thar be in hym ony mortall thyng,
And syne abuf the starnys thou him bryng:
I sall alsso heich ony of hys kyn,
Quhilk of thar proper vertu lyst do wyn
Perpetuall lovyng by dedis honorabill,   55
And doith contemp the wrachit warld onstabill;
Thame in lyke wys abufe the hevynnys hie
I sal do place and deify,' quod he.
The goddis abuf alhaill gave thar consent,
Nor ryall Juno, at that tyme present,   60
Lyst not contrary, bot gan perswaid full evyn
To bryng the gret Ene up to the hevyn,
And frendly wordis of hym carpys thar.
Than Venus slaid discendand throw the ayr
And socht onto the feildis Lawrentan,   65
Neir by quhar that Numycus throu the playn,

104

That fresch ryver, flowys to the see,
Dekkyt abowt with redis growand hie;
Quharin the body of hir son sa deir
Scho maid do wesch, and under the stremys cleir   70
All that was mortale or corruptibill thyng
Gart do away; and syne, at hir lykyng,
The recent happy sawl with hyr hynt sche
And bair it up abuf the ayr full hie
Onto the hevyn, quhar reuthfull Eneas   75
Amyd the starnys chosyn has his place;
Quham the famyll and kynrent Julian
Doith clepe and call amangis thame every ane
Indigites, quhilk is alsmekill to say
As god induellar, at thar sudiornys ay;   80
And, in remembrans of this ilk turn,
Thai gan hys templis wirschip and adorn.

Explicit liber decimus tertius Eneados

Conclusio

Now is my wark all fynyst and compleit,
Quham Jovis ire, nor fyris byrnand heit,
Nor trynschand swerd sal defas ne doun thryng,
Nor lang proces of age, consumys al thyng.
Quhen that onknawyn day sal hym addres,   5
Quhilk not bot on this body power hes,
And endis the dait of myn oncertan eld,
The bettir part of me salbe upheld
Abufe the starnys perpetualy to ryng,
And heir my naym remane, but enparyng;   10
Throw owt the ile yclepit Albyon
Red sall I be, and sung with mony one.
Thus up my pen and instrumentis full yor
On Virgillis post I fix for evirmor,
Nevir, from thens, syk materis to discryve: 15
My muse sal now be cleyn contemplatyve,

105

And solitar, as doith the byrd in cage,
Sen fer byworn is all my childis age,
And of my days neir passyt the half dait
That natur suld me grantyn, weil I wait.   20
Thus sen I feill down sweyand the ballans,
Heir I resyng up yingkeris observans:
Adew, gallandis, I geif you all gud nycht,
And God salf every gentill curtas wight! Amen.

THE PALICE OF HONOUR

[*Prologue, ll. 1–45*]

QUHEN paill Aurora with face lamentabill
Hir russat mantill, borderit all with sabill,
Lappit about the hevinly circumstance,
The tender bed and arres honorabill
Of Flora, quene till floures amiabill,   5
In May I rais to do my observance,
And enterit in a gardyne of plesance,
With sol depaint as paradice amiabill,
And blisfull bewis with blomed varyance.

Sa craftely dame Flora had ovirfret   10
Hir hevinly bed, powderit with mony a set
Of ruby, topas, perle and emerant;
With balmy dew bathit and kyndlie wet,
Quhill vapours hote, richt fresche and weill ybet,
Dulce of odour, of fluour maist fragrant,   15
The silver droppis on daseis distillant;
Quhilk verdour branches ovir the alars yet,
With smoky sence the mystis reflectant.

The fragrant flouris blomand in thair seis
Ovirspred the levis of Natures tapestreis;   20
Abone the quhilk with hevinly harmoneis
The birdis sat on twystis and on greis,
Melodiously makand their kyndlie gleis,
Quhais schill noitis fordinned all the skyis.
Of repercust air the echo cryis   25
Amang the branches of the blomed treis,
And on the laurers silver droppis lyis.

Quhill that I rowmed in that paradice,
Replenischit and full of all delice,
Out of the sey Eous alift his heid: 30
I mene the hors quhilk drawis at device

The assiltrie and goldin chair of price
Of Tytan, quhilk at morrow semis reid.
The new collour that all the nicht lay deid
Is restorit; baith foulis, flouris and rice   35
Recomfort was throw Phebus gudlyheid.

The dasy and the maryguld unlappit,
Quhilks all the nicht lay with thair levis happit
Thame to reserve fra rewmes pungitive.
The umbrate treis that Tytan about wappit   40
War portrait and on the eirth yschappit
Be goldin bemis vivificative,
Quhais amene heit is maist restorative.
The greshoppers amangis the vergers gnappit,
And beis wrocht materiall for thair hyve.   45

From Part I

All in ane fevir out of my muskane bowre   [646]
On kneis I crap and law for feir did lowre.
Than all the court on me thair heidis schuik,
Sum glowmand grim, sum girnand with visage sowre;
Sum in the nek gave me feil dyntis dowre.   50
'Pluk at the craw', thay cryit, 'deplome the ruik!'
Pulland my hair, with blek my face thay bruik.
Skrymmorie Fery gave me mony a clowre;
For Chyppynutie ful oft my chaftis quuik.

.   .   .   .

Enthronit sat Mars, Cupid and Venus.   55 [664]
Tho rais ane clerk, was cleipit Varius,
Me till accusen of a deidlie crime,
And he begouth and red ane dittay thus:
'Thow wickit cative, wod and furious,
Presumpteouslie now at this present time   60
My Lady heir blasphemit in thy rime;
Hir sone, hirself, and hir court amorous
For till betrais awaitit heir sen prime.'

Now God thow wait, me thocht my fortune fey.
With quaikand voce and hart cald as a key,   65

108

On kneis I kneillit and mercie culd imploir,
Submittand me but ony langer pley
Venus mandate and plesure to obey.
Grace was denyit and my travell forloir,
For scho gave charges to proceid as befoir.   70
Than Varius spak richt stoutlie me to fley,
Injoynand silence till ask grace ony moir.

He demandit my answer, quhat I said.
Than as I mocht, with curage all mismaid,
Fra time I understude na mair supplie,   75
Sair abaisit belive I thus outbraid:
'Set of thir pointis of crime now on me laid
I may me quite, giltles in veritie,
Yit first agane the Judge quhilk heir I se,
This inordinate court and proces quaid   80
I will object, for causis twa or thre.'

Inclynand law, quod I, with peteous face,
'I me defend, Madame, pleis it your Grace.'
'Say on,' quod scho. Than said I thus but mair:
'Madame, ye may not sit in to this cace,   85
For ladyis may be judges in na place;
And mairatouir I am na seculair.
A spirituall man, thocht I be void of lair,
Cleipit I am, and aucht my lives space
To be remit till my judge ordinair.   90

'I yow beseik, Madame, with bissie cure,
Till give ane gratious interlocuture
On thir exceptiounis now proponit lait.'
Than suddanelie Venus, I yow assure,
Deliverit sone, and with a voice sa sture   95
Answerit thus: 'Thow subtell smy, God wait!
Quhat, wenis thow to degraid my hie estait
Me to decline as judge, curst creature?
It beis not sa. The game gais uther gait!

109

'As we the find, thow sall thoill judgement.   100
Not of a clerk we se the represent
Saif onlie falset and dissaitfull taillis.
First quhen thow come, with hart and haill intent
Thow the submittit to my commandement.
Now, now, thairof me think to sone thow faillis.   105
I wene na thing bot folie that the aillis.
Ye clerkis bene in subtell wordis quent,
And in the deid als schairp as ony snaillis . . .

          .   .   .   .

'Have done,' quod scho. 'Schir Varius, alswyith   [727]
Do write the sentence. Lat this cative kyith   110
Gif our power may deming his misdeid.'
Than God thow wait gif that my spreit was blyith.
The feverous hew intill my face did myith
All my male-eis, for swa the horribill dreid
Haill me ovirset; I micht not say my creid.   115
For feir and wo within my skin I wryith.
I micht not pray, forsuith, thocht I had neid.

Yit of my dcith I set not half ane fle.
For greit effeir me thocht na pane to die.
Bot sair I dred me for sum uther jaip,   120
That Venus suld throw hir subtillitie
In till sum bysning beist transfigurat me,
As in a beir, a bair, ane oule, ane aip.
I traistit sa for till have bene mischaip,
That oft I wald my hand behald to se   125
Gif it alterit, and oft my visage graip.

From Part III

Ye Musis nine, be in my adjutorie,   [1288]
That maid me se this blis and perfite glorie.
Teiche me your facund castis eloquent,
Len me a recent, schairp, fresche memorie   130
And caus me dewlie till indite this storie.
Sum gratious sweitnes in my breist imprent
Till mak the heirars bowsum and attent,

Reidand my writ, illuminate with your loir,
Infinite thankis randerand yow thairfoir.   135

Now breiflie to my purpois for till gone:
About the hill lay wayis mony one,
And to the hicht bot ane passage ingrave,
Hewin in the roche of slid, hard marbell stone.
Agayne the sone like to the glas it schone.   140
The ascence was hie, and strait for till consave.
Yit than thir Musis, gudelie and suave,
Alichtit doun and clam the roche in hie
With all the rout, outtane my Nimphe and I.

Still at the hillis fute we twa abaid.   145
Than suddanelie my keipar to me said,
'Ascend, Galland'; than for feir I quoik.
'Be not affrayit,' scho said, 'be not dismaid,'
And with that word up the strait rod abraid.
I followit fast, scho be the hand me tuik.   150
Yit durst I never for dreid behind me luik.
With mekill pane thus clam I neir the hicht,
Quhair suddanelie I saw ane grislie sicht.

As we approchit neir the hillis heid,
Ane terribill sewch, birnand in flammis reid,   155
Abhominabill and how as hell to se,
All full of brintstane, pick and bulling leid,
Quhair mony wretchit creature lay deid,
And miserabill catives yelland loude on hie,
I saw—quhilk den micht weill compairit be   160
Till Xanthus, the flude of Troy sa schill,
Birnand at Venus hest contrair Achill.

Amid our passage lay this uglie sicht,
Nocht braid bot sa horribill to everie wicht,
That all the warld to pas it suld have dreid.   165
Weill I considderit, na uppermair I micht,
And to discend, sa hiddeous was the hicht,
I durst not aventure for this eird on breid.
Trimbland I stude, with teith chatterand gude speid.

My Nymphe beheld my cheir, and said, 'Let be.   170
Thow sall nocht aill, and lo the caus,' quod sche.

'To me thow art commit, I sall the keip.
Thir pietous pepill amid this laithlie deip
War wretchis quhilks in lustie yeiris fair
Pretendit thame till hie honour to creip,   175
Bot suddanelie thay fell on sleuthfull sleip,
Followand plesance, drownit in this loch of cair.'
And with that word scho hint me be the hair,
Caryit me till the hillis heid anone,
As Abacuk was brocht in Babylone.   180

'As we bene on the hie hill situait,
Luik doun,' quod scho, 'consave in quhat estait
Thy wretchit warld thow may considder now.'
At hir command with mekill dreid, God wait,
Out ovir the hill sa hiddeous, hie and strait,   185
I blent adoun, and felt my bodie grow.
This brukill eird, sa litill till allow,
Me thocht I saw birne in ane fyrie rage
Of stormie sey quhilk micht na maner swage.

That terribill tempest, hiddeous wallis huge,   190
War maist grislie for to behald or judge,
Quhair nouther rest nor quiet micht appeir.
Thair was ane perrellous place folk for to ludge.
Thair was na help, support, nor yit refuge.
Innumerabill folk I saw flotterand in feir,   195
Quhilk pereist on the walterand wallis weir.
And secundlie I saw ane lustie barge,
Ovirset with seyis and mony stormie charge.

This gudelie carvell, taiklit traist on raw,
With blanschite saill, milk quhite as ony snaw,   200
Richt sover, ticht, and wonder stranglie beildit,
Was on the boldyn wallis quite ovirthraw.
Contrariouslie the busteous wind did blaw

In bubbis thik, that na schipis sail micht weild it.
Now sank scho law, now hie to hevin upheildit,   205
At everie part swa sey and windis draif,
Quhill on ane sand the schip did brist and claif.

It was ane pieteous thing, alaik, alaik,
To heir the dulefull cry quhen that scho straik;
Maist lamentabill the pereist folk to se,   210
Sa fameist, drowkit, mait, forwrocht and waik;
Sum on ane plank of firre, and sum of aik,
Sum hang upon a takill, sum on ane tre,
Sum fra thair grip sone weschin with the see.
Part drownit, part to the roche fleit or swam,   215
On raipis or burdis, sine up the hill thay clam.

Tho at my Nimphe breiflie I did inquire
Quhat signifyit tha feirfull wonders seir.
'Yone multitude,' said scho, 'of pepill drint
Ar faithles folk, quhilks quhill thay ar heir   220
Misknawis God and followis thair pleseir.
Quhairfoir thay sall in endles fire be brint.
Yone lustie schip thow seis pereist and tint,
In quhome yone pepill maid ane perrellous race,
Scho hecht the Carvell of the State of Grace.   225

.   .   .   .

'This may suffice,' said scho, 'tuitchand this part.   [1396]
Returne thy heid, behald this uther art.
Considder wonders, and be vigilant,
That thow may better endyten efterwart
Things quhilkis I sall the schaw or we depart.   230
Thow sall have fouth of sentence and not scant.
Thair is na welth nor weilfair thow sall want.
The greit Palice of Honour sall thow se.
Lift up thy heid, behald that sicht,' quod sche.

At hir command I raisit hie on hicht   235
My visage, till behald that hevinlie sicht.

Bot to discrive this mater in effek
Impossibill war till ony eirdlie wicht.
It transcendis sa far abone my micht,
That I with ink may do bot paper blek.   240
I mon draw furth the yok, lyis on my nek,
As of the place to say my leude avise,
Pleneist with plesance like to paradice.

I saw ane plane of peirles pulchritude,
Quhairin aboundit alkin thingis gude,   245
Spice, wine, corne, oyle, tre, frute, flour, herbis grene,
All foullis, beistis, birdis, and alkin fude;
All maner fisches, baith of sey and flude,
War keipit in pondis of poleist silver schene,
With purifyit water as of the cristall clene.   250
To noy the small the greit beistis had na will,
Nor ravenous foulis the lytill volatill.

Still in the sessoun all things remanit thair,
Perpetuallie but outher noy or sair.
Ay rypit war baith herbis, frute and flouris.   255
Of everie thing the names to declair
Unto my febill wit unpossibill wair.
Amid the meid, repleit with sweit odouris,
A palice stude with mony royall towris,
Quhair kyrnellis quent, feil turrettis men micht find,   260
And goldin thanis waifand in the wind.

    .   .   .   .

And to proceid, my Nimphe and I furth went   [1900]
Straicht to the hall, throwout the palice gent,
And ten stages of topas did ascend.
Schute was the dure; in at a boir I blent,   265
Quhair I beheld the glaidest represent
That ever in eirth a wretchit cative kend.
Breiflie this proces to conclude and end,
Me thocht the flure was all of amatist,
Bot quhairof war the wallis I not wist.   270

114

The multitude of precious stanis seir
Thairon sa schane, my febill sicht but weir
Micht not behald thair verteous gudlines.
For all the ruif, as did to me appeir,
Hang full of plesand lowpit sapheiris cleir,   275
Of dyamontis and rubeis, as I ges;
War all the buirdis maid of maist riches,
Of sardanis, of jasp, and smaragdane:
Traistis, formis, and benkis war poleist plane.

Baith to and fro amid the hall thay went,   280
Royall princes in plait and armouris quent,
Of birneist gold, couchit with precious stanis.
Enthronit sat ane God omnipotent,
On quhais glorious visage as I blent,
In extasie be his brichtnes atanis   285
He smote me doun, and brissit all my banis.
Thair lay I still in swoun with colour blaucht,
Quhill at the last my Nimphe up hes me caucht.

.   .   .   .

'Yone war,' said scho, 'quha sa the richt discrives,   [1963]
Maist vailyeand folk, and verteous in thair lives.   290
Now in the court of Honour thay remane
Victoriusly, and in all plesance thrives.
For thay with speir, with swords and with knives,
In just battell war fundin maist of mane.
In thair promittis thay stude ever firme and plane.   295
In thame aboundit worschip and lawtie,
Illuminat with liberalitie.

'Honour,' quod scho, 'to this hevinlie ryng
Differris richt far fra warldlie honoring,
Quhilk is but pompe of eirdlie dignitie,   300
Gevin for estait of blude, micht or sic thing.
And in this countrie prince, prelate or king
Allanerlie sall for vertew honourit be.
For eirdlie gloir is nocht bot vanitie,
That as we se sa suddanelie will wend,   305
Bot verteous honour never mair sall end.'

NOTES

The Prologue of Book I

THERE are several conventions in this prologue: the aureate diction; the praise of Virgil (cf. V, prol. 28 ff. and IX, prol. 63 ff.); the excessive modesty (note ll. 19 ff., 31 ff., and 408). Douglas began to compose a marginal commentary to the poem, beginning with the Prologue. It appears in the Cambridge MS.; a few notes have been copied in the Lambeth and Bath MSS. The first note refers to I, prol. 97: 'Innatyve is alsmekil to say as inborn, or that quhilk cumis till ony person be thar natural inclination of kynd throw thar forbearis.' A typical explanatory note accompanies I. i. 28: 'Samo is an ile in Trace quhar Juno was weddit and born, as sais Servius [fourth-century commentator on Virgil], and ther, as witnessyth Sanct Jerom, stud the farest tempil of Greçe, dedicat to Juno.'

7–8. The carbuncle was anciently supposed to shine in the darkness; hence it is a symbol for anything illustrious. St. Edmund, for instance, is called 'charboncle' and 'ruby of martyrs' by Lydgate ('To St. Edmund', *Minor Poems*), who also describes St. Denis as the 'lodestar of Paris', St. Anne as a 'sugarcane', and the Virgin Mary as a cypress, cedar, carbuncle, emerald, and sapphire. Chaucer is 'the lodesterre . . . of our language' (*Fall of Princes*, I, prol. 252).

8. *A per se.* 'A' standing by itself; hence most excellent or unique.

11. *I meyn.* A common tag in Douglas, as are 'I wyss' (for 'ywis', certainly), 'as I ges', and 'but baid'.

15. *do wryte.* The periphrastic auxiliary *do* is a notable feature of sixteenth-century Scots: cf. l. 73.

21. Cf. 'rurall vulgar gros', l. 43, and 'burall bustuus thocht', l. 48.

30. *invane.* Compounds of this kind are very common in the Cambridge MS. of the poem, and have been preserved here. Cf. 'forto', 'salbe', 'siclyke', 'tobeseik', below.

60–61. Douglas's doubts and hesitations are well dramatized by the wavering, interrupted flow of the sentence.

67. *Macrobius.* Ambrosius Theodosius Macrobius (fl. 400), a Latin scholar best known for his commentary on *Somnium Scipionis*. See his *Convivia Saturnalia*, I. xxiv ('de laudibus variaque eruditione Vergilii') and III–VI *passim.*

82. *febill of rent.* Of trifling value.

86. Henry, third Lord Sinclair, succeeded to the title in 1488/9, and was killed at Flodden, 9 September 1513. Since his mother was Elizabeth, daughter of Archibald, fourth Earl of Angus, he was third cousin twice removed to Gavin Douglas. Douglas seems to have modelled his 'character' on that of Chaucer's Knight: cf. ll. 95 ff. with *CT* A, ll. 45–46, 72.

88. *Homeir*. This is hardly to be taken as evidence that Douglas knew Greek. He knew that there were borrowings from Greek into Latin (I, prol. 115), but it is improbable that his knowledge went much further.

100. *Ptholome*. Ptolomæus Philadelphus (285–247 B.C.), King of Egypt and patron of scholars at Alexandria.

102. 'Quhat so it be' depreciates this book, not his nobility.

103. *Scottis*. This is one of the earliest occasions on which English and Scots are so distinguished; earlier 'Scottis' meant Gaelic. The author of *Wallace*, for instance, calls his tongue 'Inglis' (IX. 297).

106. *Beis*. The pl. imperative commonly ends in -*is* (cf. 171, 267), but not always: note 'considir', l. 107, 'traste weill', l. 198.

109 ff. Cf. Richard Rolle's method as a translator (Hope Emily Allen, *English Writings of Richard Rolle . . .*, Oxford, 1931, p. 7 and n.): 'In this werk I seke no strange Inglish, bot lightest and comunest and swilke that es mast like vnto the Latyn, so that thai that knawes noght Latyn, be the Inglis may cum tille many Latyn wordes. In the translacioun I folow the letter als mekil als I may, and thare I fynde na propir Inglys I folow the witte of the word, so that thai that sal rede it, tham thar noght dred errynge.'

112. In Middle Scots, when the verb is separated from its personal pronoun, it regularly ends in -*is*: cf. ll. 185, 283.

118–19. The assertion that Scots is not *really* scant seems to be a patriotic afterthought. Cf. I, prol. 359; and cf. the plea of the author of the *Complaynt of Scotlande* (ff. 13*b*–14*a*) to 'al philosophouris, historigraphours, & oratours of our scottis natione to support & til excuse my barbir agrest termis; for i thocht it nocht necessair til hef fardit ande lardit this tracteit witht exquisite termis . . . it is necessair at sum tyme til myxt oure langage vitht part of termis dreuyn fra lateen, be rason that oure scottis tong is nocht sa copeus as is the lateen tong'.

127. *Lawrens of the Vaill*. Laurentius Valla (1405–57), author of *De Lingua Latinae Elegantia Libri Sex . . ., Facecie Morales, Invectivarum Libri Sex* against his fellow humanist Poggio, &c.

138–40. Caxton in 1490 translated from the French the *Livre des Eneydes* (ed. W. T. Culley and F. J. Furnivall, EETS ES 57, 1890). Neither it nor Caxton's version of it is very close to Virgil. Douglas returns to the attack on Caxton in V, prol. 49 ff.

149. *goldyn versis mair than gilt.* That is, made of real gold, not just gilded.

165. *Bocas.* Boccaccio: the *Livre des Eneydes* draws on his *De Casibus Virorum Illustrium.*

186. '*That* holds'. The relative is often omitted in Middle Scots and Northern English: cf. I. iii. 46.

195–7. The syntax is hard, for there seems to be no verb: 'For so the poets [are accustomed] to hide . . .'?—unless 'tohyde' is an intensive pl., 'hide completely'?

204–5. Boccaccio, *De Geneologia Deorum*, Lib. IX, cap. xxxiii, gives a naturalistic account of the descent of Hercules into Hell to rescue Theseus.

206. *Recolles of Troy. Le Recueil des Histoires de Troy*, by Raoul Lefevre, translated by Caxton; for the story of Theseus, v. *The Recuyell of the Historyes of Troye* (ed. H. Oskar Sommer, London, 1894), pp. 321 ff.

211–12. Kings xxviii [= 1 Sam.], as Douglas's marginal note points out.

217. Second sight and other supernatural powers come by a compact with the devil or converse with demons or fairies: thus in an age of firm faith there are fewer 'illusions'.

222–40. Caxton wrote 'Tonyre' (in the EETS edition, p. 120, l. 26; p. 130, l. 24); Douglas may have meant 'Tyra', the largest tributary of the Danube. Though 'Tanais' is mentioned in l. 239, there seems to be no manuscript authority for reading 'Tonyr' here.

254. Douglas occasionally makes Aeneas sound like the hero of a medieval romance.

260. *A twenty devill way*: 'in the devil's name': cf. 'a devill way', *OED*, s.v. 'devil' 19.

262. The comparison is proverbial: cf. *The Kingis Quair*, st. cx:

> Vnlike the mone is to the sonne schene;
> Eke Ianuarye is vnlike vnto May;
> Vnlike the cukkow to the phylomene . . .
> Vnlike the crow is to the papeiay.

269–70. *Franch . . . Franchly.* Small glosses 'frenschlie' as 'frankly', but it probably means 'lies like a Frenchman'.

274. Caxton died in 1491.

309. 'My brain, intent on grasping Virgil's meaning. . . .'

319–20. 'The sun's light is not the worse because the bat flees his beams.'

332. 'A' and 'Ane' are used indifferently in the manuscripts of the poem; 'ane' means 'one' or 'a' depending on context.

345. Chaucer, *Legend of Good Women*, ll. 1002–3; cf. ll. 924–7 and Douglas, I, prol. 413.

350. Servius has a note to *Aeneid* I. 96: 'oppetere, ore terram petere.'

366. 'And even then [they are] poorly expressed'.

367. Cf. the *Complaynt of Scotlande*, f. 15*a*, for the 'homo/animal' contrast; and *passim* for the idea that 'oure scottis tong is nocht sa copeus as is the lateen tong'.

395. *Sanct Gregor*. Pope Gregory I the Great. 'Dum enim verba custodiunt, et sensus minime attendunt, nec verba intelligi faciunt, et sensus frangunt.' *Epistolarum Lib. VII*, Indict. xv, Epist. xxx, *P.L.* 77, 887.

400–4. Horace, *De Arte Poetica*, 133–4, 'Nec verbo verbum curabis reddere fidus interpres.'

414. Chaucer, *LGW*, ll. 925–7:

> I shal, as I can,
> Folwe thy lanterne, as thow gost byforn,
> How Eneas to Dido was forsworn.

416. e.g. Aeneas to Dido 'a traytour was' (*House of Fame*, l. 267, *LGW*, l. 1328); he has to be excused 'of gret trespas' (*HF*, l. 428); 'Eneas to Dido was forsworn' (*LGW*, l. 927).

431. Cf. *Aen.* I. 534, 553–4.

452 ff. This is conventional religious language. 'The prince of poets' is Christ here, Virgil in l. 418.

460 ff. Such renunciation of pagan inspiration is commonplace. Cf. in Douglas III, prol. 41–45, V, prol. 60, VI, prol. 145 ff., X, prol. 151 ff. Cf. Lydgate, the envoy to Book II of the *Fall of Princes*; Lyndsay, *The Prolog of the Miserabill Estait of this World*, ll. 216 ff.; and *The Eclogues of Alexander Barclay* (ed. Beatrice White, EETS 175, 1928), I. 113 ff.:

> Another rewarde abideth my labour,
> The glorious sight of God my sauiour,
> Which is chiefe shepheard and head of other all,
> To him for succour in this my worke I call,
> And not on Clio nor olde Melpomene.

468–9. Deep significance was attached by medieval poets to the breasts of the Virgin. Cf. 'A Prayer to the Blessed Virgin', *The Wheatley Manuscript* (EETS 155, 1921):

> Schewe hym thi pappis for my trespas,
> That he soked whenne he ȝonge was. (ll. 229–32.)

Other examples may be seen in *Political, Religious and Love Poems* (ed. F. J. Furnivall, EETS 15, 1866); 'The Virgin's Complaint and Comfort', l. 38; 'The Stacyons of Rome', l. 424; and 'Quia Amore Langueo', l. 46.

478. 'Say forth.'

480. Cf. Eph. iii. 17.

490. 'Virgil stood so well before, that the worse, i.e. my translation, can be set aside, beyond the mark, or over the score.' See *OED*, s.v. 'score', s. 2*b*.

499–500. Cf. in Matt. vii. 3. Douglas appears to interpret Vulg. *trabem* ('beam') as 'ship'—a sense that *trabs* bears in Virgil and *beam* in English (*OED*, s.v. II. 14).

504. At this point Douglas leads into the poem, translating the first four Latin lines usually rejected from modern editions; then in l. 509, 'The batalys and the man I will discryve' stands for 'Arma virumque cano'.

Book I, ch. i, ll. 1–61, translating I. 1–33 (p. 14)

1. It is interesting to compare Chaucer's translation of the same passage:

> I wol now singen, yif I kan,
> The armes, and also the man
> That first cam, thurgh his destinee,
> Fugityf of Troy contree,
> In Italye, with ful moche pyne
> Unto the strondes of Lavyne. (*HF*, I. 143–8.)

23. Douglas apparently translated from an edition of Virgil in which the text of the poem was surrounded by the explanatory commentaries of Servius and of Jodocus Badius Ascensius (1462–1535), an eminent printer and scholar mentioned in VI, prol. 73. Ascensius's work is an expanded prose paraphrase and explanation of the poem: Douglas habitually draws from it the explanatory material he presumably thought his readers required. This explanatory material makes his version longer than the original. In this line the phrase 'full of sculys seyr' was probably suggested by Ascensius's 'laus ab arte'; in ll. 27–28 the information that Samo was Juno's native land comes from Ascensius's explanatory phrase, 'Samo in qua nata dicitur'. Only important examples of such expansion will be noted here. Passages for which there are no Virgilian equivalents are annotated 'Not in V.'.

33. 'The fatale sisteris' are the three Fates.

48–49. Not in V. Ascensius, '... propter Dardanum Iovis ex Electra Iunonis pellice filium'; and Servius, 'Electra pellex fuit Iovis exqua Dardanus natus est a quo Troiani ducunt originem'.

51. Not in V.; Servius, '. . . ministerium pocolorum . . . est remota Hebe Iunonis filia'.

57. *quhilk now is Italy*. Not in V.; Ascensius, 'Latio i. ab Italia'.

Book I, ch. iii, ll. 1–51, translating I. 92–123 (p. 16)

This storm passage is a lively example of Douglas's 'drumly' style.

6. *bytand the erd*. V., 'oppetere'; Ascensius, 'oppetere scilicet terram mordicus'.

7. *Diomed*. V., 'Tydide'; Ascensius, 'idest Dyomedes'. Douglas ordinarily simplifies patronymics (cf. 'Achillis' for 'Aeacidae' in l. 11).

10. *losit the swete*. V., 'iacet': 'the sweet' is life.

35. Not in V.; Ascensius, 'socios Pandari'.

37. *from the north wynd*. Not in V.; Ascensius, 'ab Aquilone'.

39. *the skippar clepit Lewcaspis*. V., 'magister'; Ascensius, 'Leucaspis'.

43. *salaris*. V.'s 'nantes' misread as 'nautae'?

Book I, ch. ix, ll. 27–56, translating I. 595–610 (p. 17)

Dido has met the Trojan survivors of the storm. She has just expressed a wish to meet their king. He has been present, though Venus has made him invisible. At this point, he appears, and introduces himself.

48. *sa nobill a queyn!* Not in V.

53. *conteyn*. V., 'pascit'; Ascensius, 'sustinebit', i.e. bear or support.

Book II, ch. i, translating II. 13–56 (p. 18)

In the translation, Douglas has shifted Virgil's opening lines to the end of Book I. In all of Book II, Aeneas is the speaker.

10. *walit by cut*. V., 'furtim', secretly; Douglas's meaning (*v.* Glossary) is suggested by Virgil's 'sortiti' and Ascensius's 'sortes trahuntur'.

22. V., 'nos abiisse rati'.

39. *cheif palyce*. V., 'arce'; 'arx' is also translated 'cheif temple' (II. i. 53), 'prowde palice' (II. i. 79), 'hallowit place' (II. iv. 47), &c.

49. *Quhat nedis mair?* Not in V. Douglas introduces similar tags at II. iv. 61 and XII. xiv. 110 (below).

52. *prest*. Not in V. Ascensius, 'sacerdos'.

58. V., 'dolis'; Ascensius, 'dolis, fraudibus, & insidiis'.

59. V., 'sic notus Ulixes?'; Ascensius, 'calliditate & fraude illius viri'.

74. The Loeb edition translates '. . . had *our* mind not been perverse'; Virgil has no pronoun.

Book II, ch. iv, translating II. 199–249 (p. 20)

2. *be sik hunder.* V., 'maius . . . multoque'. The meaning is 'a hundred times more'. For the construction cf. Dunbar, *Amendis to the Tailȝouris and Sowteris*, l. 27, 'And fassoun him bettir be sic thre', and Chaucer, *Book of the Duchess*, l. 408.

38. Not in V.

57–60. Expanded from *Aen.* II. 232–3; suggested by Ascensius, 'Conclamant simulachrum ducendum sup. esse, ad sedes, s. templi divae, s. Palladis, oranda i. supplicationibus & orationibus placanda sup. esse'.

65. *of this ilke bysnyng jaip.* Not in V.

68. V., 'feta armis'; Ascensius, 'pregnans & gravida armis'.

70. *dansand in a ryng.* Not in V. Ascensius, 'per circuitum'.

76. *ful of joy.* Not in V. Ascensius, 'dulcis'.

84. *drug and draw.* A common alliterative tag.

88–90. *Aen.* II. 246–7; the passage is expanded on the model of Ascensius, 'Cassandra . . . aperit dico ora non credita unquam Teucris i. Troianis iussi i. voluntate dei, s. Apollonis, qui quod promiserat donum vaticinandi illi contulit, sed quia ab ea stupro compromisso fraudatus erat credulitatem & fidem abstulit vaticinio eius ut licet vera diceret ei non crederetur'.

94. *as in May,* Not in V.

95. *fest and ryot maid.* Not in V. Ascensius, 'festum agimus'.

96. *for myscheif was glaid.* Not in V. Ascensius, 'extremum gaudium luctus occupat'.

Book II, ch. v, translating II. 250–97 (p. 23)

7. The meaning 'All were inside and still' seems forced. Read 'waryn' ('they were'), as in the Lambeth and Bath MSS.

22. *Thersander.* Some old editions of Virgil have 'Thersandrus' where modern ones read 'Thessandrus'; cf. 'Athamas' for the modern 'Acamas' in the next line.

29. *liggyng on the wall.* Not in V.

32, 36. Not in V.

47. *of hym Achillys.* For the usage, cf. Chaucer, *CT* A, l. 1333, 'For jalousie and fere of hym Arcite'.

50. Not in V. Ascensius, 'Protesilai qui . . . interfectus est ab Hectore'.

78. Not in V. Ascensius, 'fata . . . noluntque patriam defendi'.

82. Not in V.

91. V., 'Vestam'; Servius explains 'deam ignis que terra est diversa'.

Book II, ch. ix, translating II. 506–58 (p. 26)

28. *for it is won.* Not in V. Ascensius, 'cum serum sit'.

32. V., 'sic ore effata'.

33. *but ony threte.* Not in V.

39. *come to seik reskew.* Not in V. Suggested by Ascensius, 'quem se reciperet'?

87–88. V., 'sine nomine corpus'; the addition is suggested by Ascensius, 'corpus sine nomine, id est ignobile dicitur sine nomine aut ad sui cognitionem mortales invitat, ut cognoscant quia ablato capite etiam regis sit sine nomine, i. non enim agnoscitur'.

Book II, ch. xi, translating II. 679–759 (p. 28)

1. *sche. sc.* Creusa, wife of Æneas. Ll. 1–2 are expanded from V.'s 'Talia vociferans gemitu tectum omne replebat'.

21. *help.* 'auxilium' of old editions (mod. edns. 'augurium').

25. V., 'laevum'; Ascensius, 'pars septentrionales'.

31. *quhidder at we suld spur.* Not in V.

36. *our bute.* Not in V. Ascensius, 'rei bone significativum'.

74. V., 'succedoque oneri'; Ascensius, 'suscipio patrem'.

78. *secret wentis and quyet rewys.* V., 'opaca locorum'.

82. *causyt grow.* 'Made me shudder.'

93–94. *I ran befor the laif.* V., 'excedo'; Ascensius, 'excedo id est ante eo insequentes'.

102. *mote of Ceres.* V., 'antiquae Cereris sedemque sacratam': it is seldom that Douglas condenses.

118. *every streit and way.* Not in V.

Book II, ch. xii, translating II. 760–804 (p. 32)

4. *thocht it was gyrth.* Not in V.

14–15. *with mony . . . sayr.* Some old editions complete II. 767, ' et tacitis implent mugitibus aures'.

32. ' This chance has not befallen contrary to the will of the gods.'

38. *sail.* V., 'arandum'; Ascensius explains the metaphor, 'navibus non aratro'.

54. *for ay we mon dissevir.* Not in V.

58. 'And many words I would have said.'

63. *or the son beym.* Not in V.

77. *the day starn, Lucifer the brycht.* V., 'Lucifer'; Ascensius, 'stella matutina lucem ferens'.

From the Prologue of Book IV (p. 34)

The sermon on love is a conventional part of medieval moralizing; cf. St. Augustine, *De Civitate Dei*, Lib. XIV, cap. xvi–xxii; Gower, *Confessio Amantis*, *ad fin.*; Chaucer, *The Parson's Tale*, 'De Luxuria'; *Le Livre du Chevalier de la Tour-Landry, pour l'enseignement de ses filles*; and cf. the moralizing about false lovers in Hoccleve, 'A Letter of Cupid to Lovers, his Subjects' (EETS ES 61, pp. 72 ff.); or John Audelay, 'Poem Number 1' (EETS 184).

36. *cheyn of luf.* For the turn of expression, cf. *CT* A, l. 2988, and *Romance of the Rose*, ll. 4809–12, 'Love . . . is . . . Annexed and knet betwixe tweyne, . . . male and female, with oo cheyne'.

36–44. Cf. *CT* A, ll. 1785–9, and the beginning of 'The Cuckoo and the Nightingale' (Skeat, *Chaucerian and Other Pieces*, p. 347):

> The god of love, a! benedicite!
> How mighty and how greet a lord is he!
> For he can make of lowe hertes hye,
> And of hye lowe, and lyke for to dye,
> And herde hertes he can maken free, [&c.].

42. By Harrowing Hell between the Crucifixion and the Resurrection Christ released the virtuous Jews from Hell and 'plenyst paradyce' with them: cf., for example, *Piers Plowman* XVIII (B) 260–404.

43. For reference to the power of love, cf., for example, Lydgate, *Reason and Sensuality* (EETS ES 84, 1901), ll. 1475–1534, where it is asserted that Venus makes the covetous spend their goods, the proud to incline to humility, the haughty to be debonair, the sullen to be fairspoken, the envious to be amiable, the angry to be biddable, cowards to be manful, the brave to be cowardly; even the gods obey her.

45. *Jonathas, Davy.* Jonathan and David, in Samuel.

46. *Alexander.* Alexander the Great was infatuated with Roxane.

47. *Jacob.* Gen. xxix. 20–28.

48. *Hercules.* Deianira persuaded Hercules, her husband, to surrender to him his warlike tasks while he assumed her domestic ones.

107. 'Lust is not really love, though people generally like it.'

108–9. False concords of this kind, 'flambe . . . ar', are not uncommon in late ME.

112–34. St. Augustine, *De Civitate Dei*, Lib. XV, cap. xxii, as Douglas's note in the Cambridge MS. points out. The idea that it is inordinate to love anything more than God also appears, e.g. in St. Augustine, *Sermo* cccxlix: 'Non dico ut non diligas uxorem; sed plus delige Christum. Non dico ut non diligas patrem, non dico ut non diligas filios; sed plus dilige Christum.'

114. Medieval medicine saw a connexion between fever and love; *v.* Lydgate, 'Fabula Duorum Mercatorum' (*Minor Poems*, EETS 192, 1934), ll. 348–50:

> thes lechys
> Konne of this man noon othir ffevir espye
> Bot that for love was hool his malladye.

119–20. This is part of Renaissance medical theory: *v.* Sir Thomas Elyot, *The Castel of Helth* (1541), ff. 38ᵛ–39ʳ: 'Chyldren wold be noryshed with meates and drynkes, whyche are moderately hotte and moyst. . . . Olde men in whome naturall heate & strength semeth to decay, shuld vse alway meates, whiche are of qualitie hotte and moyste. . . .'

137. Cf. Ps. x. 6: 'Qui diligit iniquitatem odit animam suam'.

Book IV, ch. i, translating II. 1–53 (p. 36)

1. *Be this.* 'By this time'—after hearing the tale of Æneas' sufferings.

14. *and the ayr new schrowd.* Not in V.

21. V., 'quem sese ore ferens!' ('How noble his mien!', Loeb).

22. *O God, quhat wondir thing!* Not in V.

27–28. Expanded from V.'s 'degeneres animos timor arguit' in accordance with Douglas's aristocratic opinions.

30–31. Expanded from V.'s 'quae bella exhausta canebat'; suggested by Ascensius, 'laboribus . . . exhausta i. iam expleta & gesta atque pacta . . . gravissima & maxime formidanda'.

38. *Genyus chalmyr.* V., 'thalami'; Douglas apparently has misunderstood Ascensius's explanation, 'i. thori genialis'.

40. V., 'uni . . . culpae'; Ascensius, '. . . esset transuendo ad secundas nuptias'.

42. *sory.* Not 'contemptible', but 'wretched' (for V.'s 'miseri').

47. V., 'veteris flammae'; Servius, 'martialis coniugii ardorem'.

52–53. *hellis holl . . . nycht.* V., 'Erebi'; Ascensius, 'i. loci obscurissimi in inferno'.

56. *your.* I.e. of Pudor, named by Virgil but not by Douglas.

58. V., 'amores abstulit'; Ascensius, 'abstulit primos amores meos'; Servius, 'a cum illo consumpta sunt desideria & voluptates'.

62–63. *or scho wist, sa mot I thryve.* Not in V.

65. *alane in wedowhed.* V., 'sola'; Ascensius, 'i. viduatate'.

70. V., 'id . . . curare'.

72. *thy lord new ded.* V., 'aegram'; Ascensius, 'idest tristem propter maritum'.

74. Douglas omits 'non ante Tyro'.

87–88. V., 'hinc deserta siti regio'; Ascensius, 'propter aquarum penuriam'; Servius, 'intelligit Xerolibyen'.

110. Not in V.

112. *byd . . . aik.* Not in V.

Book IV, ch. ii, translating IV. 54–89 (p. 39)

7. Not (of course) in V.

8. *benevolence and gude luk.* V., 'pacem'; Ascensius, 'idest pacationem, conciliationem & beneuolentiam'.

12. *law ledar.* For V.'s 'legiferae', law-giver.

13. *Bachus.* V., 'patrique Lyaeo'; Ascensius, 'seu Baccho', a characteristic simplification of mythology.

19. *ontamyt.* Not in V. Douglas misunderstood Ascensius's 'intacte'.

24. *And rych gyftis geif Trojanys.* V., 'instauratque diem donis'; Servius, 'aut donabat tyriis vel Troianis'.

27. Not in V.

28. Not in V. Ascensius, 'consilium expedit'.

29–38. Douglas has expanded *Aen.* IV. 65–67.

50–51. *offerit . . . commandment.* (V., 'urbem paratum'.) Suggested by Ascensius, '. . . quod signum est coniugalis amoris'?

59. V., 'post ubi digressi'.

64. V., 'vacua'; Ascensius, 's. amato'.

66–68. *thinkis . . . be.* V., 'auditque videtque'; Ascensius, 'audit & videt s. per fantasiam & imaginationem illum s. amatum absentem'.

69. *the page.* Not in V.; little additions of this kind give the translation something of the flavour of a medieval romance: cf. l. 77, where V.'s 'minaeque murorum ingentes' is represented by the tapestry-like 'pynnakillis hie'.

75. 'Nor safe war-turrets. . . .'

78. *towris.* V., 'machina'; Ascensius, 'edificii aut turris'.

Book IV, ch. iii, translating IV. 90–128 (p. 41)

27. *al Lyby land.* Not in V. Ascensius, 'in Libyam hoc est in Carthaginem'.

30–31. *the Trojane kynd, And weris tocum.* V., 'regnum'.

38. V., 'sed fatis incerta feror' ('But the Fates send me adrift', Loeb).

65. Not in V.

Book IV, ch. iv, translating IV. 129–72 (p. 43)

16. V., 'picto . . . limbo'.

38. *of lawrer.* V., 'fronde'; Ascensius, 'scilicet lauri'.

46–55. Expand *Aen.* IV. 152–5: Douglas often enlarges such scenes of action.

65–66. V., 'insequitur commixta grandine nimbus'.

72. Not in V. Ascensius, 'i. tegmina & speluncas per agros, i. que & quas intervenire poterant'.

75–76. *al thame alane . . . rane.* Not in V.

83. *glaidnes.* V., 'leti' ('death', Loeb); Ascensius, 'i. laeticie & voluptatis'. Cf. Chaucer, *LGW* 1230–1.

Book IV, ch. v, translating IV. 173–278 (p. 45)

13. *last.* 'Last-born.'

26–27. *nobillis, princis.* Not in V. The flavour is medieval.

42. *est, west, north and sowth.* V., 'passim'.

64. *Bachus.* V., 'Lenaeum'; Ascensius, 'Bacchicum'; unfamiliar mythological allusions are almost always simplified.

82. *Becaus.* V., 'quippe'; 'and yet' would have been a better translation.

83. *invane.* V.'s 'inanem' has been misread as an adverb, under the influence of the neighbouring 'frustra' in Servius?

84. *at hame.* Not in V. A characteristic 'hamelie' touch.

109. 'Though the honour of such great things doesn't stir him. . . .'

122. *weyngis.* V., 'talaria'; Servius, 'pennae'.

128. V., 'Tartara'; Ascensius, 'i. loca profundissima & obscurissima in inferno'.

131. *brekis the stryngis tway.* Not in V. Suggested by Ascensius, '. . . lumina id est pupillas quas aufert'. See *OED*, s.v. 'eyestring': 'The eyestrings were formerly supposed to crack at death.'

143. *stern and grisly.* V., 'rigida'.

144. V., 'paribus nitens Cyllenius alis'; Ascensius, 'idest Mercurius', as in ll. 151, 185, and elsewhere.

176. *fremmyt.* V., 'Libycis'; Ascensius, 'inimicas'.

187. *I wait nevir quhar.* Not in V.

Book IV, ch. vi, translating IV. 279–361 (p. 50)

5. *ful laith.* This contradicts the sense of V., 'ardet . . . relinquere terras'.

17. *Cloanthus.* 'Cloanthum' of old editions (mod. edns. 'Serestum').

24. Not in V. Ascensius, 'abire velit'.

35. Not in V. Ascensius, 'nam res est solliciti plena timoris amor'.

41. *nunnys of Bachus.* V., 'Thias'; Ascensius, 'sacerdos Bacchi'.

42. *bankis, brays and bus.* Not in V.

43. Douglas omits 'commotis excita sacris'.

47–48. *of hir fre will, Eftir lang musyng.* Not in V. Ascensius, 'post longam cogitationem . . . non exigentem eius compellationem'.

51. *myne onwyttyng.* V., 'tacitus'; for the construction with the possessive pronoun, see *OED*, s.v. 'unwitting' 3 a.

59. *I put the cace.* V., 'quid'; Ascensius, 'quin etiam'.

61. 'To no unknown lands would you need to go, nor to any strange or desolate places, even if Troy were standing; should you then leave . . .?'

63. *leif this weilfair and joy.* Not in V. Suggested by Servius, 'ac si dicat Cartago iam tibi nota est'.

85–86. Douglas is more vivid than V. IV. 324, 'Hoc solum nomen quoniam de coniuge restat'.

87. V., 'quid moror?'; Ascensius, 'i. quid differo mortem?'

88. Not in V.

100. *in febil estate.* Not in V.

115. *quhat nedis you sa tofeyn?* Not in V. Ascensius, 'ne dicas eam ex opinione tua fugam'.

118. *ne frendschip in Cartage.* Not in V.

126. *at now fallis.* Not in V. Ascensius, 'post cassum'.

137. V., 'invidia'; Ascensius, 'invidia idest iniuria'.

Book IV, ch. vii, translating IV. 362–407 (p. 55)

1. *aggrevit.* Not in V. Ascensius, 'indignata & irata'.

11–12. V., 'Hyrcanaeque admorunt ubera tigres'; Servius, 'Arabicae ab Hyrcania Arabiae sylva'.

18. *Na, not to yeir.* Not in V. Ascensius, 'etiam minima'.

42. V., 'supplicia hausurum'; Ascensius, 'idest luiturum & daturum . . . punitionem perfidie'.

57. V., 'linquens multa metu cunctantem'.

62. *apon rych carpettis spred.* Not in V. Ascensius, 'tapetibus instratis'.

76. *gret mastis.* Not in V. Ascensius, 'pro malis'.

Book IV, ch. viii, translating IV. 408–73 (p. 57)

4–6. V., 'cum litore fervere late', considerably expanded.

17. Not in V. Ascensius, 'unde convenit Annam sororem suam'.

20. V., 'vocat iam carbasus auras', i.e. 'the canvas calls the breezes'.

30–31. IV. 427, 'Alone thou knowest the hour for easy access to him' (Loeb).

41. *from hys behufe.* Not in V.

56–58. Where modern editions in IV. 436 have 'dederit' and 'remittam', some old editions have 'dederis' and 'relinquam'.

57. *weil twentyfald.* Not in V. Ascensius, 'copiose'.

68. Not in V.

84–85. V., 'magno presentit pectore curas'.

106. *carpettis and ensens.* Not in V. Servius, 'laneis vittis . . . oleo'.

128. *farcis,* 'tragedies'. V. 'scaenis agitatus'.

129. *Rowpyt and sung.* Not in V. Ascensius, 'actus & . . . exhibitus'.

131. *grisly goddis fed.* Not in V.

Book IV, ch. ix, translating IV. 474–521 (p. 61)

1–3. V., 'Ergo ubi concepit furias evicta dolore decrevitque mori'; Ascensius, 'tum vero infelix fatis exterrita Dido mortem orat.'

24. *in the gardyngis.* Not in V. Ascensius, 'quod in hortis . . . est'.

26. *goldyn.* V., 'sacros ramos'; Ascensius, 'aurea'.

28. *to quykkyn his spreit.* Not in V. Ascensius, 'conservativum cerebri & humorum draconis'; the translation should be 'to calm'.

56. *pail as ony wall.* Not in V. It is impossible to say whether the simile means 'pale as a whitewashed wall' or 'pale as a foamy wave'.

78. *Proserpina.* V., 'Hecaten'; Ascensius, 'i. Proserpinam', and so also in IV. xi. 50. She is 'thrynfald' because she is often merged with Diana and Luna.

82. Not in V. Ascensius, 'i. lacus ad introitum inferni'.

88. This lump is a love-charm, which Dido takes to persuade her sister she is intent on recapturing Aeneas' love.

91–92. *bandis . . . weyd.* V., 'in veste recincta'.

Book IV, ch. x, translating IV. 522–83 (p. 63)

23. V., 'inrisa'.

49. *and a new rays.* Not in V.; 'race' here probably means 'journey' rather than 'a division of mankind'.

79. *quham thou knawys.* Not in V. Ascensius, 'tibi nota'.

86. V., 'turbari trabibus'.

88. *Reddy to byrn thi schippys.* Not in V. Ascensius, 'ad naves tuas comburendas'.

112. *ankyrris uphynt and rave.* Not in V.

Book IV, ch. xi, translating IV. 584–641 (p. 67)

13. *vavengeour stranger.* V., 'advena'.

22. *werdis.* 'Fata' of old editions (mod. edns. 'facta').

27. The grammar would be improved if it were *quha* here and in l. 29. The *quham* may be modelled on V.'s 'quam . . . aiunt portare . . . quem subisse . . .'.

47. *clengis.* V.'s 'lustras' probably should be taken as 'you observe'.

50. *by our gentile lawys.* Not in V.; *v.* Glossary, *s.v.* 'gentile'.

52. *with mony mudy wight.* Not in V. Ascensius, 'querentibus frequentatis'.

53. V., 'Dirae ultrices'; Ascensius, 'idest furiae eumenides ultrices s. scelerum'.

55. V., 'morientis Elissae'; Ascensius, 'i. in quarum potestatem ventura est Elissa'.

57–58. V., 'meritumque malis avertite numen' (mod. edns. 'advertite'); Ascensius, 'i. a malis quod mali merentur habere infestum: & ita se innocentem indicat'.

68. *help.* V., 'complexu', misread as 'complice'?

76. *hevand up my handis.* Not in V.

101. *broun.* V., 'ater', i.e. 'black'; the idea of burying is not in Virgil.

110. *Pluto.* V., 'Iovi Stygio'; Ascensius, 'idest Plutoni'.

Book IV, ch. xii, translating IV. 642–705 (p. 70)

15. V., 'dulcis exuviae'.

17. *that on flocht is.* Not in V.

32. Not in V.

34. Not in V. Ascensius, '& eo dicto statim in gladium incubuit'.

42. *furthsprent.* V., 'sparsas'; Servius, 'aut perfusas sanguine aut morte resolutas'.

53. *baith but and ben.* Not in V. A homely Scottish touch.

77. *with my counsell.* Not in V. Ascensius, 'consilio meo'.

80. *(I) distroyt.* Cf. 'extinxi' of old editions (mod. edns. 'exstinxti', 2nd sg. perf.).

82. *hald hir in myne arm.* Not in V.

117. *to Pluto consecrate.* V., 'Diti sacrum'; Ascensius, 'consecratum . . . Plutoni'.

Book VI, ch. iv, translating VI. 236–94 (p. 73)

7. *als blak as ony craw.* Not in V.

26. Not in V.

58. V., 'Chaos'; Ascensius, 'origio rerum confusa'.

59. V., 'Phlegthon'; Ascensius, 'i. ardoris infernalis fluvius'.

66–67. *oneth . . . went*. Not in V.

80. *that causys folk be seik*. V., 'pallentes'; Ascensius, 'i. pallidos facientes'.

86. *diseysful Pane*. Not in V.

88. V., 'mala mentis Gaudia'; Ascensius, 'i. immodica aut nociva gaudia mentis'.

92. *that wondryng maist crewell*. Not in V.

103. *dowbil porturat*. V., 'biformes'.

107. V., 'flammisque armata'; Ascensius, 'quia mons est cuius cacumen ardet'.

110. Not in V. Servius, 'Eryli & Gerionis'.

Book VI, ch. vii, ll. 55–108, translating VI. 450–76 (p. 76)

96. *curage, face nor bre*. V., 'vultum'.

106–8. A loose expansion of V.'s 'prosequitur lacrimis longe et miseratur euntem'.

Book VI, ch. xiii, ll. 71–110, translating VI. 788–807 (p. 78)

93. *Assery*. Not in V. Ascensius, 'ad fines Assyriorum'.

94. *Scithya*. Not in V. Ascensius, 'idest scythia ubi est Meotis'.

100. *wynd swift*. V., 'aeripedem', or 'brazen-footed'; Ascensius, 'i. habentem aereos pedes i. veloces'; the phrase should be read as 'wind-swift'.

The Prologue of Book VII (p. 79)

For the description of winter, correlated with the poet's mood, cf. Henryson, *The Testament of Criseyd*; Dunbar, 'Meditatioun in Wyntir'; Chambers and Sidgwick, *Early English Lyrics*, p. 169; and Barnabe Googe's translation of the Preface to the 1560 edition of Marcellus Palingenius, *The Zodiake of Life* (ed. with introd. by Rosemund Tuve, New York, 1947):

> When as syr Phebe with backward course.
> The horned gote had caught, [&c.]

The reader should beware of attributing to Douglas an originality and nervous energy that he does not have.

2 ff. That is, the sun is low (the opposite of its highest position in the sky), scarcely above the horizon, for it is the third day after the sun entered Capricorn at the winter solstice.

14–15. *brumaill, brym.* Notice the mild pun. Douglas would be aware that there is no etymological connexion between 'brumaill' (< L 'brumalis' < 'brume', contr. 'brevissima', shortest, i.e. the shortest day of the year) and 'brym' (< OE 'breme', famous, celebrated).

22. The lion is part of the poetic scenery, not of Scottish fauna.

25, 29. Mars and Saturn are generally malefic in their astrological influences.

33. Astrologically, Hebe or Ganymeda is identified with Aquarius: the sun enters Aquarius on 21 January, so the allusion to Hebe does not square with l. 8. The point may be that Hebe, as the goddess of youth, has no role to play in the aged year.

37 ff. Note the amount of alliteration here and in the following lines, e.g. 67–70.

38. 'Mountain tops covered with snow hide or are hidden.'

89. *warm stovis.* If 'stove' means a heating apparatus (as 'fyris' suggests), not a room so heated, then this is an earlier occurrence of the sense than any in *OED*.

94. *a bed.* 'Abed.'

98. *I dyd tak kepe.* 'I observed, I noticed.'

100. *watry lycht.* Either pale or portending rain (*OED*, *s.v.* 'watry', 3 and 6 c).

101–4. The moon is in opposition to the sun (the angular distance subsisting between them is 180°), always an evil aspect astrologically.

105. *Hebowd.* (Fr. 'hibou'. Evidently an uncommon word since the manuscripts read 'he bowd', &c. 1553 ed. 'The horned byrd'.) *DOST* gives only this example.

113. *Phebus crownyt byrd.* So called because the cock rises with the sun. Lydgate calls it 'Embasiatour of Phebus fyry lyght' in *Isopes Fabules*, 86.

119. *Palamedes byrdis.* Philostratus credits Palamedes with the invention of the Greek letters v, ϕ, and χ, v representing cranes in flight, and ϕ representing a single crane standing on one leg. (Cf. Martial xiii. 75, and Ausonius, *Opuscula XII*, xiii.)

136. 'By nature cold or chilly.'

150. *the yok lyis on thy nek.* Proverbial for onerous difficulty: cf. *Richard III*, IV. iv. 111, and below, l. 158.

152. Proverbial, perhaps ultimately from Lucan (*Pharsalia* II. 657), 'Nil actum credens, cum quid superesset agendum'.

162. Douglas here adds six lines requesting that the letters of this

prologue should be illuminated in black, to reflect the departure from
the Underworld in Book VI.

Book VII, ch. i, ll. 1–44, translating VII. 25–44 (p. 84)

Douglas transferred the first twenty-four lines of Book VII to the
end of Book VI, apparently feeling that they have a strong logical
connexion with the preceding material.

4. *brown sanguane*. 'Brownish red.' V., 'lutea'; Ascensius, 'sub rudens
interminato s. croceo'.

7. V., 'in lento . . . marmore'; the sea is marmoreal in its calm.

16. *in the clewis*. Not in V. Ascensius, 'a parte superiori'.

24. V., 'opaco'; Ascensius, 'umbroso silvis decumbentibus obtecto'.

30. *arrivyn*. Infinitive.

Book VII, ch. x, translating VII. 601–40 (p. 85)

2. *ancyent Latyum*. V., 'Hesperio in Latio'; Servius, 'hoc est in
antiquo'.

9. *with ostis plane*. V., 'manu'; Ascensius, 'cum novis hostibus'.

22. *slottis*. V., 'robora', that is, strength; Ascensius, 'i. repagula
fortia'.

23. V., 'aeterna'; Ascensius, 'i. inconsumptibilia'.

28. V., 'consul'.

31. *fut syde*. 'Reaching to the feet.' Not in V. Ascensius, 'circumcin-
gente altera extremitate'.

38. Not in V. Suggested by Ascensius, 'vir severus & venerandus'?

43. *nor brek his heist*. Not in V. Suggested by Ascensius, 'contra foedus
& amicitiam fidemque Aeneae datam'.

44. *ganestud thar requeste*. Not in V. Ascensius, 'vitavit & refutavit'.

50. Not in V.

54. *into fury bellicall*. Not in V. Ascensius, 's. ardore . . . bellico'.

71. Not in V. Ascensius, 'bene muratae'.

74. Not in V.

76–77. Expanded from V.'s 'aut levis ocreas lento ducunt argento'.

78–88. Expanded from 635–7 and made more lively.

82. 'The desire for such tools (and such work) was all gone.'

90. Not in V.

The Prologue to Book VIII, ll. 79–117 (p. 88)

For the alliterative form in Scotland, *v.* Sir William Craigie, *The Scottish Alliterative Poems*, 1942. The speaker is an anonymous stranger whom Douglas meets in a dream. The criticism of contemporary society is conventional: cf., for example, Dunbar, 'Tydingis fra the Sessioun'. The language of this prologue is often exceedingly difficult.

81. 'Tricks and dangerous deceptions are considered sound policy or sagacity.'

84. The topsy-turvy world, in which lords are landless, and peasants and tradesmen rich, is a common late medieval theme: see Helen C. White, *Social Criticism in Popular Religious Literature of the Sixteenth Century* (New York, 1944), particularly Chapter V, 'Submission'.

85. 'Merchants bring home the booth to breed at home'?—if the merchant who has but one trading-booth works at home at night, then his booth will reproduce.

86. 'Kowhubeis' is an obscure term of abuse, 'simpleton'? For 'plukkyt crawis' cf. Lyndesay, *Complaint*, l. 230.

92. A difficult line. Perhaps 'Some who, against the law, spend plated brass freely, get little esteem thereby'. Ruddiman suggests 'Some, contrary to all law and reason, take mixt metal, copper or brass, which they *leep*, i.e., put into molten tin or silver, that so it may pass for true silver though truly it is of small value'. Small suggests 'Some illegally circulate a base metal, held in little estimation', or 'Some plated money, against the law, leaps about or circulates, though held in low esteem'.

94–95. An allusion to alchemists. Chaucer in the 'Canon's Yeoman's Tale' regards alchemy as a fraud; it is impossible to determine Douglas's attitude, unless only a foolish man 'gowkis' where a clever one would 'gaze' or the like.

96. 'This one who announces the destruction of the world lives by his wits', an allusion to violent apocalyptical preachers.

97. 'Some hoarder clips the coinage and keeps cornstacks.' Douglas probably means that the hoarder hoarded corn until time of scarcity in order to get an inflated price, an act as anti-social as coin-clipping: cf. Sir William Forrest, *Pleasaunt Poesye of Princelie Practise* (EETS ES 32), ll. 92–95:

> In tyme of plentie the riche too vpp mucker
> Corne, Grayne, or Chafre hopinge vppon dearthe:
> for his pryuate wealthe so daylye too hucker:
> this criethe for vengeaunce too heauyn from the earthe.

98. 'Some haggle for pennies, some flatter with a private promise.'

99. 'Some push with a Jedburgh staff to pierce through black jackets.'

100. 'What a feigned course!'

105. 'Priests, who should be sayers of Paternosters.' Evidently 'pat-terers' is meant in no derogatory sense.

106. *papis of patermon.* 'Pope' is here used figuratively for one who is considered to have authority analogous to that of a pope.

107-8. Ironic: 'The tithes of ten parishes are a mere trifle, but if he can take a kingdom of parish churches and benefices—ah, how fine!'

113-15. 'The members of no social rank, knights, clerks, commons, burgesses or barons, are contented with their present style.' 'Thar stile' is either the style of living adopted by the clergy, or the rank and titles enjoyed by the complainers themselves.

116-17. 'All would have those at the bottom raised to the top, and have the present order turned upside-down.'

The Prologue to Book IX, ll. 21–76 (p. 89)

21. *the ryall style.* William Webbe speaks of 'the princelie part of Poetry' ('Of English poetry', *Elizabethan Critical Essays*, ed. G. G. Smith, vol. i, pp. 255-6), and Puttenham defines the epic as 'long histories of the noble gests of kings & great Princis entermedling the dealings of the gods . . .' (ibid., vol. ii, p. 26). But the *Aeneid* is pre-eminent among epics, and is described as *'the wark imperiall'* in l. 56 below.

33-35. Based on the beginning of *Georgics* II? If 'myne authour' is not Virgil, the reference may be to Horace, *Ars Poetica*, 19 ff. and 156 ff. Cf. Alexander Barclay, *Eclogues* (ed. Beatrice White, EETS 175, 1928), I. 83–88:

> It were not fitting a heard or man rurall
> To speake in terms gay and rhethoricall.
> So teacheth Horace in arte of poetry,
> That writers namely their reason should apply
> Mete speeche appropring to euery personage,
> After his estate, behauour, wit and age.

40-41. Apparently a mild joke: the first 'gait' is 'way', the second 'goat'.

44. 'No knight should read anything but a knightly tale.'

49. The mastiff is a mean dog: cf. *Petite Pallace . . .* (ed. I. Gollancz, vol. ii, p. 85), 'As the saying is, the mastiff never loveth the greyhound'.

59-62. Luke ii. 1-5, the taxing by Augustus.

63-76. For the modesty, and the praise of Virgil, both highly con-ventional, cf. I, prol. 1 ff., V, prol. 28 ff., &c.

The Prologue to Book XII, ll. 175-266 (p. 91)

The 1553 edition calls this 'ane singular lernit Proloug' and L. M. Watt says it is 'vibrant with the freshness of the living air'; it is, in fact, entirely within a medieval and Renaissance tradition. Cf. Chaucer, *BkD*, ll. 291-320; *The Kingis Quair*, lxv; Dunbar, 'The Thrissil and the Rois', 'The Golden Targe', and 'The Merle and the Nychtingaill'; Lyndsay, the prologue to 'Ane Dialog Betwix Experience and ane Courteour', &c.

187-8. Doryda is Doris, the nymph daughter of Thetis; the Naedes are the Nereides (Douglas's form may be due to association with Dryades).

197-200. These might be real songs, or simply joyful remarks. Cf. Chaucer, *FranklT*, ll. 853-4: 'Is ther no ship, of so manye I se, Wol bryngen hom my lord? Thanne were myn herte Al warisshed of his bittre peynes smerte'; this is not a song.

213-24. Notice the lively dialogue.

252 ff. This kind of address is a common device of rhetoric: cf. Chaucer's addresses to summer, *ParlF*, ll. 680-92, and *LGW*, ll. 170 ff. For the device of *repetitio*, cf. Chaucer, *ComplMars*, ll. 290-6; or Hawes, *Passetyme of Pleasure*, ll. 4050-74.

Book XII, ch. xiv, ll. 80-154, translating XII. 919-52 (p. 93)

99. 'The Rutulians started up, groaning together.'

100. V., 'gemitu'.

129. V., 'cunctantem'.

138. The belt is unfriendly to Turnus because it reminds Aeneas of the death of his young friend and protégé Pallas; and Turnus was unfriendly to Pallas; the double sense is in the Latin.

154. *with disdeyn*. V., 'indignata'.

The Prologue to Book XIII (p. 95)

Book XIII is a rather dull fifteenth-century addition by Mapheus Vegius (1407-58): *v.* Anna Cox Brinton, *Mapheus Vegius and his Thirteenth Book of the Aeneid* (Stanford University Press, 1930).

The *Prologue*: Interviews with persons who suggest the course the author should follow are very common in Lydgate's *Fall of Princes* (ed. Bergen, Washington, 1923), e.g. I. 3844-4212, where Thyestes and Atreus demand that Boccaccio (the work is a loose translation of Boccaccio's *De Casibus*) should tell their stories.

2, 4. *in the Crab Appollo held hys sete . . . and supper doyn*. That is, when it was summer, and evening.

16. *Phegon.* For Phlegon, one of the four horses of the sun: Boccaccio (*De Geneologia Deorum*) likewise has the form.

61-62. *Philomeyn.* Philomele sings 'from the spleen' because she was violated by her brother-in-law, and was then changed into a nightingale. The form in -*n(e)* is the usual one before Spenser.

76. '*Who* said. . . .' For the dream-interlocutor cf. VIII, prologue.

93. 'I, who never saw you before, fain would know. . . .'

98. 'But otherwise, this seat [i.e. your position] will be salt [i.e. uncomfortable].'

102. '. . . not in the least fond of you.'

115. 'Also, father, trust me, some people consider. . . .'

118. Ascensius has a note at the beginning of Book XIII, 'unde frustra quidem quadrigis rotam quintam addidit'.

122. Jerome, *Epist.*, xxii. 30.

127-8. Ps. xiv. 1, 4.

144. 'By the soul of the father who begot me.'

152. In honour of God and the twelve Apostles 'in the numbir od', that is, twelve apostles and God adding up to thirteen.

182. *the joly day now dawys.* 'Now the day dawis' is mentioned as the tune of 'commone menstrallis' by Dunbar in 'To the Merchants of Edinburgh', l. 30. A similar song occurs in the late fifteenth-century Fairfax MS. and is printed in E. Flügel, *Neuenglisches Lesebuch*, p. 159.

191. 'My speech and my writing are the same, i.e. both vernacular.'

Book XIII, ch. viii, ll. 37–108, translating XIII. 461–89 (p. 101)

42. Not in Mapheus.

46. *palys, bowr and hall.* Mapheus, 'regia'; the locution 'bower and hall' (i.e. private and public rooms) is a romance tag for 'everywhere'.

55-57. Expanded from Mapheus, 'sidereos deiecta oculos'.

64. *na litill apperans.* Not in Mapheus. The idea is: if the first glance could astonish Aeneas, long association could well move Turnus.

67-68. The phrasing suggests 'courtly love' in Douglas, not in Mapheus, 'Qui haud parva spe ductus ovans in proelia tantos civisset motus . . .'.

69. *to abbryge our mater.* Not in Mapheus. As a matter of fact, Douglas, ll. 69-80, are expanded from Mapheus XIII. 474-7; 73 has no parallel in Mapheus; 75-76 are expanded from Mapheus, 'plausus fremitusque'; 80-93 are expanded from Mapheus, XIII. 478-82. Douglas frequently amplifies courtly scenes of this sort.

81. 'And the celebration of the crowd continuing. . . .'

Book XIII, ch. xi, translating XIII. 593–630 (p. 103)

1–6. Expanded from Mapheus, XIII. 593–4.

9. Mapheus has simply 'res hominum'.

42–43. Mapheus has 'Junone secunda'.

56. Douglas has misunderstood Mapheus, 'gestis praestantibus orbem exornent'.

73. *recent.* That is, 'newly dead'.

75–76. *quhar reuthfull Eneas . . . chosyn has his place.* Not in Mapheus.

80. Not in Mapheus. Ascensius, 'invenies per tabulam'.

Conclusio (p. 105)

1–10. These lines translate Ovid, *Metamorphoses*, xv. 871–6.

6. That is, it has no power over the soul.

16–17. Douglas subsequently devoted his time to the political fortunes of his family, and to writing letters that might improve them.

THE PALICE OF HONOUR

This work, usually dated *c.* 1501, is an allegorical dream-poem, modelled in part on Chaucer's *House of Fame*. Douglas's theme is a moral one, an inquiry into the nature of honour, but this theme is overlaid and often obscured by his taste for lavish set-pieces of description, and by the desire, as it seems, to include within his poem almost every theme and motif of the courtly love tradition. The style is florid and exuberant, the language thick with rhetorical ornament, with mythological allusion, and, particularly in the more ceremonial passages, with fashionable Latin neologisms. These extracts illustrate something of the diversity of his style as of his subject-matter.

I. Douglas's opening is traditional: a description of a spring morning, notable for its learned, aureate diction, and for the artifice of its imagery. Parts of this description were later re-worked, and included, with much extra detail, in Prologue XII of the *Aeneid*.

1–2. *lamentabill . . . sabill.* An allusion to Aurora's mourning for the death of her son, Memnon.

6. *observance.* Rites and ceremonies in honour of May. Cf. Chaucer, *CT* A, ll. 1043 ff.:

The sesoun priketh every gentil herte . . .
And seith, 'Arise, and do thyn observaunce'.

8. *amiabill*. The repetition of this word is surprising, since Douglas
is usually careful in the construction of his elaborate rhyme scheme.
A sixteenth-century reader who made numerous corrections to the
National Library of Scotland's copy of R has substituted 'dilectabill';
but his authority is dubious, and metrically it is hardly an improvement.

14–18. The syntax is obscure. Unless the text is corrupt, *distillant* is
perhaps elliptical for *war distillant*; *Quhilk* probably refers to *vapours*
rather than *droppis*.

20. Cf. *Aen.* Prol. XII. 101–2:

> The lowkyt buttonys on the gemmyt treis
> Ourspredand leyvis of naturis tapestreis.

30. *Eous*. Named by Ovid as the second of the four 'volucres . . . equi'
that draw the chariot of the sun (*Met.* ii. 153–4). Cf. *Aen.* Prol. XII. 25–26:

> Eous the steid, with ruby hamys red,
> Abuf the sey lyftis furth hys hed.

32. Cf. *Met.* ii. 107–8: 'aureus axis erat, temo aureus, aurea summae /
curvatura rotae. . . .'

39. *rewmes pungitive*. Night mists or vapours, which were thought
particularly harmful to the health.

46 ff. The poet dreams that he is transported from the garden to a
desert, 'combust, barrant, unblomit and unleifit'. Three processions pass
before him—of Minerva, Diana, and Venus—and in fear he hides in the
stump of an oak tree. He is discovered by the followers of Venus, when
he sings, somewhat tactlessly, a 'ballet of inconstant love'.

51. *Pluk at the craw*. The name of a game in which the 'craw' appears
to have been subjected to much rough horseplay. Cf. Winzet, 'sum . . .
imagin thame to rug of his clathis, as thai war playng with him,—pluk
at the craw.' *Certain Tractates*, ed. J. K. Hewison (STS), ii. 81.

53–54. *Skrymmorie* and *Chyppynutie* were probably local Scottish
nicknames given to malicious goblins—'browneis' or 'bogillis'; no other
instance of their use is known, although *DOST* records the form 'chipe-
nute' as a man's nickname.

55 ff. The trial scene was a familiar motif in courtly allegory. Douglas
almost certainly knew Henryson's use of it in the *Fable of the Sheep and
the Wolf* and in the *Testament of Cresseid*, where Cresseid, like Douglas,
is condemned for blasphemy against the deities of love. Douglas's treatment is characterized by a humorous fidelity to some of the procedures

of Scottish criminal law. After hearing the 'dittay' or indictment, he makes a request for mercy. This being refused, he protests his innocence —a recognized formality—and begins his defence proper with an 'exceptioun declinatour' (ll. 79 ff.), i.e. an objection to the competency of the court to try him. (See Balfour, 'Anent exceptiounis and essonzies', *Practicks: or a system of the more ancient law of Scotland*, Edinburgh, 1754, p. 343.)

86. 'Ane woman is forbiddin of the law to be ane Judge.' Balfour, op. cit., p. 283.

87–90. 'He that is within ordouris sall not answer befoir ane prophane Judge, bot sall be remittit to his Judge ordinar.' Balfour, op. cit., p. 682, quoting one of the 'Auld lawis be the Kingis of Scotland'. Douglas claims the right to be tried by an ecclesiastical court.

92. *interlocuture*. The sentence 'interlocuture' was an interim judgement passed by the judge on the validity of exceptions 'proponit' by the defendant; it was distinguished from the sentence *definitive* or final judgement in a case, which is referred to in l. 110 below.

101. *not*. 'Nothing.'

107. *Ye* (C); *Yit* (R).

122 ff. There is evidence elsewhere in the *Palice* of Douglas's reading of the *Metamorphoses*, and he may here be recalling such 'transfigurations' as that of Callisto into a bear (*Met*. ii. 470 ff.) and that of Ascalaphus into an owl (*Met*. v. 538–50).

127 ff. This invocation begins the third and last book. The dreamer has reason to be grateful to the Muses since it was through their intercession that he obtained pardon from Venus. He is assigned to the care of a Nymph in their court, and after a celestial journey arrives at the foot of a high mountain.

140. Perhaps reminiscent of the mountain 'lyk alum de glas' on which stood Chaucer's House of Fame (l. 1124).

145. Douglas's hesitation resembles that of Dante at the foot of the mountain of Purgatory (*Purgatorio* iii).

154 ff. Possibly influenced by the *Inferno*, but there is no close parallel and there are many similar passages in the medieval legends of Hell.

162. A confused recollection of *Iliad* XXI. The river Xanthus, enraged by Achilles' slaughter of the Trojans, rushed towards him in spate, and was halted by the *hest* not of Venus but of Hera, who ordered Hephaestus to set the river on fire, in order to help Achilles, not harm him.

180. *Abacuk*. The Jewish prophet whom the angel of the Lord miraculously carried by the hair of his head to Babylon, bearing food for Daniel in the lions' den. (*Bel and the Dragon*, 33–39.)

183 ff. Douglas briefly experiences *contemptus mundi*. His vision of the

pettiness of the world resembles that of Troilus at the end of *Troilus and Criseyde* (V. 1814 ff.).

197 ff. The allegorical ship had become a commonplace with medieval homilists and preachers. Douglas's analogy between the perils of a storm at sea and the moral and spiritual dangers of the world is a familiar one; he is more original in making the ship represent the 'state of grace'. In the Prologue to *Aen.* XI he shows his interest in the doctrine of grace, adopting an Augustinian standpoint.

202. *boldyn* (C); *bairdin* (R); *bairdin* is meaningless in this context; *boldyn* is an epithet commonly applied to tumultuous waves.

212. *firre* (C); *fir tre* (R); C's reading is metrically preferable; R's *tre* was probably caught from the line beneath.

218. *tha* (C); *that* (R).

219. *drint* (C); *drownit* (R); the rhyme shows that C's reading is correct.

239. *sa far* (C); *far* (R).

241. Cf. *Aen.* Prol. VII. 150.

262 ff. After passing through the outer courts of the palace the poet finally achieves his goal: he sees, however imperfectly (through a *boir*), the Court of Honour, and learns that it is identical with the Kingdom of God.

Descriptions of magnificent palaces, glittering with jewels, abound in courtly allegory, but this account is clearly reminiscent of St. John's vision of the New Jerusalem (Rev. xxi).

267. *a* (C); *I* (R).

283 ff. Cf. Rev. iv. 2: 'And behold there was a throne set in heaven, and one sitting upon the throne.'

288 ff. When the dreamer recovers from his swoon the nymph rallies him—'thou hes ane wyifes hart / That for a plesand sicht was sa mismaid'. Stung by her taunt, he 'maid a busteous briad':

> 'Carling', quod I, 'quhat was yone that thow said?'
> 'Soft yow,' said scho, 'they are not wys that stryifis,
> For kirkmen war ay gentill to thair wyifis.'

289–97. A reply to the poet's question as to 'Quhat folk thay war' within the hall. The ultimate source is probably St. Paul's allegory of the Christian soldier—'Put on the whole armour of God . . .' (Ephes. vi. 11). Douglas shows his interest in this theme in the Prologue to *Aen.* XI. 62 ff.:

> Paule witnessith that nane sall wyn the crown
> Bot he quhilk dewly makis hym reddy bown
> To stand wightly, and feght in the forfront.

292. *Victoriusly* (C); *Verteouslie* (R). R's reading gives a weaker sense, and may well have been caught from the adjective used in l. 290.

298. *ryng* (C); *King* (R). Both readings make sense, but C's leads more logically to the phrase 'in this countrie' (302), and avoids the repetition of the rhyme word.

299. *honoring* (C); *governing* (R). C's reading is preferable. Douglas is making a crucial distinction between 'verteous honour' and 'eirdlie gloir', between the spiritual and the *warldlie* conceptions of honour. He is also making a rhetorical play on the different forms of the word.

306. The action of the poem ends with the nymph and dreamer leaving the paradisal garden by a narrow bridge. In his fear the dreamer falls into the water below. The shock, and bird song, waken him 'In the garding qhuair I first doun fell'. Sitting under a tree he writes a balade in commendation of honour and virtue, which concludes the work.

GLOSSARY

This glossary lists words that are dialectal or obsolete, or used in some special sense, or spelt in a way that might present difficulty to the modern reader. It is not a complete word-list. Words are listed in the inflexional forms in which they appear. But present participles (in *-and*), plurals (in *-is*), past tenses and participles (in *-it*) are not usually registered if the verb occurs in the glossary in other forms; nor are the plurals (in *-is*) of nouns listed in singular forms.

a, *adj.* one, sole (as in II. xi. 53).
A per se, A standing by itself; hence something unique, a paragon.
abaid, lingered.
abraid, started.
abaisit, abasit, abashed, discouraged, dismayed.
abone, aboyn, above, higher than.
aboutspech, circumlocution.
accordyng, agreeing with.
acquart, turned in the wrong way, sideways.
addres, arrange, prepare, direct.
adew, (*interj.*) adieu; (*adv.*) gone, departed.
adherdand, adhering.
adjutorie, help, assistance.
adornyt, worshipped, adored.
adyll, putrid liquid.
afald, single, comprising but one, single-minded.
affeir, (*v., n.*) fear.
afferys, affairs, used in vague reference to things in general.
affrayit, frightened.
agrys, frighten.
aik, oak.
alanerly, only, merely.
alars, alders.
albayr, quite bare.
albedene, at once.
albyrn, burn completely.
ald, (*adj.*) old; (*n.*) old man.
algait, algatis, always, in any case.
alhaill, whole; wholly.
alift, raised.
alkin, alkyn, all kind of, of every kind.
allanerlie, solely.

allow, commend.
alquhar, everywhere.
alsweill, as well.
alsswyth, alswyith, at once, as fast as possible.
altymys, always.
aluterly, completely.
amatist, amethyst.
amene, pleasant.
amerant, emerald-coloured.
amiabill, pleasant, delightful.
amorus, (*adj.*) amorous; (*n.*) the amorous.
and, if; and if; also.
annelit, annealed.
anorn, adorn.
anys, once.
arekit, reached.
aris, oars.
armouris, armour.
arras, remove, rip.
arres, arras, tapestry hangings of the kind made at Arras, in Artois.
arrivyn, to arrive.
art, region, part, neighbourhood; direction; quarter of the heavens.
ascence, ascent.
aspy, spy, observer.
assay, try, make first use of, attempt.
assiltre, assiltrie, axle, the axis of the earth.
assis, assys, (funeral) ashes.
astabillit, established, stabilized.
at, that.
atanis, atanys, at once (usually padding).
athis, oaths.
atour, beyond.

attechyng, accusing.
attempyt, attempted, attacked.
attent, attentive.
Austyne, Augustine.
availl, advantage.
aventur, chance, outcome, accident.
avise, avys, judgement, opinion, advice.
awa, away.
awalk, awoik, awake; awoke.
ay, always.
aynd, breath.
ayr, earlier.

baid, delay.
bail, beacon-fire.
baill, misery, sorrow.
bair, boar.
bak, bat; back.
bald, bold.
ballyngar, ballyngare, ship (orig. whaling-ship).
band, promise, contract.
barbour, barbarous, rude.
bargan, battle.
barknyt, hardened, clotted.
barmkyn, battlement.
barrant, barren.
barys, boars.
bassyn, made of bass or woven fibres.
bawdry, immorality.
bawkis, cross-beams of houses; hence, houses? (VIII, prol. 85).
bay, the song of birds.
bayn, bone.
be, (*v.*) be; (*p.p.*) been; (*pa. sjv.* **war**; *imp. see* **beis, beys**).
beche, beech tree, beech wood.
bedene, straightway, quickly.
bedovyn, bedowyn, plunged, soaked.
beft, beaten.
begouth, began.
begrat, wept, bewailed.
behest, promise, vow.
behufe, well-being, advantage, benefit.
behufis, behufyt, (*impers.*) behove; 'me behufyt', it behoved me, it was incumbent upon me.
beild, shelter, protection, shelteringplace.
beildit, built.

beir, bear.
beir, rasping noise, cry.
beis, beys, *imp.* be.
beit, repair, prepare.
bekend, known, familiar.
belappit, embraced.
beld, shelter, protection.
beleve, expectation, hope, trust.
belive, belyve, at once, immediately.
bellicall, warlike.
bemyng, sounding, buzzing.
bend, bendis, headband, draping; cloths, fillets.
benedicite, (*L. imp., interj.*) bless you!
benkis, benches.
bereif, rob, deprive of.
beris, (1) cries out, roars (as in II. xi. 1); (2) bears.
beryall, crystal-clear.
beseik, beseech.
beseyn, arranged, equipped.
bestiall, animal-kind.
bet, (*v., p.p.*) built; constructed, made; beat, beaten.
betald, told.
betauch, yielded, entrusted.
betis, overcomes by blows.
betrais, betray.
betrump, deceive.
bewavit, stirred up; blown away.
bewis, bewys, boughs.
bewry, surrounded.
beyn, comfortable, genial.
beyt, prepare.
birne, burn.
bla, blue, bluish from cold.
blaitly, dully, stupidly.
blanchit, faded, bleached.
blason, praise, extol.
blastrand, blowing in blasts.
blaucht, pale; lit., bleached (*PH*, l. 287).
blaw, blow; blew; blown.
blek, (*v.*) blot, make dirty; (*n.*) filth.
blenk, glance.
blent, glanced, gazed.
bles, (*v.*) blaze; (*n.*) torch.
blissit, ~yt, blessed.
blomed, flowery, covered with flowers.
blowt, bare, naked.

boddom, a low-lying stretch of ground.

bogill, a supernatural creature.

boir, chink, crevice.

boldyn (*p.p.* **boldyn(nyt)**), swell.

bos, hollow, concave.

bost, boastfulness, threatening and arrogant manner or speech.

bothe, booth.

boun, ready, prepared.

boundis, limits; the area enclosed by limits.

bourd, (*v.*, *n.*) joke, jest.

bow, bend, curve.

bowbardis, bowbartis, sluggards, rustics.

bowkis, carcasses.

bown, ready, prepared (to go).

bownys, makes ready; betakes; hastens.

bowr, bower, inner chamber.

bowrd, joke.

bowsum, tractable, disposed to listen.

boyr, hole made by boring; chink.

boys, (*adj.*) hollow, concave; (*n.*) knob, boss.

brace, embrace.

bradis, bursts forth.

brag, boast, defiant sound.

braid, (*adj.*) broad; evident, unmistakable; (*n.*) sudden movement, leap.

brandysis, ∼ys, threatens, acts conspicuously or violently.

brasand, embracing.

bratland, ∼yng, rattling.

bray, brayt, roar; (*pr. p.* **brayng**).

bre, brow.

breid, breadth; *on* ∼, abroad, wide-open, at large.

brimell, thorny, crude.

brint, burnt.

brintstane, brimstone.

brissit, bruised.

brist, break asunder.

brokkettis, young stags.

bromys, broym, the broom plant.

bruik, besmear.

bruke, enjoy, use.

brukill, fragile.

brumaill, wintry.

brusyt, embroidered.

bruyt, fame; clamour.

brym, fierce, violent.

bryntstane, brimstone.

bryt(t)nyt, cut up, sacrificed.

bub (*pl.* **bubbis**), blast, squall.

buirdis, boards, planks; tables.

bukleris, small, round shields.

bullyrrit, bubbled (*pr. p.* **bullerand, bulling**).

burall, rustic, rude.

burgeonys, sprays, blossoming boughs.

burgionyt, blossomed.

burnys, brooks.

burnys, burnish.

buskis, bushes.

buskit, made ready, prepared.

bussart, the buzzard hawk.

busteous, bustuus, rough, violent.

but, without.

but and ben (*advv.*, used as *nn.*) the outer and inner parts of a house.

bute, remedy, help.

by, buy.

byd, wait.

byg, build.

byggyngys, buildings.

byke, hive, den.

bylgis, the lower parts of ship hulls, hence any ship-like space.

byng, heap.

byr, a strong gust of wind.

byrdyng, burden.

byrne, cuirass.

bysning, ∼yng, threatening, foreboding, monstrous.

bysprent, sprinkled, spotted.

byt, bite.

bywaif, bywave, blown about, wafted away.

cace, in, if.

cachit, drove, tossed; driven.

cairfull, full of care, sad.

callour, fresh.

camscho, crooked.

carpis, speaks.

carvell, carvel, a light, fast ship.

caryand, carrying; travelling.

cast, rhetorical figure, device, stratagem, trick of speech.

catchit, driven, tossed.

cative (*pl.* **catyvis**), wretch, worthless person.

caucht, catch.

causay, causeway.

ceptour, sceptre.

chaftis, jaws.

chair, chariot.

char, turn; *on* ~, on the turn, ajar.

charbukkill, carbuncle stone; fig., anything excellent.

charris, turns, causes to turn back.

chawmyr, room, chamber.

cheir, expression.

chekis, cheeks; side-pieces.

chesbow, the poppy plant.

Chiron, the constellation Sagittarius.

chop, strike forcibly against.

chos, choice, select.

chowpis, mumbles.

chymmys, buildings; chief dwellings (astrol.).

Chyppynutie, the name of a sprite or goblin.

chyrmys, chirps. **~ing,** twittering.

circumstance, surroundings.

claif, split asunder.

clam, climbed.

claws, clause, speech, remark.

clekkyt, bore, gave birth to.

clenge, clengis, cleanse.

clepe, call, cry; name.

clewis, ~ys, valleys, gorges.

clos, (*adj.*) shut in; (*n.*), courtyard.

closeris, bars, enclosing walls.

clowre, lump, swelling caused by a violent blow.

clynk, sing, make a clinking sound.

clynty, stony.

collour, device of rhetoric, literary embellishment.

commendis, benefices.

commonyng, talking, conversation.

commovyt, excited.

compar, comparison; equal or rival.

compasis, plans. **~ing,** examining, considering.

complenyng, lamenting.

complexioun, combination of humours, temperament.

complyng, compline, the last service of the day.

conding, condyngly, (*adj., adv.*) worthy, suitable; suitably.

conjunct, joined, connected.

consait, understanding; device of rhetoric, idea, fancy.

consave, perceive.

considder, contemplate.

contak, conflict.

contemp, despise.

contrar, oppose, contradict.

controvit, contrived.

contryfate, counterfeit.

convenabill, suitable, fitting.

cors (*pl.* ~ys), body.

cost, the side of a person or animal; (*pl.*) entrails; coast.

couchit, cowchit, covered with layers, inlaid.

couth (*past* of **can**), knew; the sense passes imperceptibly to 'could', 'did'.

covert, conceal.

cowp, cup.

cowschet, the wood-pigeon.

Crab, Cancer, a sign of the Zodiac.

crachour, hoarder.

craftely, skilfully.

crafty, characterized by craftsmanship, skilful.

crap, crept.

craw, crow.

creisch, grease, tallow.

croppys, tops.

crowdis, coos, sings.

crowpyng, crying harshly.

croyn, groan, rumble.

croys, cross-sail, square sail.

crynys, clips, reduces in size.

cullour, colour; sense, flavour; literary embellishment.

cultyris, the coulters of a plough.

culyeis, cuddles.

cummyn, (*p.p.*) come; (*vbl. n.*) coming, arrival.

cumpas, circle, circuit.

cundyt, conduit; well-spring, source.

cunnand, understanding, agreement.

cunnyng, skill, knowledge.

cuplyng, uniting, as in marriage.

cuppillys, leashes for dogs.

cur(e), carefulness, care; function, charge; (*pl.*) cares.

curage, mind, spirit, disposition; courage.

curs, course.

cury, cooking, concoction.

GLOSSARY

curyus, elegant, subtle.

cut, lot.

cuyr, cure; office, function; care, anxiety; *in* ～, in charge.

cuyrbulye, leather hardened by boiling.

dang, struck.

dante, esteem, favour.

dantit, tamed, domesticated.

darn, dark, secret.

darth, dearth.

daw, sluggard, sloven.

days, does, female deer.

de, die.

debait, war, strife.

declynyng, a bending downwards, as from the zenith towards the horizon.

decrete, decree, ordain.

ded, (1) deed; (2) death.

dedenyt, deigned.

dedly, dying.

defend, forbid; protect.

deill, part; *sum* ～, somewhat.

deir, (*n.*) harm, injury; (*v.*) harm, injure.

dekkit, covered, sheltered, clothed.

deming, judge.

depaint, brightly painted.

depayntar, painter.

deplome, strip of feathers, de-plume.

depulye, dispoil.

deray, disorder, revelry.

dereyn, engage in battle, undertake.

dern, secret(ly).

destane, (*trisyll.*) destine.

devaill (*3 pr. sg.* **devalis**), descend, fall.

device, devyce, plan; *at al* ～, properly, according to plan, with perfect skill.

deys, dais.

dichis, ditches.

diffynys, describes.

dirk, dark.

discend, descended.

discrepans, disagreement.

discrive (*3 pr. sg.* **discryvis**), describe.

disdenye, disdain, scorn.

dissave, deceived, forsworn.

dissevir, separate.

dissoverit, separated, kept apart.

disteyn, stain, spoil.

distillant, distilling.

dittay, indictment.

dolly, sad, dismal.

donk, (*adj.*, *n.*) damp; (*pl.*) damp places, marshes.

dosk, dark, dusky.

doutsum, doubtful.

dowe, is of worth or value.

dowis, doves.

dowkit, ducked.

downbet, beaten down.

dowr, dowre, stern, resolute, hard, harsh.

doym, judgement.

draglit, bedraggled.

draucht trumpet, war trumpet, one drawing to war.

draw, (*v.*, *p.p.*) draw; drawn.

dreid, fear; doubt; reverence.

drery, gloomy; cruel.

dressyt, made ready, prepared.

drewch, drew.

dreys, endures.

drint, drowned.

drowkit, drenched, soaked.

drug, drag.

drumly, cloudy, gloomy; muddy.

drynchit, drowned; overwhelmed, buried.

dryve, (*v.*, *p.p.*) drive; driven.

dubbis, puddles.

dubbyt, consigned, condemned.

dulce, sweet.

dulefull, mournful.

dung, struck.

dure, door.

duschit, struck.

duyl, duyll, dule, mourning, lamentation.

dwynys, fades away.

dyall, a clock; a measure of excellence.

dyamontis, diamonds.

dycht, dyght, prepared, dressed.

dyng, worthy.

dyng, strike.

dynt, stroke, blow, the force of a blow.

dyseys, disease; dis-ease, any disturbance of a sound condition.

dyttit, stopped up.

dyvulgat, divulged, made common knowledge.

e (*pl.* eyn), eye.
edderis, serpents.
edify, build.
effeir, terror.
effek, n. effect; *in* ~, in fact, in reality.
efferis, befits, is suitable.
eft, aft.
eik, also.
eild, age; old age.
eird, earth. ~lie, earthly.
eith, easy.
ekit, added.
elbok, elbow.
eld, age; old age.
elrich, weird, uncanny.
emerant, emerald.
emmotis, emmets, ants.
emptyve, empty.
endlang, beside, along.
endyt, endyten, endyte, (*v.*, *p.p.*) put into writing; endite, compose; (*n.*) composition, literary or artistic writing.
Ene, Enee, Aeneas. Eneadan, (*adj.*) of the *Aeneid*. Eneadanys, (*n.*) men of Aeneas. Eneadon, Eneados, The *Aeneid*.
enewch, enough.
enforcyng, exerting, applying (oneself).
enfyrit, set on fire.
engyne, ingenuity.
ennoyt, annoyed.
enparyng, diminution.
ensenye, ensign, flag; warcry.
ensew, ensewys, follow.
ententis, wills, designs.
entertenyr, entertain.
entonyng, (*3 pr. pl.*) intone.
entre, entres, entry, gate; permission or right to enter.
entring, (*3 pr. pl.*) enter.
envolvyt, enveloped, wrapped.
erd, earth.
errit, wandered away.
errour, wandering, travelling; error.
eschamyt, affected with shame.
eschevit, achieved, performed (for L 'gesta' IV. i. 31).
Esperus, Hesperus, the evening star.
essonyeis, excuses.

estait, state; ~ *of blude*, rights and privileges obtained by birth.
etlys, ettill (*pa.* ~it), attempts, plans, intends; directs one's course.
exceptiounis, pleas by defendant against a charge, defences.
excersyt, exercised, employed, occupied in.
exemplis, *exempla*, typical instances.
expreme, express, explain, state.
expres, expressly, definitely.
eyk, also.
eyr, earlier.

facund, eloquent.
fader (*g.* fader, ~is), father.
faid, company of hunters.
fair, course, faring.
fait, feat, deed.
fald, enclosure; *be firth and* ~, everywhere.
faldyn, folded.
fallow, fellow, companion.
falset, falsehood.
falyeit, failed.
fame, (1) fame; (2) foam.
fameist, famished.
fane, fain, glad.
fantasy, understanding, mental apprehension; product of the imagination; habit of self-delusion.
far, on, at a distance.
fard, journey, flight.
farnys, ferns.
fasson, fashion, manner.
fatale, fated, caused by fate, fateful.
fawch, pale brown or yellow.
fax, hair.
faym, foam.
fayn, fain, inclined, disposed.
fays, foes.
fed, fede, anger, vengeance, hatred.
feddyrame, feathered wings, plumage.
feil, many.
feilabill, capable of being felt, producing emotion.
feild, (battle-)field.
feir, in, *see* infeir.
fell, fierce, ruthless.
fellon, felloun, fierce, savage; monstrous; very great.
fendit, defended.

fensabill, able-bodied.
fenye, feign; ~ *it,* feigned, false.
fermans, enclosure.
fery, fairy.
ferys, companions.
fettysly, elegantly.
fewlume, a species of bird.
fey, fated; fated to die; unhappy; bringing evil fortune.
feyn, feign.
feyr, a companion.
fild, defiled.
firth, wooded country; *see* **fald.**
flaggis, flashes of lightning.
Flagiton, Phlegethon.
flane, arrow.
flat, flatter.
flaukartis, thigh-armour.
flaw, a blast, or squall of wind.
fle, flee, fly.
fleit (*v., pa. t.*), float(ed).
fley, put to flight, scare, frighten.
fleym, drive out, expel.
flocht, *on* ~, in a state of excitement or dismay.
flodderit, flooded, overflowed.
flokkyng, (*3 ps. pl.*) they flock.
floschis, watery swamps, marshes.
flotterand, floating awkwardly, floundering.
flude, river.
fluour, smell, scent.
flure, floor.
flyte, wrangle, scold.
folys, foal's.
fordoverit, overcome by sleep.
fordryvis, scatters, drives away.
fordynnand, deafening; **fordynnyt, fordinned,** deafened, filled with noise.
forfeblit, rendered feeble.
forgane, forgayn, against.
forgyar, builder, maker.
forleit, abandoned, forsaken.
forlo(i)r, lost, wasted, forlorn.
forrydar, forerunner.
forsis, matters to, concerns.
forvay, err, depart from a path, go astray.
forwrocht, exhausted with toil.
foryeld, recompense, reward.
foryet, (*v., p.p.*) forget; forgotten.

fostyr, fosterer.
fouth, fowth, plenitude, abundance.
fownys, fawns.
frawart, hostile, perverse.
frawart, ~**is,** away from.
fredom, liberality, generosity; freedom.
freklyt, spotted, flecked.
fremmyt, (*adj.*) strange, unfriendly, unfamiliar; ~**ly,** (*adv.*) hostilely, strangely.
frontis, foremost parts; cliffs.
fructuus, fruitful.
fude, food.
fulderis, thunderbolts.
fundin, found.
fundrit, submerged in; stumbled.
fur (*pl.* **furris**), furrow.
furthsprent, stretched out, spread out.
furthstrekit, stretched out; put forth.
furthyet, pour(ed) or throw(n) forth.
fut hait, fute hait, immediately.
fut syde, of a garment, reaching to the feet.
fylit, fylyt, defiled.
fyne, end, purpose.
fyreslauch, fyreslaucht, a flash of lightning.
fyrryn, made of fir.

gabbyng, lying.
gaistis, ghosts, spirits.
galys, (of birds) calls or sings.
gan, began, used as an auxiliary (cf. mod. 'did') followed by infin.
ganand, fit, suitable.
ganestud, withstood.
ganys, befits.
garrand, causing (something to be done).
gart, caused.
garth, garden, yard.
gastis, ghosts.
gayn, gone.
gaynyeld, reward, recompense.
gent, beautiful.
gentile, ~**is,** (*adj.*) of a family or kindred, gentilitial; *our* ~ *lawys,* our own laws; (*n.*) gentile, heathen, the heathens.
germane, having the same parent.
gersis, grasses.

ges, believe.
get, got.
girgand, jarring, creaking.
girnand, grinning, baring the teeth in anger.
gladyng, gladdening.
glaid, (1) gladden; (2) glided.
glavys, swords.
gled, kite, the species of bird.
gleis, melodies.
gleyd, a live coal, flame.
glotnyt, clotted, clogged.
glowmand, frowning, scowling.
gnappit, nibbled, bit in short, abrupt bites.
gobbettis, small pieces of raw flesh.
godly, sacred, divine.
goldspynk, goldfinch.
gone, gone; (3 ps. pl.) they go; (inf.) PH, l. 136.
gousty, gowsty, dismal, dreary.
gowkis, gawks, stares.
gowlyng, yelling.
graip, handle, touch.
graith (p.p. **grathit**), prepare.
graith, instruments, equipment; clengyng ~, cleansing equipment.
granys, branches.
grape, search, examine.
gravys, groves.
grayn, branch.
grayth, grey-beard, old man.
gre (pl. **greis**), degree, pre-eminence; first place; levels; on greis, one above the other.
Gregion, Gregioun, (adj., n.) Greek.
greif, steward, overseer.
grekyng, daybreak, dawn.
gresy, grassy.
greting, weeping.
Grew, (adj., n.) Greek.
gromys, grooms, servants.
grow, shake, shudder, shrink in fear.
gude douchtyr, daughter-in-law.
gudelie, beautiful.
gudlyheid, goodness, excellence.
gukgo, cuckoo.
gum, mist, fog.
gurl, stormy.
gylty, gilded, golden.
gymp, quibble.
gyrth, place of sanctuary.

gys, guise, custom.

habirgyon, short coat of mail.
habyte, garments, costume.
haddir, heather.
hailsum, wholesome.
hair, hoary, frosty.
hait, hot.
hait, hecht, (is) named or called.
haitrent, hatred.
haldis, safe places, forts.
halfdeill, halfway.
halfettis, sides of the head, temples.
hals, throat(s).
hang, hung (PH 213).
hankis, twists, loops.
hant, hantis, frequents, follows as a custom.
happit, wrapped up.
har, hoary, frosty.
harmys, pain, suffering.
harnes, harness, armour.
harsk, harsh, ungraceful, disagreeably rough.
hasard, grey.
haw, bluish, livid.
hawbrik, coat of mail.
he, high.
hechis, the hatches on a ship.
hecht, promise; see hait.
hed, (1) head; (2) heed.
heich, high.
heich, raise.
heildit, covered.
heist, promise.
heit, heating (XIII, prol. 129).
hepit, heaped up.
herbry, shelter, dwelling-place.
heris, lords, chiefs.
heris, (v. ind. & imp.) hear.
heroner, heron-catcher, a falcon trained to fly at the heron.
hertis, (1) hearts; (2) harts.
hesit, raised, hoisted.
hespis, hasps for securing a door.
hest, command.
het, hot.
hethyng, scorn.
hevand, raising, lifting.
heynd, gentle, agreeable, courteous.
hicht, highest point.
hidlis, hiding-places.

hie, high.
hirst, doorsill, threshold.
hirstis, hillsides.
holk, hull, large ship.
holkit, hollowed.
holl, hollow, sunken, deep.
holtis, groves, woods.
honeste, honour, virtue, chastity.
hovand, waiting, remaining stationary.
hovir, hovyr, a state or position of indecision.
how, hollow.
howchis, the middle joints of the hind leg of an animal.
howt, holt, wood.
hug, great.
hukis, sickles.
husbandis, farmers.
hy, hie, hasten.
hychit, walked jerkily.
hycht, height; *cry on* ~, cry aloud.
hydlys, hiding-places.
hyght, height; *on* ~, on high.
hyndir, later, recently past.
hyne, hence.
hynt, took.
hynys, hinds, farm labourers.
hyrd, herdsman, shepherd.
hyrnys, recesses, hiding-places.

ilk(e), same. ~**ane,** each one.
illuminate, enlightened spiritually.
imprent, stamp, imprint.
incompetabill, incompetent.
inconsumptive, inconsumable, eternal.
indigens, lack, poverty.
indigites, a deified hero.
indurand, induryng, lasting, enduring, going on.
inequale, unequal; inequitable, unjust.
infeir, inferis, together.
inflambit, took fire.
ingil, hearth, altar.
ingynys, genius, abilities.
inhy, in haste.
innatyve, innate, inborn.
inordinate, irregular.
interlocuture, interim judgement pronounced by the presiding judge.
interprys, undertake.
intertrike, disarrange.

intill, in.
invane, in vain.
involvyng, wrapping. ~**yt,** wrapped.
irk, weary; *thocht* ~, became weary.
irkit, grew tired.
ische schouchlis, ise schokyllis, icicles.
ischis, issues.
ithand(ly), eager(ly).

jaip, trick, piece of enchantment.
jakkis, jackets, jerkins.
jarris, pushes.
jasp, jasper.
jaw, a dashing or breaking wave.
jawys, jaws; entrance.
jed staf, a Jedburgh staff, a kind of battle-axe.
Jherom, St. Jerome.
jonyngs, joints.
jowellis, jewels; any costly articles.
Jubar, the day star.
juncturis, joints.

kan, can; as auxil., equivalent to the mod. 'did'.
katchit, drove; driven.
kaucht, catch.
kavill(ys), lot, chance, oracle.
kays, jackdaws.
keip, attention, care.
kend, knew; known, instructed.
knoppis, flower heads.
ky(i)th, show, make known or manifest.
kynd, nature; species, race. ~**lie, ~ly,** natural; belonging to one by virtue of one's kind or race; naturally (*PH*, l. 13).
kyndlys, catches fire.
kynrayd, race, kindred.
kyrkis, churches.
kyrnellis, battlements.
kytlys, excites, arouses.

laggerit, bemired.
laid stern, a star that shows the way, a guide.
lair, lore, learning.
laith, loath, unwilling. ~**lie,** loathsome.
lakar, worse.

lakkyn, dispraise, reproach.
lamentabill, mournful; grief-inspiring.
landbrist, surf.
langis, along, beside.
langis, belongs.
langsum, tedious.
lappit, surrounded, enwrapped, folded.
laser, leisure, opportunity.
latit, plated or covered over with metal.
laton, latton, brass.
lauchyng, laughing.
laurers, laurels.
lave, the rest, the remainder.
law, low.
lawdis, laud, praises.
lawly, humbly.
lawrer, laurel.
lawte, lawtie, loyalty, fidelity.
lawyd, laud, esteem?
lawyst, thou lowerest.
lech, leech, physician.
ledderyn, leathern.
ledis, peoples, nations.
leful, lefull, lawful.
lege, liege lord.
leid, (1) speech, language; (2) lead.
leifand, leaving.
leir, learn.
lemand, gleaming.
lemman, sweetheart.
len, lend, grant. lent, given.
lent, lenyt, leaned, inclined.
les, lies; but ~, without lying, truly.
lesum, lawful.
let, delay, hindrance.
lethis, joints.
lettron, lectern.
leude, ignorant.
levyn, light; lightning.
levyt, lived.
lew, lukewarm.
lewch, laughed.
lewit, ~yt, unlearned, untaught.
lewytnes, ignorance.
leyd, language.
ley(i)s, leas, pastures.
leyn, they lie, tell falsehoods.
leyndis, dwell, remain.
lift, sky.
liggyng, lying.

lippyn, trust.
loch, lake.
loif, praise.
loir, instruction.
lomys, tools, implements.
lovyng(is), praising, praise.
lovys, praises.
lowch (pl. lowys), lake.
lowis, loose.
lownyt, calmed.
lowpit, looped, twisted, coiled in loops.
lowre, crouch.
lowys, loose, free.
lowys, lows.
Lucyn, Lucinia, the moon.
luffit, praised.
lugyng, lodging-place, house.
lurkit, peered furtively.
lust, desire, pleasure, delight. ~y, pertaining to lust, amorous; lively, pleasing; pleasure-loving.
lychtly, treat lightly, undervalue.
lyddir, slow, lazy; cum ~ speid, make slow headway.
lyft, sky.
lyge, league.
lyggis, lies.
lyk, lick.
lykand, agreeable, likeable.
lykis, (impers.) it pleases.
lykly, make attractive, embellish.
lynd, the linden or lime tree.
lynnys, waterfalls.
lyntquhite, the thistle finch.
lyre, flesh.
lys, lessen.
lyssouris, pastures, meadows.
lyst, hem.
lyst, (impers.) have pleasure in, desire; the ~, it gives you pleasure, you take pleasure in.
lyte, little.
lyve, life.

ma(l)gre, in spite of; ~ thar hed, in spite of them.
ma(il)talent, ill-will, rage.
mairatouir, maratour, moreover.
mait, weary, exhausted.
malapert, impudent.
male-eis, uneasiness, discomfort.

man, must.
mane, strength.
mannans, menace.
mannasis (*pr. p.* **mannysand**), menaces.
mansioun, dwelling; astrological position.
mantemys, possesses.
manuyr, cultivate.
mark, murky.
marrasis, marshes.
Martys, Mar's.
mastys, mastiff.
matyn, one of the canonical hours, sung at daybreak.
mavys, the song-thrush.
may, maiden.
mayn, strength.
maynsweryng, perjury. **maynsworn,** perjured.
meid, medis, meadow, meadows.
meirswyne, dolphin or porpoise.
meit, proper, suitable.
meki(l), large.
meldyr, flour for a sacrifice.
melle, skirmish, fight.
menskles, ungracious.
menstralis, minstrels.
menye, train, company.
merch, bone-marrow.
merl, the blackbird.
mery, pleasant, sweet.
mesyng, calming.
meyn, (1) method, means; (2) think, intend.
meys, (1) mess, feast; (2) assuage, calm.
mischaip, deformed.
misknawis, are ignorant of.
mismaid, disturbed, troubled.
moblis, furniture, goods.
mocht, might.
modyfy, limit, keep within bounds.
mon, must.
monyst, admonished, warned. **~syngis,** admonitions, warnings.
mortfundeit, chilled, benumbed with cold.
mot, might. *sa~ I thee*; a mild oath.
mowe, funeral pile; heap.
moy, mild, gentle.
mudy, ill-humoured, complaining.

muggis, earthenware vessels.
muldis, funeral ashes.
muris, moors.
murnand, mourning.
musis, waits or looks expectantly; muses.
muskane, rotten, decaying.
must, musty.
myddill (*p.p.* **mydlit**), mingle.
mygeis, midges, gnats.
myith, reveal.
mynys, diminish.
myrthfull, joyous.
mysseym, myssemyng, mis-seem, misbecome.
mystir, need. **~full,** needy, in need of.

nanys, in *for the~*, for the nonce, for the present.
nate, end, purpose.
necessiteis, state of deprivation.
neddir, lower.
netheles, nevertheless.
nevis, fists.
nevo, nephew; grandson; posterity.
newlyngis, just now, anew.
nocht, noth, not.
nold, would not.
not, know not.
notis, uses, offices, practices.
notyfys, makes evident or conspicuous.
noy, (*n., v.*) harm.
nummyn, taken, captured.
nyce, nys, strange, rare, uncommon; ignorant; exact, precise.

observance, ritual ceremonies.
ocht, anything.
oly, oil.
ombeset, ombyset, beset, surround(ed).
omdo, undo.
on ane, onan, anon, quickly.
oncunnandnes, ignorance.
ondantit, unsubdued.
ondoyn, undone, ruined.
ondreich, in a state of grief or trouble.
oneith, oneth, scarcely.
onerdyt, unburied.
onfenyt, unfeigned.

onkowth, strange, unnatural, novel.
onleill, unloyal, treacherous.
onlesum, unlawful.
onmeit, unequal.
onrestles, restless.
onrycht, unrightly, erroneously.
onsikkyr, unsafe.
onsilly, unfortunate, unhappy.
onsound, unhealthy, wounded.
onsterit, undisturbed.
ontretabill, unhearing, stubborn.
onwaryit, uncursed.
onweldy, incapable, awkward.
onwemmyt, unstained.
onwrokyn, unavenged.
onyrkyt, untroubled.
or, ere, before.
oriyont, the orient, the east, the morning.
orlager, proclaimer of the hours. **orlege**, timepiece; hence, a measure of excellence.
our, o'er, excessively; over.
ourfret, cover over with ornaments or embroidery.
ourheildis, ourheld, cover(ed).
ourhippit, passed over, skipped.
ourset, beset, oppressed.
ourseyn, examined, looked over.
ourspynnerand, spinning over.
ourtane, overtaken, overcome.
ourvolvyt, laid aside.
ourweltrand, overriding.
ouryeid, passed over, travelled through.
outbraid, burst into speech.
outbullyrand, boiling out.
outquent, quenched.
outtane, except.
outwith, outside of, beyond.
ovirfret, richly embroidered.
ovirset, threw into confusion; overturned, capsized.
ovirthraw, overturned.
owtak, except.
owthir, owder, either.
oys, use.

pacient, patient, invalid.
pailyeon, a large tent.
pal, rich cloth.
palmys, palms; the blades of oars.

palustrall, athletic.
palys, palings, fence.
pane, trouble, exertion.
papyngay, parrot.
parage, equality.
parroch, (used attrib.) parish.
pastans, pastime, recreation.
patermon, patrimony.
patro(u)n, lord, master.
patterraris, sayers of the Pater Noster.
pawkis, deceptions, wiles.
pelit, peeled, bereft of hair.
pendes, pendants, ornaments.
penys, beats out or forges.
per de, by God!
pereist, perished.
pertryk, partridge.
peteous, pitiful, mournful.
pew, the melancholy chirp of a bird.
peyr, pour.
peys, cup, wine-cup.
Phenyssane, Phoenician.
pick, pitch.
pieteous, pitiful, mournful.
pight, decorated, as with jewels.
pilis, pointed blades of grass.
plait, plate-armour.
plakkis, small copper coins.
plane, open, level; smooth; honest.
plat, flat, level.
plays, games, amusements.
pled, plea, pleading.
plenyst, filled up, stocked.
plet, wove, twined.
pleuch, plough.
pley, plea, pleading.
pleyn, complain, lament.
poill, pole star.
poleist, polyst, polished.
pollecy, polycy, prudence, sagacity.
portis, ports; gates.
postponyt, set aside.
pot, pit.
powder, dust. ~**it**, sprinkled.
poynt, arrangement, order; *in* ~ *to*, ready to.
practike, difficult, requiring skill.
prattis, tricks.
prekis, spurs.
pres, press to, make haste.
pretendit, professed.
previte, private, privacy.

prevy, secret.

price, great value.

prik, standing up, erect.

prime, the first hour of the day.

promit, promise; vow.

pronuba, an assistant in the ceremonies of marriage.

properte, proper use of words, propriety; property.

propir, one's own, personal.

proponyng, proposing.

prospir, prosperous.

prunyeit, decked out, adorned.

prygpenny, haggle?

prynnyt, sewed, embroidered.

pulchritude, beauty.

pulder, dust, powder. ~**it,** sprinkled.

pungitive, sharp, pungent.

punytioun, punishment.

purvayt, provided, arranged in advance.

puyr, pure, clear.

pyg, an earthenware bottle.

pyk, the act of sticking with something pointed.

pyle, hair, hide.

pyne, pain, effort.

pynsellis, standards, banners.

pyrkis, perches.

quaid, wicked.

quaikand, quaking.

(to) quakyng, to quake (violently).

quayf, coif, head-dress.

quellys, oppresses, vanquishes.

quent, knowing, cunning; skilled; strange, odd; elegant, skilfully made; proud, fierce.

queym, closed against the wind.

quha(y), who. **quhais,** whose. **quham,** whom. **quhamto,** to whom.

quhalis, whales.

quhar, where. ~**in,** wherein. ~**for,** wherefore.

quhat, what. ~**sumever,** whatsoever.

quheill, wheel.

quhelmyt, turned upside down.

quhen, when.

quhete, wheat.

quhew, the sound of a rapid passage through the air.

quhidder, whether (*sts. interrog.*).

quhidderand, rushing.

quhil(l), until.

quhilk(is), which, who.

quhilum, at times, once.

quhirlit, whirled.

quhirrand, whirring.

quhislyng, whistling.

quhite, white.

quhitstanys, whetstones.

quhow, how.

quhoyn, few.

quhy, why.

quhyn, a hard, dark-coloured stone.

quite, clear oneself, prove one's innocence.

quod, quoth.

quoik, quuik, trembled.

quy, heifer.

quyk, vital, living.

quynchyng, to die out, be extinguished; to quench.

quynt essens, quintessence.

quyt, quyte, repay; recompensed.

quytteris, quivers.

race, course, journey.

ragment, gibberish, rigmarole.

raid, road, a piece of water where ships may anchor.

raif, tore, broke apart.

raik, proceed at a rapid pace; ~ *on raw,* proceed in order.

raipis, ropes.

rak, fog, mist.

rakis, walks rapidly; *see* **raik.**

rakles, reckless, careless.

ralys, rails, enclosures.

rammale, brushwood, underwood.

randerand, rendering.

rangis, rows or ranks of hunters, fighters, or animals.

raparal, rebuild, repair.

raport, obtain, get for oneself.

rave, drag, tear; tore, pierced.

ravenous, rapacious; ~ *foulis,* birds of prey.

raxit, raised or stretched oneself.

rayr, roar.

rays, roes.

rays, course taken by a moving body.

rebald(-)daill, ribald or vulgar people or doings.

rebutyt, repulsed, driven back.
recent, fresh, not affected by decay.
recollect, collect, gather.
recontyr, meet, encounter in battle.
red, advice, counsel.
reduce, lead or bring back; recall; translate, render.
redymyte, ornate, beautiful.
reffell, revelry.
reflectant, turning away.
regester, a regulating device; hence, a fixed standard.
reguler, regulator.
reif, theft, spoliation.
reke, reach, hand over, stretch.
reknys, reckons.
releschand, singing.
remeid, remedy.
renk, course, race.
renownye, renown.
rent, profit, value.
repair, retreat, the act of returning or going to a place.
repar, repair, go. **~ar,** restorer.
reparalyt, repaired, refitted.
repatyrrit, fed.
repercust, driven back, reflected.
represent, sight.
rerd, roar, noise. **~it,** echoed, resounded.
reserve, preserve, keep safe.
restorative, capable of restoring health.
resyng, resign.
retrograde, (of the planets) apparently moving backwards.
reuth, ruth, mercy, pity. **~full,** pitying, compassionate.
revertis, of plants, springs up afresh.
revis, steals.
revist, ravished, seized.
revolve, turn over in the mind.
rewmes, harmful moisture, mists.
rewys, streets.
rice, twigs, small branches.
riggyng, back.
roche, rochis, rock(s); mountain.
rocht, cared for.
rod, path, road.
rokis, clouds.
ro(l)kis, rocks.

ronk (*adj.*), rank.
ronnys, ronys, brambles, thickets.
rouch, roucht, rough.
roundis, round-dances.
rout, rowt(is), company, crowd, army.
rovis, in ships, the plates on which the point of a rivet is beaten down.
rowmed, wandered.
rown, whisper.
rowpit, ~yt, called, summoned, invoked loudly.
rowt, blow.
rowt, roar, resound.
ruif, roof.
ruik, rook.
rumland, rumbling.
rummys (*pa.* **rumys(i)t,** *pr. p.* **~ing),** rumble, roar.
rungeand, chewing, gnawing.
russat, reddish brown.
ryfe, common, widespread.
rym, fog, chill mist.
rynd, hoar-frost, frozen mist.
ryng, reign, kingdom. **ryng** (*v.*), reign; ring, resound.
ryngis, circular dances.
rynk, a course in a tournament.
rype, search thoroughly, open up.
ryvand, tearing.

sa, (1) so; (2) say.
sacryfy, offer a sacrifice to.
saill, hall.
sal(l), shall; in compounds *salbe, salbeir, saldo,* &c.
salf (*pr. p.* **salvand**), saved.
salus, greet.
same, lard.
samekil(l), so great, so large.
sammyn, together.
sand, sand-bank.
sanguane, a blood-red colour.
sapheiris, saphires.
sardanis, sardonyx.
sauch tre, the sallow or willow tree.
scaill, scatter, pour down.
scaithfull, harmful.
scald, be scorched or burned.
schaik, shake, shaken; (*all*) *to* **~** shaken up violently.

schald, shallow, shoal.

schane, shone, sparkled.

schape, shaped, arranged.

schaw, (1) grove; (2) show.

schayn, shone.

sched, the parting of the hair.

schene, bright.

schent, destroy; fouled, desecrated, ruined.

schet, shut.

scheyn, shining, beautiful.

schill, (1) shrill; (2) chill.

schippit, shipped, took aboard ship.

schirris, sirs.

schort, shorten, beguile.

schot (wyndo), a window that can be opened and shut.

schrewis, wicked people, male or female. schrewit, vicious, fierce.

schydis, chips, split pieces of logs.

schyne, shine; shone.

schyre, bright; brightly.

screik, shriek.

scroggis, brushwood.

scry, cry.

scryke, shriek.

scuggis, shadows.

seculair, a layman.

see, (1) dwelling-place, seat, (pl.) seis, places, positions. (2) see sey.

sege, seat.

seir, several, separate; different.

sekyng, they seek (IV. ii. 9).

selis, seals as proofs of authenticity.

sellet, a light leather helmet.

selvyn, self.

semabill, like, similar.

sembland, semblance, appearance.

semmys, seams.

semys, (impers.) it seems.

sence, sens, incense.

sentence, sentens, sense, substance, thought. ~cyus, full of wisdom.

senyeory, lordship, rule. ~eis, king-doms.

sermond, conversation, any kind of speech.

sersand, sersyng, searching.

serve, deserves.

sermonys, ceremonies.

sesyng, to cease.

se(y)syt, placed, fixed, established.

set, although.

set, set, a jewelled ornament placed on garments.

set, set; inclined, having a specific disposition.

setis, men posted to intercept game.

sewch, gulf.

sey, see, seyis, sea, stormy waves.

seyll, joy.

seyr, several, many.

sik, such; as in compounds, ~ane, ~lyke.

sike, brook, stream.

sikkyr, sure, safe. ~ly, surely.

silly, innocent, helpless.

skaill, skalis, skalys, scatter(ed), spread.

ska(i)th, harm, injury.

skugg, shadow. ~yt, shaded.

skyrlys, screams.

slaid, slid.

slaw, slain.

sle, cunning, skilful.

sleipryfe, bringing sleep.

slekit, smoothed, sleek, polished.

slevit, slit, cut; thrust.

slid, slippery.

sloggorn, battlecry.

slottis, door-bars.

slottry, sluggish.

sloyk, slake, quench.

slycht, trick, ruse.

smaragdane, emerald.

smy, rogue, knave.

snell, bitter, keen, severe.

snog, sleek, smooth.

snyppand, biting, cutting.

socery, sossary, sossery, sorcery.

sokkis, ploughshares.

sol, soil, ground.

soles, solace.

somys, the ropes or chains attaching a draught-horse to a plough.

sone, sun.

soppis, soppys, little clouds.

sort, assortment, group.

sory, unhappy, wretched.

sover, sovir, safe, sure, secure. ~ly, surely.

sown, sound.

spamen, prophets.

span, grasp, lay hold of.

spayit, foresaw, prophesied.

speir, (1) spear; (2) sphere; (3) ask, inquire.

spelys, climbs.

spill, spilt, (*intrans., trans.*) fall; destroy; spoiled.

spirituell, ecclesiastical, religious.

sprauch, cry, scream.

spreitles, swooning.

sprent, sprinkled.

spreth, plunder.

sprutlit, speckled.

spulye, spoil, plunder. **~it,** dispoiled, plundered.

spyll, damage, destroy.

stages, steps.

staill, position, place of ambush.

stair, (*v., n.*) gaze, stare.

stait, estate, rank.

stanchit, satisfied.

standyn, stood.

stangis, stings, as of a serpent.

startling, capering.

starve, die.

ste(i)d, place, stead.

steid, horse.

steir, stir.

stelit, made of steel.

stent, ~is, ~it, set up; erect; placed; decorate; decorated.

sterage, movement, motion.

sternys, stars.

sterve, die.

stevin, (*n.*) prow, stem; (*v.*) steer.

stevynnys, voices.

stoir, domestic animals collectively; abundance, supplies.

storour, store-keeper.

stottis, (*n.*) steers.

stour (*pl.* **stowris**), battle; tumult, storm.

stouth, an act done by stealth.

stoutlie, resolutely.

stowris, (1) rises in a cloud; (2) *see* **stour.**

stra, straw; **~** *for to spek* . . ., a mild imprecation.

straik, blow.

strait, narrow.

strekis (*pa.* **strekyt**), reaches, stretches.

strenys, constrains.

strive, strife.

strynkil, strynklis (*pr. p.* **~and**), sprinkle; sprinkling.

stuffit, furnished.

sture, harsh.

stuthis, knobs, studs.

styddeis, anvils.

styf, stout, stalwart.

stykkyt, garnished.

stynt, stop; stopped.

stythly, stiff, unyielding.

suave, gracious, kindly.

subtell, cunning. **subtillitie,** cunning.

sudiornys, sojourns.

sudron, Southern English as distinguished from Scots.

suguryt, sugared, sweet.

suld, should.

sulye, soil, land.

sum, summyn, some.

supple, supplie, aid, assistance.

suppowellyng, supplying, support.

swage, abate, grow calm.

swak, (*n.*) blow, violent dash; (*v.*) strike, throw.

sweit, (1) sweat; (2) sweet.

swelly, swallow, drink in.

swelth, whirlpool.

swete, sweet; what is sweet, hence 'life'.

swevyn (*pl.* **~nys**), dream, dreams.

sweyand, swaying, swinging.

swik, cheat, ensnare.

swith, quickly.

swokand, making the sucking noise of waves.

swouchand, swowchand, whistling.

swowch, a breathing sound or whistle.

swyre, valley.

swyth, at once.

Syche, Sychey, Sicheus, the first husband of Dido.

syde, large, extensive.

sykkyn, such, of that kind.

syld, concealed.

symmyr, summer.

syndry, asunder, apart.

syne, afterwards; since.

syng, sign.

sypir, cypress.

sys, times.

syt, sit; endure, put up with.

taiklit, furnished with tackle.

158

taill, account, tale.

takill, tackle, part of the rigging of a ship.

tallonyt, tallowed, greased.

targettis, light, round shields.

tary (*pa.* **tareit**), delay. **~sum,** slow in coming.

tayll, tail; *in the* **~,** along behind.

tayn, taken.

tays, takes; weighs, poises, aims.

tayt, cheerful, nimble.

techrys, water-drops.

tendis, tithes.

tent, attention, notice.

teyn, anger.

tha, thai, those.

thak, thatch, thatched roof.

than, in that case, sometimes, at the same time, then.

thanis, fanes.

thankful, thanks-deserving, agreeable.

tharto, in addition, moreover.

the(e), thigh.

the, prosper; v. *mot.*

thewes, manners, customs, virtues.

thir, these.

thoch(t), though.

thocht, (*impers.*) me**~,** it seemed to me.

thochtfull, melancholy, pensive.

thoill, tholis, endure, suffer.

thrang, (*n.*) bustle, crowding; (*v.*) see **thryng.**

thraw, (*n.*) moment, trice; twist, turn; (*v.*) **thrawis, thrawyn,** twists; twisted, awry.

thraw, throw.

threpe, complain, scold.

threw, twisted.

thringis, throngs, thrusts.

thristis, thrusts.

throwand, (*v., pr. p.*) twisting, writhing; (as *n.*) one who is twisting and turning.

throwgangis, passages.

thrynfald, triple, three-ply.

thryng (*pa.* **thrang**), thrust, push, throng, spread.

thuddis, blows, blasts of wind.

thusgatis, thus, in this way.

thy, this.

thyftuusly, stealthily.

thyne, thence.

ticht, water-tight, well caulked and pitched.

tint, lost.

Titan, Tithonus, consort of Aurora.

tobald, over-bold.

to-, the first element of infinitives, e.g. **tobeseik,** to beseech.

toppyt, (high-)topped, lofty.

toyn, tune.

traist, firmly, securely; **traste,** faithfull.

traistis, trestles.

traistit, expected.

transfigurat, transform.

trastis, believe.

trat, old woman, crone.

tratlys, idle talk, gossip.

travel(l), travail, labour; travel.

trays, course, route.

tre, wooden vessel, barrel.

tretabill, compliant, tractable.

trety, treatise.

trimbland, trembling.

trowit, ~yt, believed, expected, trusted.

trubly, troubled, stormy.

trufis, trifles, jests.

trump, trifle.

tryg, trim, neat.

trygland, trickling.

tryne, train, procession.

trynschand, piercing; pierced; *all to trynschit,* completely pierced through.

tuitchand, concerning.

tume, empty.

turs, carry. **~and,** carrying.

tuskyt, having teeth.

twichit, touched.

twyntris, sheep or cows two years old.

twystis, shoots, branches, twigs.

tychirris, small spots.

tyd, betided.

tydy, in good condition, plump.

tyndis, the pointed branches of deer horns.

tynt, lost.

tysche, tissue; a girdle of rich fabric.

tyste, entice.

tyte, quickly, soon.

ugsum, ugly. **~nes,** ugliness.

umbrage, shadow.

umbrate, shady.
umquhile, once, formerly.
Ungary, Hungary.
unlappit, unfolded.
upheildit, uptilted.
uphynt, draw up, take up.
uppermair, higher up.
upstowryng, stirring up.
upwalxis, waxes, grows.
upwark, cessation of work.
upwelt, stir up, throw up.
upwrelis, pulls up, raises.
Ursis, Ursa, the Great Bear.

vailyeand, valiant.
varyance, variety.
vassalage, strength, prowess, courage.
vavengeour, vagabond.
veilys, 'veals', calves.
ventositeis, blasts of wind.
verdour, verdurous.
vergers, gardens, orchards.
verray, true.
verteous (*adj.*), possessing magical or medical powers (of jewels). **vertew** (*n.*), virtue.
vivificative, vivifying, life-giving.
void, voyd, empty; hence, meaningless or foolish; destitute, lacking.
volatill, birds, esp. wild-fowl.
voydyt, emptied, cleared.
vrusum, apparently an error for *unrusum*, restless (XIII, prol. 57).
vulgar, (*adj.*) vulgar, common; vernacular; (*n.*) the vernacular.
vysseys, visits.

wachand, watching, keeping watch.
waik, weak.
waist, desolate.
wait, (1) wet; (2) know.
wak, watery, wet.
walit, chosen.
walking, they walk (VI. iv. 66).
walkryfe, sleepless, wakeful.
walkynnaris, those who awaken or stir up.
wallaris, wall-builders.
wallis, (1) waves; (2) walls.
wallowit, (*v., p.p.*) withered.
wally, wave-y, swelling.

walterand, surging, tossing.
wame, belly, womb. **wamyt,** wombed.
wanthrift, lack of thrift or economy.
wappit, wrapped.
ward, courtyard, compartment.
wareit, cursed.
warly, carefully, cautiously.
warp, throw, cast.
warpit, wrapped (by metathesis).
warryn, were.
weid, clothing, garment.
weif, woven.
weild, endure.
weir, (1) war; (2) doubt, confusion.
weirly, warlike.
welch, sickening to the taste.
weltir, roll, toss. **weltrit,** overturned.
weltis, roll, turn over.
wemmys, scars, injuries.
went, path, course; usage, order.
wenys (*pa.* **wenyt**), believes.
werd, fate, fortune.
wernour, warner.
weschin, weschyn, washed.
weyr, *see* **weir** (2).
wicht, wyght, creature, person.
widdyrsyns, in a direction opposite from the usual.
wight, (*adj. used as a n.*) the strong; any individual, man or woman.
wil, will, (*adj., adv.*) strange, astray, lost. **~sum,** wandering, strange, unknown.
wily coyt, an under-coat.
wirschip, sense of honour; credit.
wiskis, whisks, goes quickly.
with, by.
withhawd, withhold.
without, without; outside of.
wittering, knowledge.
wo, grieved, sorrowful.
wod(e), mad.
wolx, waxed, became.
womentyng, lamenting.
worschip, honour.
worth, became.
woyd, mad.
wrablis, warblings.
wra(i)k, destruction, disaster.
wreil, twist.
wrek(is), avenge.

write, (*n.*) writing, poem; (*p.p.*) written.
writh, twist, turn.
wrokyn, avenged.
wryblis, warblings.
wyfly, womanly, female.
wymp(il)lis, garments folded to envelop the head; folds or wrinkles.
wymplit, twisted up, enfolded.
wyndill strays, dry stalks of coarse grass.
wyrin, made of wire; like wire.
wys, wise, manner.
wys, in *I ~*, as a quasi-verb, from *gewis*, certainly.
wysnyt, wizened, thin.
wyte, blame, reproach.

yald (*~in*), yielded; surrendered.
yarn, carefully, eagerly.

y-, the sign of the past participle, e.g. in **ybet,** made, constituted, **yschappit,** depicted, **ysowpit,** soaked.
ye, yhe, ye, you.
yee, (*interj.*) yes.
yeld, barren.
yelloch, yell.
yellyt, honoured by cries.
yet, yettis, gate; gates.
yet, pour(ed).
ygrant, granted.
ying, young.
yingker, yongker(is), young man, men.
yoir, yor, formerly, long ago.
yow, ewe.
yowle, yell.
yowthed, youth.
yoyd, went.
yschit, issued.

PRINTED IN GREAT BRITAIN
AT THE UNIVERSITY PRESS, OXFORD
BY VIVIAN RIDLER
PRINTER TO THE UNIVERSITY